D0517163

Step by Step

Microsoft® Office
Outlook® 2003

Online Training Solutions, Inc.

PUBLISHED BY
Microsoft Press
A Division of Microsoft Corporation
One Microsoft Way
Redmond, Washington 98052-6399

Library of Congress Cataloging-in-Publication Data
Microsoft Office Outlook 2003 Step by Step / Online Training Solutions, Inc.
      p. cm.
    Includes index.
    ISBN 0-7356-1521-7
    1. Microsoft Outlook.   2. Time management--Computer programs.   3. Personal information management--Computer programs.   4. Electronic mail systems--Computer programs   I. Online Training Solutions (Firm)

   HF5548.4.M5255M52   2003
   005.369--dc21   2003052658

Printed and bound in the United States of America.

2 3 4 5 6 7 8 9   QWE   8 7 6 5 4 3

Distributed in Canada by H.B. Fenn and Company Ltd.

A CIP catalogue record for this book is available from the British Library.

Microsoft Press books are available through booksellers and distributors worldwide. For further information about international editions, contact your local Microsoft Corporation office or contact Microsoft Press International directly at fax (425) 936-7329. Visit our Web site at www.microsoft.com/mspress. Send comments to *mspinput@microsoft.com*.

Acquisitions Editor: Alex Blanton
Project Editor: Aileen Wrothwell

Body Part No. X09-71457

Contents

Contents

iv

What's New in Microsoft Office Outlook 2003

You'll notice some changes as soon as you start Microsoft Office Outlook 2003. Many of the familiar program elements have been reorganized to give you better access to the features you use most, and many new features have been added to make it easier to access the tools you use most often.

New in Office 2003

Some of the features that are new or improved in this version of Outlook won't be apparent to you until you start using the program. To help you quickly identify features that are new or improved with this version, this book uses the icon in the margin whenever those features are discussed or shown.

The following table lists the new features that you might be interested in, as well as the chapters in which those features are discussed.

To learn how to	Using this feature	See
Quickly access your mail, calendar, contacts, tasks, and other Outlook items	Navigation Pane	Chapter 1
Open attachments without opening the item	Reading Pane	Chapter 1
Access Word's e-mail-related toolbar buttons from one convenient location	Word as your e-mail editor simplifications	Chapter 1
Read and respond to an e-mail message without closing other applications	Desktop Alerts	Chapter 1 Chapter 9
Post attachments for group input	Live Attachments	Chapter 1
View your messages in any of 13 pre-defined views	Arrangements	Chapter 2
Quickly mark messages for follow-up	Quick Flags	Chapter 2
Assign a different signature to each Outlook account	Unique signature per account	Chapter 2
View your messages in a new way	Arrange by Conversation	Chapter 2
Collect and automatically update related information in virtual folders	Search Folders	Chapter 3
Create and organize rules in an easier way	Rules	Chapter 3

To learn how to	Using this feature	See
View your Calendar and the Date Navigator in a new, streamlined format	Calendar View	Chapter 4
View multiple calendars at the same time	Side-by-side calendars	Chapter 4
Add a picture to an Address Book entry	Contact Picture	Chapter 6
See a list of contacts with whom you can share information	View SharePoint Team Services contacts	Chapter 6
Connect directly to Outlook over the Internet	Exchange Server access through the Internet (RPC over HTTP)	Chapter 8
Store a local copy of your mailbox on your computer	Cached Exchange Mode	Chapter 8
Quickly switch between panes in the Navigation Pane	Go menu	Chapter 9
Create a Personal Folders file	New Data File Type (.pst)	Chapter 9
Display the individual names of Distribution List members to edit the recipients of a message	Expand Distribution Lists in an e-mail message	Chapter 9
Create messages with restricted permission to prevent messages from being forwarded, printed, copied, or edited by unauthorized people	Information Rights Management	Chapter 9
Block or allow external Web content such as pictures or sounds to display in e-mail messages, and prevent Web beacons from validating your e-mail address to junk mail senders	Enhanced privacy features	Chapter 9
Receive e-mail notifications when SharePoint site content changes	Create and manage alerts	Chapter 9

Getting Help

Every effort has been made to ensure the accuracy of this book and the contents of its CD-ROM. If you do run into problems, please contact the appropriate source for help and assistance.

Getting Help with This Book and Its CD-ROM

If your question or issue concerns the content of this book or its companion CD-ROM, please first search the online Microsoft Press Knowledge Base, which provides support information for known errors in or corrections to this book, at the following Web site:

www.microsoft.com/mspress/support/search.asp

If you do not find your answer at the online Knowledge Base, send your comments or questions to Microsoft Press Technical Support at:

mspinput@microsoft.com

Getting Help with Microsoft Office Outlook 2003

If your question is about Microsoft Office Outlook 2003, and not about the content of this Microsoft Press book, your first recourse is Outlook's Help system. This system is a combination of help tools and files stored on your computer when you installed The Microsoft Office System 2003 and, if your computer is connected to the Internet, help files available from Microsoft Office Online.

To find out about different items on the screen, you can display a *ScreenTip*. To display a ScreenTip for a toolbar button, for example, point to the button without clicking it. Its ScreenTip appears, telling you its name. In some dialog boxes, you can click a question mark icon to the left of the Close button in the title bar to display the Microsoft Office Outlook Help window with information related to the dialog box.

When you have a question about using Outlook, you can type it in the "Type a question for help" box at the right end of the program window's menu bar. Then press `Enter` to display a list of Help topics from which you can select the one that most closely relates to your question.

Another way to get help is to display the Office Assistant, which provides help as you work in the form of helpful information or a tip. If the Office Assistant is hidden when a tip is available, a light bulb appears. Clicking the light bulb displays the tip, and provides other options.

If you want to practice getting help, you can work through this exercise, which demonstrates two ways to get help.

BE SURE TO start Outlook before beginning this exercise.

1 At the right end of the menu bar, click the **Type a question for help** box.

2 Type **How do I get help?**, and press ⌷Enter⌷.

A list of topics that relate to your question appears in the Search Results task pane.

You can click any of the help topics to get more information or instructions.

3 In the **Search Results** task pane, scroll down the results list, and click **About getting help while you work**.

The Microsoft Office Outlook Help window opens, displaying information about that topic.

Maximize

4 At the right end of the Microsoft Office Outlook Help window's title bar, click the **Maximize** button, and then click **Show All**.

The topic content expands to provide in-depth information about getting help while you work.

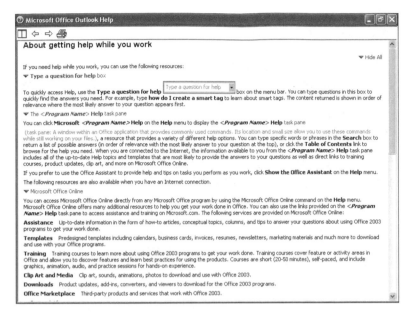

Close

5 At the right end of the Microsoft Office Outlook Help window's title bar, click the **Close** button, to close the window.

6 On the **Help** menu, click **Microsoft Office Outlook Help**.

7 In the Outlook Help task pane, click **Table of Contents**.

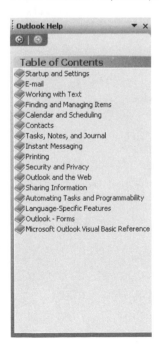

The task pane now displays a list of help topics organized by category, like the table of contents in a book.

Back

8   On the toolbar at the top of the task pane, click the **Back** button.

Notice the categories of information that are available from the Microsoft Office Online Web site. You can also reach this Web site by clicking Microsoft Office Online on the Help menu.

More Information

If your question is about a Microsoft software product, including Outlook 2003, and not about the content of this Microsoft Press book, please search the appropriate product support center or the Microsoft Knowledge Base at:

support.microsoft.com

In the United States, Microsoft software product support issues not covered by the Microsoft Knowledge Base are addressed by Microsoft Product Support Services. The Microsoft software support options available from Microsoft Product Support Services are listed at:

support.microsoft.com

Outside the United States, for support information specific to your location, please refer to the Worldwide Support menu on the Microsoft Product Support Services Web site for the site specific to your country:

support.microsoft.com

Using the Book's CD-ROM

The CD-ROM included with this book contains all the practice files you'll use as you work through the exercises in this book. By using practice files, you won't waste time creating sample content with which to experiment—instead, you can jump right in and concentrate on learning how to use Microsoft Office Outlook 2003.

What's on the CD-ROM?

In addition to the practice files, the CD-ROM contains some exciting resources that will really enhance your ability to get the most out of using this book and Outlook 2003, including the following:

- *Microsoft Office Outlook 2003 Step by Step* in e-book format.
- *Insider's Guide to Microsoft Office OneNote 2003* in e-book format.
- *Microsoft Office System Quick Reference* in e-book format.
- *Introducing the Tablet PC* in e-book format.
- *Microsoft Computer Dictionary, Fifth Edition* in e-book format.
- 25 business-oriented templates for use with programs in The Microsoft Office System.
- 100 pieces of clip art.

Important The CD-ROM for this book does not contain the Outlook 2003 software. You should purchase and install that program before using this book.

Minimum System Requirements

To use this book, you will need:

- **Computer/Processor**

  Computer with a Pentium 133-megahertz (MHz) or higher processor

- **Memory**

  64 MB of RAM (128 MB recommended) plus an additional 8 MB of RAM for each program in The Microsoft Office System (such as Outlook) running simultaneously

- **Hard Disk**

    - 245 MB of available hard disk space with 115 MB on the hard disk where the operating system is installed

    - An additional 20 MB of hard disk space is required for installing the practice files

    Hard disk requirements will vary depending on configuration; custom installation choices may require more or less hard disk space

- **Operating System**

    Microsoft Windows 2000 with Service Pack 3 (SP3) or Microsoft Windows XP or later

- **Drive**

    CD-ROM drive

- **Display**

    Super VGA (800 × 600) or higher-resolution monitor with 256 colors

- **Peripherals**

    Microsoft Mouse, Microsoft IntelliMouse, or compatible pointing device

- **Software**

    Microsoft Office Outlook 2003, Microsoft Office Word 2003, and Microsoft Internet Explorer 5 or later

Installing the Practice Files

You need to install the practice files on your hard disk before you can open them in Outlook for use in the chapters' exercises. Follow these steps to copy the CD's files to your computer:

1   Insert the CD-ROM into the CD-ROM drive of your computer.

The Step by Step Companion CD End User License Agreement appears. Follow the on-screen directions. It is necessary to accept the terms of the license agreement in order to use the practice files. After you accept the license agreement, a menu screen appears.

Important   If the menu screen does not appear, start Windows Explorer. In the left pane, locate the icon for your CD-ROM drive and click this icon. In the right pane, double-click the StartCD executable file.

2   Click **Install Practice Files**.

3   Click **Next** on the first screen, and then click **Yes** to accept the license agreement on the next screen.

4   If you want to install the practice files to a location other than the default folder (*My Documents\Microsoft Press\Microsoft Outlook 2003 SBS*), click the **Browse** button, select the new drive and path, and then click **OK**.

5   Click **Next** on the **Choose Destination Location** screen, click **Next** on the **Select Features** screen, and then click **Next** on the **Start Copying Files** screen to install the selected practice files.

6   After the practice files have been installed, click **Finish**.

Within the installation folder are subfolders for each chapter in the book.

7   Close the Step by Step Companion CD window, remove the CD-ROM from the CD-ROM drive, and return it to the envelope at the back of the book.

Opening the Practice Data Files in Outlook

Chapters 1 through 7 each have an accompanying Outlook data file containing the practice files pertinent to that chapter. You need to open the chapter's data file in Outlook before you can use the practice files. Follow these steps prior to beginning each chapter:

1   Start Outlook.

2   On the **File** menu, point to **Open**, and then click **Outlook Data File**.

The Open Outlook Data File dialog box appears.

3   On the **Places** bar, click **My Documents**.

4   In the folder list, double-click **Microsoft Press**, **Outlook 2003 SBS**, and then the appropriate chapter folder and subfolder (if applicable).

Tip   See "Using the Practice Files," below, for the list of chapter folders, subfolders, and practice files.

5   Click the Outlook data file, and then click **OK**.

The data file opens in Outlook and is visible at the bottom of the Navigation Pane.

Using the Practice Files

Each exercise is preceded by a paragraph or paragraphs that list the files needed for that exercise and explains any file preparation you need to take care of before you start working through the exercise.

The following table lists each chapter's practice files.

Chapter	Folder	Subfolder	Files
Chapter 1: Working with Outlook	Working	Attach	SBSWorking Attachment
Chapter 2: Managing E-Mail Messages	Managing		SBSManaging
Chapter 3: Finding and Organizing E-Mail Messages	Organizing		SBSOrganizing
Chapter 4: Managing Your Calendar	Calendar		SBSCalendar
Chapter 5: Scheduling and Managing Meetings	Meetings		SBSMeetings
Chapter 6: Creating and Organizing a List of Contacts	Contacts		SBSContacts
Chapter 7: Keeping Track of Information	Tasks		SBSTracking
Chapter 8: Working from Multiple Locations	No practice files		
Chapter 9: Customizing and Configuring Outlook	No practice files		

Uninstalling the Practice Files

After you finish working through this book, you should uninstall the practice files to free up hard disk space.

1   On the Windows taskbar, click the **Start** button, and then click **Control Panel**.

2   In Control Panel, click **Add or Remove Programs**.

3   In the list of installed programs, click **Microsoft Office Outlook 2003 Step By Step**, and then click the **Remove** or **Change/Remove** button.

4   In the **Unistall** dialog box, click **OK**.

5   After the files are uninstalled, click **Finish**, and then close the Add or Remove Programs window and Control Panel.

Important   If you need additional help installing or uninstalling the practice files, please see "Getting Help" earlier in this book. Microsoft Product Support Services does not provide support for this book or its CD-ROM.

Conventions and Features

You can save time when you use this book by understanding how the *Step by Step* series shows special instructions, keys to press, buttons to click, and so on.

Convention	Meaning
Microsoft Office Specialist	This icon indicates a topic that covers a Microsoft Office Specialist exam objective.
New in Office 2003	This icon indicates a new or greatly improved feature in Microsoft Office Outlook 2003.
	This icon indicates a reference to the book's companion CD.
BE SURE TO	These words are found at the beginning of paragraphs preceding or following step-by-step exercises. They point out items you should check or actions you should carry out either before beginning an exercise or after completing an exercise.
USE OPEN	These words are found at the beginning of paragraphs preceding step-by-step exercises. They draw your attention to practice files that you'll need to use in the exercise.
CLOSE	This word is found at the beginning of paragraphs following step-by-step exercises. They give instructions for closing open files or programs before moving on to another topic.
1 2	Numbered steps guide you through hands-on exercises in each topic.
●	A round bullet indicates an exercise that has only one step.
Troubleshooting	These paragraphs show you how to fix a common problem that might prevent you from continuing with the exercise.
Tip	These paragraphs provide a helpful hint or shortcut that makes working through a task easier.
Important	These paragraphs point out information that you need to know to complete a procedure.

Convention	Meaning
❎ Close	The first time you are told to click a button in an exercise, a picture of the button appears in the left margin. If the name of the button does not appear on the button itself, the name appears under the picture.
Ctrl + Home	A plus sign (+) between two key names means that you must hold down the first key while you press the second key. For example, "press Ctrl + Home" means "hold down the Ctrl key while you press the Home key."
Black bold characters	In steps, the names of program elements, such as buttons, commands, and dialog boxes, are shown in black bold characters.
Blue bold characters	Anything you are supposed to type appears in blue bold characters.
Blue italic characters	Terms that are explained in the glossary at the end of the book are shown in blue italic characters.

Taking a Microsoft Office Specialist Certification Exam

As desktop computing technology advances, more employers rely on the objectivity and consistency of technology certification when screening, hiring, and training employees to ensure the competence of these professionals. As a job seeker or employee, you can use technology certification to prove that you have the skills businesses need, and can save them the trouble and expense of training. Microsoft Office Specialist is the only Microsoft certification program designed to assist employees in validating their Microsoft Office System skills.

About the Microsoft Office Specialist Program

A Microsoft Office Specialist is an individual who has demonstrated worldwide standards of Microsoft Office System skill through a certification exam in one or more of the Microsoft Office System desktop programs including Microsoft Word, Excel, PowerPoint®, Outlook®, Access and Project. Office Specialist certifications are available at the "Specialist" and "Expert" skill levels. Visit *www.microsoft.com/officespecialist/* to locate skill standards for each certification and an Authorized Testing Center in your area.

What Does This Logo Mean?

This Microsoft Office Specialist logo means this courseware has been approved by the Microsoft Office Specialist Program to be among the finest available for learning Outlook 2003. It also means that upon completion of this courseware, you might be prepared to become a Microsoft Office Specialist.

Selecting a Microsoft Office Specialist Certification Level

When selecting the Microsoft Office Specialist certification(s) level that you would like to pursue, you should assess the following:

- The Microsoft Office System program ("program") and version(s) of that program with which you are familiar

- The length of time you have used the program

- Whether you have had formal or informal training in the use of that program

Candidates for Specialist-level certification are expected to successfully complete a wide range of standard business tasks, such as formatting a document or spreadsheet. Successful candidates generally have six or more months of experience with the program, including either formal, instructor-led training or self-study using Microsoft Office Specialist-approved books, guides, or interactive computer-based materials.

Candidates for Expert-level certification are expected to complete more complex, business-oriented tasks utilizing the program's advanced functionality, such as importing data and recording macros. Successful candidates generally have one or more years of experience with the program, including formal, instructor-led training or self-study using Microsoft Office Specialist-approved materials.

Microsoft Office Specialist Skill Standards

Every Microsoft Office Specialist certification exam is developed from a set of exam skill standards that are derived from studies of how The Microsoft Office System is used in the workplace. Because these skill standards dictate the scope of each exam, they provide you with critical information on how to prepare for certification.

Microsoft Office Specialist Approved Courseware, including the Microsoft Press *Step by Step* series, are reviewed and approved on the basis of their coverage of the Microsoft Office Specialist skill standards.

The Exam Experience

Microsoft Office Specialist certification exams for The Microsoft Office System 2003 programs are performance-based exams that require you to complete 15 to 20 standard business tasks using an interactive simulation (a digital model) of a Microsoft Office System program. Exam questions can have one, two, or three task components that, for example, require you to create or modify a document or spreadsheet:

Modify the existing brochure by completing the following three tasks:

1 Left-align the heading, *Premium Real Estate*.

2 Insert a footer with right-aligned page numbering. (Note: accept all other default settings.)

3 Save the document with the file name Broker Brochure in the My Documents folder.

Candidates should also be aware that each exam must be completed within an allotted time of 45 minutes and that in the interest of test security and fairness, the Office Help system (including the Office Assistant) cannot be accessed during the exam.

Passing standards (the minimum required score) for Microsoft Office Specialist certification exams range from 60 to 85 percent correct, depending on the exam.

The Exam Interface and Controls

The exam interface and controls, including the test question, appear across the bottom of the screen.

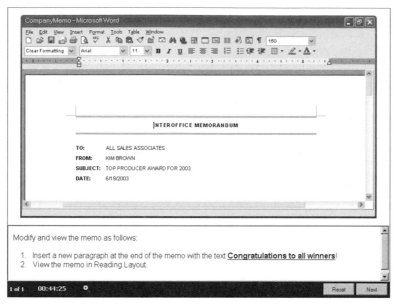

- The **Counter** is located in the left corner of the exam interface and tracks the number of questions completed and how many questions.

- The **Timer** is located to the right of the **Counter** and starts when the first question appears on the screen. The Timer displays the remaining exam time. If the Timer is distracting, click the Timer to remove the display.

   Important Transition time between questions is not counted against total allotted exam time.

- The **Reset** button is located to the left of the **Next** button and will restart a question if you believe you have made an error. The **Reset** button will not restart the entire exam nor extend the total allotted exam time.

- The **Next** button is located in the right corner. When you complete a question, click the **Next** button to move to the next question. It is not possible to move back to a previous question on the exam.

Test-Taking Tips

- Follow all instructions provided in each question completely and accurately.

- Enter requested information as it appears in the instructions, but without duplicating the format. For example, all text and values that you will be asked to enter will appear in the instructions with bold and underlined text formats (for example, text), however, you should enter the information without applying these formats unless you are specifically instructed to do otherwise.

- Close all dialog boxes before proceeding to the next exam question unless you are specifically instructed otherwise.

- There is no need to close task panes or save your work before proceeding to the next exam question unless you are specifically instructed otherwise.

- For questions that ask you to print a document, spreadsheet, chart, report, slide, and so on, please be aware that nothing will actually be printed.

- Responses are scored based on the result of your work, not the method you use to achieve that result (unless a specific method is indicated in the instructions), and not the time you take to complete the question. Extra keystrokes or mouse clicks do not count against your score.

- If your computer becomes unstable during the exam (for example, if the exam does not respond or the mouse no longer functions) or if a power outage occurs, contact a testing center administrator immediately. The administrator will restart the computer and return the exam to the point where the interruption occurred with your score intact.

Certification

At the conclusion of the exam, you will receive a score report, which you can print with the assistance of the testing center administrator. If your score meets or exceeds the passing standard (the minimum required score), you will be mailed a printed certificate within approximately 14 days.

College Credit Recommendation

The American Council on Education (ACE) has issued a one-semester hour college credit recommendation for each Microsoft Office Specialist certification. To learn more, visit *www.microsoft.com/traincert/mcp/officespecialist/credit.asp*.

For More Information

To learn more about Microsoft Office Specialist certification, visit *www.microsoft.com /officespecialist/*.

To learn about other Microsoft Office Specialist approved courseware from Microsoft Press, visit *www.microsoft.com/mspress/certification/officespecialist/*.

Microsoft Office Specialist Skill Standards

Each Microsoft Office Specialist certification has a set of corresponding skill standards that describe areas of individual, Microsoft Office System program use. You should master each skill standard to prepare for the corresponding Microsoft Office Specialist certification exam.

Microsoft Office Specialist

This book will fully prepare you for the Microsoft Office Specialist certification at the Specialist level. Throughout this book, content that pertains to a Microsoft Office Specialist skill standard is identified with the logo shown in the margin.

Standard	Skill	Page
OL03S-1	**Messaging**	
OL03S-1-1	Originate and respond to e-mail and instant messages	9, 26
OL03S-1-2	Attach files to items	20, 173, 207
OL03S-1-3	Create and modify a personal signature for messages	53
OL03S-1-4	Modify e-mail message settings and delivery options	57
OL03S-1-5	Create and edit contacts	16, 156
OL03S-1-6	Accept, decline, and delegate tasks	199
OL03S-2	**Scheduling**	
OL03S-2-1	Create and modify appointments, meetings, and events	105, 130, 136
OL03S-2-2	Update, cancel, and respond to meeting requests	138, 143
OL03S-2-3	Customize Calendar settings	99, 117
OL03S-2-4	Create, modify, and assign tasks	184, 189, 199
OL03S-3	**Organizing**	
OL03S-3-1	Create and modify distribution lists	16
OL03S-3-2	Link contacts to other items	169, 207
OL03S-3-3	Create and modify notes	205
OL03S-3-4	Organize items	44, 50, 72, 75, 162, 193, 207

Standard	Skill	Page
OL03S-3-5	Organize items using folders	67, 81, 93
OL03S-3-6	Search for items	63, 67
OL03S-3-7	Save items in different file formats	90
OL03S-3-8	Assign items to categories	111
OL03S-3-9	Preview and print items	25, 122, 176

About the Authors

Online Training Solutions, Inc. (OTSI)

OTSI is a traditional and electronic publishing company specializing in the creation, production, and delivery of computer software training. OTSI publishes the Quick Course® series of computer and business training products. The principals of OTSI are:

Joyce Cox has over 20 years' experience in writing about and editing technical subjects for non-technical audiences. For 12 of those years she was the principal author for Online Press. She was also the first managing editor of Microsoft Press, an editor for Sybex, and an editor for the University of California.

Steve Lambert started playing with computers in the mid-seventies. As computers evolved from wire-wrap and solder to consumer products, he evolved from hardware geek to programmer and writer. He has written over 14 books and a wide variety of technical documentation and has produced training tools and help systems.

Gale Nelson honed her communication skills as a technical writer for a SQL Server training company. Her attention to detail soon led her into software testing and quality assurance management. She now divides her work time between writing and data conversion projects.

Joan Preppernau has been contributing to the creation of excellent technical training materials for computer professionals for as long as she cares to remember. Joan's wide-ranging experiences in various facets of the industry have contributed to her passion for producing interesting, useful, and understandable training materials.

The OTSI publishing team includes the following outstanding professionals:

Susie Bayers
Jan Bednarczuk
Keith Bednarczuk
RJ Cadranell
Liz Clark
Nancy Depper
Leslie Eliel
Joseph Ford
Jon Kenoyer
Marlene Lambert
Aaron L'Heureux
Lisa Van Every
Michelle Ziegwied

For more information about Online Training Solutions, Inc., visit *www.otsi.com*.

Kristen Crupi

Microsoft Outlook Version 2002 Step by Step, on which this book was based, was written by Kristen Crupi, who has more than seven years' experience as a technical writer and information architect for Web-based applications. Kristen also contributed to the Microsoft Excel 2000 Step by Step courseware and served as a technical resource on the Windows 95 Resource Kit team.

Quick Reference

13 **To create a new message from the Inbox**

● On the toolbar, click the **New Mail Message** button.

13 **To create a new message from any Outlook folder**

1 Click the down arrow to the right of the **New** button.

2 On the drop-down menu, click **Mail Message**.

13 **To display the All Mail Folders list**

● On the Navigation Pane, click the **Mail** icon.

13 **To address a message**

● Type the recipient's e-mail address in the **To** box, or click the **To** button and select a name from the Address Book.

13 **To send a message**

1 Compose and address the e-mail message you want to send.

2 On the message form's toolbar, click the **Send** button.

16 **To add an entry to the Address Book**

1 On the **Tools** menu, click **Address Book**.

2 Click the **New Entry** button.

3 In the **New Entry** dialog box, click **New Contact**.

4 In the **Put this entry** drop-down list, click the address book to which you want to add the contact, and then click **OK**.

5 In the **Untitled – Contact** dialog box, type the information you want to save for this contact, and then click **Save and Close**.

16 **To create a distribution list**

1 On the **Tools** menu, click **Address Book**.

2 Click the **New Entry** button.

3 In the **New Entry** dialog box, click **New Distribution List**.

4 In the **Put this entry** drop-down list, click the address book to which you want to add the distribution list, and then click **OK**.

5 In the **Untitled – Distribution List** dialog box, in the **Name** box, type the name of the distribution list.

6 To add distribution list members from an existing address book, click the **Select Members** button. In the **Select Members** dialog box, select the contacts you want to add to the distribution list, and then click **OK.**

7 To add new distribution list members, click the **Add New** button. In the **Add New Member** dialog box, type the display name and e-mail address of the new contact, select the **Add to Contacts** check box if you want, and then click **OK.**

8 Click **Save and Close.**

20 **To attach a file to a message**

1 With the message open, on the toolbar, click the **Insert File** button.

2 In the **Insert File** dialog box, browse to the file you want to attach, click the file, and then click the **Insert** button.

23 **To check for new messages**

● On the toolbar, click the **Send/Receive** button.

23 **To delete a message**

1 Select the message.

2 On the toolbar, click the **Delete** button.

25 **To print a message**

1 Select or open the message you want to print.

2 On the toolbar, click the **Print** button.

27 **To turn on smart tags for instant messaging**

1 On the **Tools** menu click **Options.**

2 In the **Options** dialog box, click the **Other** tab.

3 In the **Person Names** area, select the **Enable the Person Names Smart Tag** and **Display Messenger Status in the From field** check boxes.

4 Click **OK.**

27 **To send an instant message from an e-mail message**

1 Open a message to or from your instant messaging contact.

2 In the message header, click the **Person Names Smart Tag** next to the contact's name, and then on the shortcut menu click **Send Instant Message.**

3   In the **Delivery options** area of the **Message Options** dialog box, select the check boxes for the options you want.

4   Click **Close**.

39   **To set the importance of a message**

1   Compose a new e-mail message.

2   On the Message form's toolbar, click the **Options** button.

3   In the **Message settings** area of the **Message Options** dialog box, click the down arrow to the right of the **Importance** box, and then click **Low**, **Normal**, or **High**.

4   Click **Close**.

44   **To sort messages**

●   Click the heading of the column by which you'd like to sort messages.

44   **To group messages**

●   On the **View** menu, point to **Arrange By**, and then click the field by which you'd like to group messages.

44   **To turn off message grouping**

●   On the **View** menu, point to **Arrange By**, and then click **Show in Groups**.

44   **To change the message view**

●   On the **View** menu, point to **Arrange By**, point to **Current View**, and then click the view you want.

44   **To customize the message view**

1   On the **View** menu, point to **Arrange By**, point to **Current View**, and then click **Customize Current View**.

2   In the **Customize View** dialog box, click the button of the element you want to customize.

3   In the resulting dialog box, make the changes you want, and then click **OK**.

4   Repeat Steps 2 and 3 for each element you want to change.

5   Click **OK** to close the **Customize View** dialog box and save your changes.

50   **To color-code messages**

1   On the **Tools** menu, click **Organize**.

2   In the **Ways to Organize** pane, click **Using Colors**.

3 Select the type of messages you want to color-code and the color you want them to be, and then click the **Apply Color** button.

53 **To create a message signature**

1 On the **Tools** menu, click **Options**.

2 In the **Options** dialog box, click the **Mail Format** tab.

3 In the **Select the signatures to use with the following account** list, click an account, click the **Signatures** button, and then click the **New** button.

4 In the **Create New Signature** dialog box, type the name of your signature, and then click the **Next** button.

5 In the **Signature Text** box, type and style your signature, and then click **Finish**.

6 Click **OK** to close the **Options** dialog box.

57 **To flag a message with the default flag color**

● In your Inbox, click the message's **Flag Status** icon.

57 **To flag a message with a flag color other than the default**

1 In your Inbox, right-click the message's **Flag Status** icon, and then click **Add Reminder**.

2 In the **Flag for Follow Up** dialog box, in the **Flag color** list, click a color.

3 Click **OK**.

57 **To mark a flagged message as complete**

● In your Inbox, click the message's **Flag Status** icon.

57 **To view all your flagged messages**

● In the **Favorite Folders** list, click **For Follow Up**.

57 **To flag a message you are composing**

1 On the message window's toolbar, click the **Message Flag** button.

2 In the **Flag for Follow Up** dialog box, in the **Flag To** list click a label.

3 In the **Due by** lists, click a date and a time.

4 In the **Flag color** list, click a color.

5 Click **OK**.

Chapter 3 Finding and Organizing E-Mail Messages

Page 64 **To find messages**

1 On the toolbar, click the **Find** button.

2 In the **Look for** box in the **Find** pane, type a word you know is in the message you are looking for.

3 Click the **Find Now** button.

64 **To assign a message to a category**

1 Select the message, and on the **Edit** menu, click **Categories**.

2 In the **Item(s) belong to these categories** box, type the name of a new category, or, in the **Available Categories** list, select the appropriate category for the message.

3 Click **OK**.

67 **To create a Search Folder from a template**

1 On the **File** menu, point to **New**, and then click **Search Folder**.

2 In the **Select a Search Folder** list, click a template.

3 If a **Choose** button appears in the **Customize Search Folder** area, click it, specify the criteria to use, and then click **OK**.

4 Click **OK** to close the **New Search Folder** dialog box.

67 **To rename a Search Folder**

1 In the **Navigation Pane**, right-click the folder, and then click **Rename** on the shortcut menu.

2 Type the new name, and then press Enter.

67 **To create a custom Search Folder**

1 On the **File** menu, point to **New**, and then click **Search Folder**.

2 In the **Select a Search Folder** list, click **Create a custom Search Folder**.

3 In the **Customize Search Folder** area, click **Choose**.

4 In the name box, type a name for the Search Folder.

5 Click the **Criteria** button, specify the search criteria, and then click **OK**.

6 Click **OK** in each of the open dialog boxes.

72 **To create a view to filter messages**

1   On the **View** menu, point to **Arrange By**, point to **Current View**, and then click **Define Views**.

2   In the **Custom View Organizer** dialog box, click **New**.

3   In the **Create a New View** dialog box, type the name of the new view, select the type of view, select the folders on which the view can be used, and then click **OK**.

4   In the **Customize View** dialog box, click the button of the element you want to customize.

5   In the resulting dialog box, make the changes you want, and then click **OK**.

6   Repeat Steps 4 and 5 for each element you want to change.

7   Click **OK** to close the **Customize View** dialog box and save your changes.

8   Click **Apply View**, and then click **Close**.

75 **To create a rule to filter messages**

1   On the **Tools** menu, click **Rules and Alerts**.

2   In the **Rules and Alerts** dialog box, click **New Rule**.

3   In the Rules Wizard, follow the instructions to create the new rule.

4   When you are done, click **Finish**, and then click **OK**.

80 **To filter junk or adult content messages**

1   On the **Actions** menu, point to **Junk E-mail**, and then click **Junk E-mail Options**.

2   Select a level of protection, and then click **OK**.

81 **To create a folder**

1   On the **File** menu, point to **New**, and then click **Folder**.

2   In the **Create New Folder** dialog box, in the **Name** box, type the name of the folder.

3   In the **Folder contains** list, click the kind of items you want to store in the folder.

4   In the **Select where to place the folder** list, click the mailbox or folder in which you want to create the new folder.

5   Click **OK**.

81 **To move a message to a folder**

1   Right-click the message, and on the shortcut menu, click **Move to Folder**.

2   In the **Move Items** dialog box, click the folder to which you want to move the message, and then click **OK**.

81 **To move a folder**

● In the **Folder List**, drag the folder to the location you want.

81 **To rename a folder**

1 In the **Folder List**, right-click the folder, and click **Rename**.

2 Type the new folder name, and then press Enter.

81 **To delete a folder**

1 In the **Folder List**, click the folder you want to delete.

2 On the toolbar, click the **Delete** button.

85 **To share a folder**

1 In the **Folder List**, right-click the folder, and on the shortcut menu, click **Sharing**.

2 Click the **Add** button.

3 Select the person with whom you want to share your folder, and then click **OK**.

4 Click **Apply**, and then click **OK**.

85 **To make someone a delegate**

1 On the **Tools** menu, click **Options**.

2 On the **Delegates** tab, click **Add**.

3 In the **Type Name or Select from List** box, select the person you want to make a delegate, and click **OK**.

4 In the **Delegate Permissions** dialog box, select the permissions you want to grant the delegate, and then click **OK**.

5 Click **OK** to close the **Options** dialog box.

90 **To save a message as an HTML file**

1 Select the message, and on the **File** menu, click **Save As**.

2 In the **Save As** dialog box, browse to the location where you want to save the file.

3 In the **Save as type** drop-down list, click **HTML**.

4 Click the **Save** button.

90 **To save a message as a text file**

1 Select the message, and on the **File** menu, click **Save As**.

2 In the **Save As** dialog box, browse to the location where you want to save the file.

3 In the **Save as type** drop-down list, click **Text Only**.

4 Click the **Save** button.

105 **To schedule an event**

1 In the Calendar, right-click the day on which you want to schedule the event, and click **New All Day Event** on the shortcut menu.

2 In the **Event** form, enter the relevant information about the event, and click the **Save and Close** button.

111 **To assign a category to an appointment**

1 At the bottom of the **Appointment** form, click the **Categories** button.

2 In the **Categories** dialog box, select the category, and then click **OK**.

111 **To move an appointment**

● In the Calendar, drag the appointment to the new time or date.

111 **To copy an appointment**

1 Right-click and drag the appointment to the new time or date.

2 On the shortcut menu that appears, click **Copy**.

111 **To delete an appointment**

1 Click the appointment you want to delete.

2 On the toolbar, click the **Delete** button.

115 **To create a calendar folder**

1 On the **File** menu, point to **New**, and then click **Folder**.

2 In the **Name** box, type the name of the new calendar.

3 In the **Folder contains** list, click **Calendar Items**.

4 In the **Select where to place the folder** list, click the folder under which you want to create the new calendar.

5 Click **OK**.

115 **To view multiple calendars**

1 Make sure the Calendar is displayed.

2 In the **My Calendars** area of the **Navigation Pane**, select the check boxes for the calendars you want to view.

115 **To view your schedule for the work week**

1 Make sure the Calendar is displayed.

2 On the toolbar, click the **Work Week** button.

115 **To view your schedule for a full week**

   1 Make sure the Calendar is displayed.

   2 On the toolbar, click the **Week** button.

115 **To view your schedule for a month**

   1 Make sure the Calendar is displayed.

   2 On the toolbar, click the **Month** button.

117 **To change your work week**

   1 On the **Tools** menu, click **Options**.

   2 On the **Preferences** tab of the **Options** dialog box, click the **Calendar Options** button.

   3 In the **Calendar work week** area of the **Calendar Options** dialog box, select the check boxes for your work days.

   4 Click **OK** in each of the open dialog boxes.

120 **To change your time zone**

   1 On the **Tools** menu, click **Options**.

   2 On the **Preferences** tab of the **Options** dialog box, click the **Calendar Options** button.

   3 In the **Calendar Options** dialog box, click the **Time Zone** button.

   4 In the **Time Zone** dialog box, click the time zone you want, and then click **OK** in each of the open dialog boxes.

121 **To manually label an appointment**

   1 Double-click the appointment.

   2 In the **Appointment** form, click the down arrow to the right of the **Label** box, and then click a label.

   3 Click **Save and Close**.

121 **To label appointments with color**

   1 On the toolbar, click the **Calendar Coloring** button, and then click **Edit Labels**.

   2 In the **Edit Calendar Labels** dialog box, select the label you want to edit and rename it as you like.

122 **To print your calendar**

   1 Make sure the Calendar is displayed, but no appointment is open.

   2 On the toolbar, click the **Print** button.

   3 In the **Print** dialog box, select a print style, and click the **Print** button.

Chapter 5 **Scheduling and Managing Meetings**

Page 130 **To plan a meeting**

1 On the **Actions** menu, click **Plan a Meeting**.

2 In the **Plan a Meeting** dialog box, click the **Add Others** button and then click **Add from Address Book**.

3 In the **Select Attendees and Resources** dialog box, select the Required and Optional attendees and the Resources, and then click **OK**.

4 In the Free/Busy area, drag the red and green bars to set the meeting time, and then click the **Make Meeting** button.

5 In the resulting meeting form, complete any additional information, and then click **Send**.

130 **To set or remove a reminder**

1 In the meeting form, select or clear the **Reminder** check box.

2 If setting a reminder, select the amount of time before the meeting that you want to be reminded.

3 Close the meeting form and save your changes.

137 **To schedule an online meeting**

1 On the toolbar, click the down arrow to the right of the **New** button, and then click **Meeting Request**.

2 On the **Meeting** form, select the **This is an online meeting using** check box.

3 Complete the remaining meeting information, and then click **Send**.

138 **To accept a meeting request**

1 In the open meeting request or in the Reading Pane, click **Accept**.

2 Choose whether to edit and send a response, and then click **OK**.

138 **To decline a meeting request**

1 In the open meeting request or in the Reading Pane, click **Decline**.

2 Choose whether to edit and send a response, and then click **OK**.

138 **To propose a new meeting time**

1 In the open meeting request or in the Reading Pane, click the **Propose New Time** button.

2 In the Free/Busy area, select the preferred time, and click the **Propose Time** button.

143 **To automatically respond to meeting requests**

1 On the **Tools** menu, click **Options**.

2 On the **Preferences** tab of the **Options** dialog box, click the **Calendar Options** button.

3 In the **Calendar Options** dialog box, click the **Resource Scheduling** button.

4 In the **Resource Scheduling** dialog box, select the check boxes for the automatic response options you want, and then click **OK** in the open dialog boxes.

143 **To reschedule a meeting**

1 Open the meeting, and click the **Scheduling** tab.

2 In the Free/Busy area, select new start and end dates and times.

3 Click the **Send Update** button.

143 **To invite others to a meeting**

1 In the meeting form, click the **Scheduling** tab, and then click the **Add Others** button.

2 Click the contacts you want to add, click the **Required** or **Optional** button, and then click **OK**.

143 **To cancel a meeting**

1 Open the meeting, and on the **Actions** menu, click **Cancel Meeting**.

2 Choose whether to send a cancellation notice to the attendees, and then click **OK**.

146 **To create a group schedule**

1 Make sure the Calendar is displayed.

2 On the toolbar, click the **View Group Schedules** button.

3 In the **View Group Schedules** dialog box, click the **New** button.

4 In the **Create New Group Schedule** dialog box, type a name for the group schedule, and then click **OK**.

5 Add the group members you want, and then click **Save and Close**.

149 **To open another person's calendar directly**

1 On the **File** menu, point to **Open**, and click **Other User's Folder**.

2 Click the **Name** button, click the name of the person whose folder you want to open, and then click **OK**.

3 Make sure Calendar appears in the **Folder** box, and then click **OK**.

150 **To save your Calendar as a Web page**

1 On the **File** menu, click **Save as Web Page**.

2 In the **Duration** area, enter the start and end dates for which you want to save the calendar.

3 In the **File Name** box, type the name and path with which you want to save the Web page.

4 Click **Save**.

152 **To start using the Microsoft Office Internet Free/Busy Service**

1 On the **Tools** menu, click **Options**.

2 In the **Calendar** area of the **Preferences** tab, click the **Calendar Options** button.

3 In the **Advanced options** area of the **Calendar Options** dialog box, click the **Free/Busy Options** button.

4 In the **Free/Busy Options** dialog box, select the **Publish and search using Microsoft Office Internet Free/Busy Service** check box.

5 Click **OK** in the open dialog boxes.

152 **To publish your schedule to an intranet location**

1 On the **Tools** menu, click **Options**.

2 In the **Options** dialog box, click the **Calendar Options** button.

3 In the **Calendar Options** dialog box, click the **Free/Busy Options** button.

4 In the **Free/Busy Options** dialog box, select the **Publish at my location** check box, and type the name of the server where your free/busy information should be stored.

5 Click in the **Search Location** box and type the name of the server.

6 Click **OK** in the open dialog boxes.

152 **To publish your free and busy times**

1 On the **Tools** menu, click **Options**.

2 In the **Calendar** area of the **Options** dialog box, click the **Calendar Options** button.

3 In the **Advanced options** area of the **Calendar Options** dialog box, click the **Free/Busy Options** button.

4 Select the **Publish at my location** check box, and in the **Publish at my location** box, type the server location and file name.

5   Close each of the open dialog boxes.

6   On the **Tools** menu, point to **Send/Receive**, and then click **Free/Busy Information** to publish your free/busy information to your server.

7   To view your published free/busy information, open your Web browser, and in the **Address** box, type the URL of the file on the server.

Chapter 6   **Creating and Organizing a List of Contacts**

Page 156   **To create a contact entry from the Contacts folder**

●   On the toolbar, click the **New Contact** button.

156   **To create a contact entry from any Outlook folder**

1   Click the down arrow to the right of the **New** button.

2   On the drop-down menu, click **Contact**.

156   **To create multiple contacts from the same company**

1   Open a contact entry from the company you want to duplicate.

2   On the **Actions** menu, click **New Contact from Same Company**.

162   **To delete a contact entry**

1   Click the contact you want to delete.

2   On the toolbar, click the **Delete** button.

162   **To assign a category to a contact entry**

1   Open the contact entry, and click the **Categories** button.

2   In the **Available categories** list of the **Categories** dialog box, select the category you want to assign to the contact entry, and then click **OK**.

169   **To link an appointment or task to a contact entry**

1   Open the appointment or task, and click the **Contacts** button.

2   In the **Look in** box of the **Select Contacts** dialog box, click the contact folder in which the contact entry you want is stored.

3   In the **Items** list, click the contact entry to which you want to link the appointment or task.

169   **To flag a contact entry for follow up**

1   Open the contact entry you want to flag.

2   On the contact form's toolbar, click the **Follow Up** button.

173   To send a vCard through e-mail

1   Open the contact entry you want to send.

2   On the **Actions** menu, click **Forward as vCard**.

3   Address the resulting e-mail message, and then click **Send**.

176   To print a contact entry

1   Open the contact entry you want to print.

2   On the **File** menu, click **Print**.

3   In the **Print** dialog box, select a print style, and click **OK**.

180   To import Windows SharePoint Services contact entries

1   In your Web browser, open the SharePoint contacts list.

2   Click **Link to Outlook**, and then click **Yes**.

Chapter 7   Keeping Track of Information

Page 184   **To create a task from the Tasks folder**

●   On the toolbar, click the **New Task** button.

184   To create a task from any Outlook folder

1   Click the down arrow to the right of the **New** button.

2   On the drop-down menu, click **Task**.

184   To create a recurring task

1   Create a new task.

2   In the task form, click the **Recurrence** button.

3   In the **Task Recurrence** dialog box, set the recurrence options you want, and then click **OK**.

184   To set or remove a task reminder

1   In the Task form, select or clear the **Reminder** check box.

2   If setting a reminder, set the date and time you want the reminder to occur.

3   Click **OK**.

184   To modify task settings

1   On the **Tools** menu, click **Options**.

2   In the **Options** dialog box, click the **Task Options** button.

3   Set the task options you want, and then click **OK** in the open dialog boxes.

200   **To stop a task from recurring**

    1   Open the task, and click the **Recurrence** button.

    2   In the **Task Recurrence** dialog box, click the **Remove Recurrence** button.

200   **To delete a task**

    1   In the **Tasks** list, click the task you want to delete.

    2   On the toolbar, click the **Delete** button.

205   **To create a note from the Notes folder**

    1   On the toolbar, click the **New Note** button.

    2   Type the note content.

    3   Click the **Close** button to save the note.

205   **To create a note from any Outlook folder**

    1   Click the down arrow to the right of the **New** button.

    2   On the drop-down menu, click **Note**.

    3   Type the note content.

    4   Click the **Close** button to save the note.

205   **To delete a note**

    1   In the Notes folder, select the note.

    2   On the toolbar, click the **Delete** button.

207   **To change your Note view**

    ●   On the **View** menu, point to **Arrange By**, point to **Current View**, and click the view you want.

207   **To assign a category to a note**

    1   Open the note, click the **Note** icon in the upper-left corner, and click **Categories** in the drop-down list.

    2   Select the check box next to the category you want, and then click **OK**.

    3   Close the note.

207   **To forward a note**

    1   Open the note, click the **Note** icon in the upper-left corner, and click **Forward** in the drop-down list.

    2   In the **To** box, type the address of the person to whom you will forward the note, and then click **Send**.

To link a note to a contact

1   Open the note, click the **Note** icon in the upper-left corner, and click **Contacts** in the drop-down list.

2   In the **Contacts for Note** dialog box, click the **Contacts** button.

3   In the Look in box of the Select Contacts dialog box, click the contacts folder where the contact entry to which you want to link the note is stored.

4   In the **Items** list, click the contact entry you want to link to the note.

5   Click **OK**, and then click **Close**.

Working from Multiple Locations

To set up a new Outlook account

1   Click the **Start** button, and then click **Control Panel**.

2   In Control Panel, double-click the **Mail** icon.

3   On the **Server Type** page, select the type of server to which you are connecting, and then click **Next**.

4   On the **Internet E-mail Settings** page, enter the user information for the account you're setting up, click **Next**, and then click **Finish**.

5   To set up a new e-mail account or change an existing account, click **E-mail Accounts**.

6   To change the location in which Outlook stores your data files, click **Data Files**.

7   To set up multiple user profiles or change an existing profile, click **Show Profiles**.

8   Click **Close**.

To set up a dial-up connection

1   On the **Tools** menu, click **E-mail Accounts**.

2   Select the **View or change existing e-mail accounts** option, and click **Next**.

3   Click your e-mail account, and then click the **Change** button.

4   Click the **More Settings** button.

5   In the dialog box that appears, click the **Connection** tab, and select the **Connect using my phone line** option.

6   In the **Modem** area, click the **Add** button.

7   On the **Type of Connection** page of the wizard, select the **Dial-up to private network** option, and click **Next**.

8 On the **Phone Number to Dial** page, type the phone number of your ISP in the **Phone Number** box.

9 If appropriate to your situation, select the smart card option you want, and then click **Next**.

10 In the **Type a name you want for this connection** box, type a meaningful name for the connection you are creating (For example, *Company Dial-Up Connection*), and click **Finish**.

11 In the **Use the following Dial-up Networking connection** list, click the connection you just created, and then click **OK**.

12 In the **E-mail Accounts Wizard**, click **Next**, and then click **Finish**.

221 **To download messages**

● On the toolbar, click the **Send/Receive** button.

225 **To turn Cached Exchange Mode on or off**

1 On the **Tools** menu, click **E-mail Accounts**.

2 Select the **View or change existing e-mail accounts** option, and click **Next**.

3 Click **Microsoft Exchange Server**, and then click the **Change** button.

4 Select the **Use local copy of Mailbox** check box.

225 **To change the Cached Exchange Mode connection setting**

1 On the **Tools** menu, click **E-mail Accounts**.

2 Select the **View or change existing e-mail accounts** option, and click **Next**.

3 Click **Microsoft Exchange Server**, and then click the **Change** button.

4 Click the **More Settings** button.

5 In the **Microsoft Exchange Server** dialog box, click the **Advanced** tab, and select the option you want.

6 Restart Outlook.

227 **To create an offline folder**

1 On the **Tools** menu, click **E-mail Accounts**.

2 Select the **View or change existing e-mail accounts** option, and click **Next**.

3 Click your e-mail account, and then click the **Change** button.

4 Click the **More Settings** button.

5 Click the **Advanced** tab, and then click the **Offline Folder File Settings** button.

6   Click the **Disable Offline Use** button, and then click **Yes**.

7   Click the **Offline Folder File Settings** button again, and then click the **Browse** button.

8   Click the down arrow to the right of the **Look in** box, and then navigate to the folder you want to use.

9   Click **OK**. If Outlook prompts you to create the *outlook.ost* file, click **Yes**.

227   **To switch between working online and offline**

●   On the **File** menu, click **Work Offline**.

231   **To synchronize an offline folder**

1   While working online, display the contents of the folder.

2   On the **Tools** menu, point to **Send/Receive**, and click **This Folder**.

Chapter 9   **Customizing and Configuring Outlook**

Page 238   **To create a desktop shortcut to a specific Outlook pane**

1   Right-click the Outlook program file (usually in *C:\Program Files\Microsoft Office\Office2003*), and click **Create Shortcut**.

2   Right-click the shortcut, and click **Properties** on the shortcut menu.

3   In the **Target** box, type a space after the end of the path, type */select outlook:*, type another space, and then type the name of a pane to which the shortcut will be directed.

238   **To customize Outlook Today**

1   On the Advanced toolbar, click the **Outlook Today** icon.

2   Click **Customize Outlook Today**.

238   **To add a shortcut to the Shortcut pane**

1   In the **Navigation Pane**, click the **Shortcuts** icon.

2   Click **Add New Shortcut**.

3   Click the folder for which you want to create a shortcut.

242   **To display or hide a toolbar**

●   On the **View** menu, point to **Toolbars**, and then click the toolbar you want.

242   **To set menu and toolbar options**

1   On the **Tools** menu, click **Customize**.

2   On the **Options** tab, select the check boxes of the options you want, and then click **Close**.

242 **To add a command to a toolbar or menu**

> **1** On the **Tools** menu, click **Customize**.
>
> **2** Click the **Commands** tab.
>
> **3** In the **Categories** list, click the command's category.
>
> **4** In the **Commands** list, click the command, and drag it to the toolbar or menu.

242 **To remove a custom command from a toolbar or menu**

> **1** On the **Tools** menu, click **Customize**.
>
> **2** Drag the command off of the toolbar or menu.

246 **To create a Personal Folder**

> **1** On the **File** menu, point to **New**, and then click **Outlook Data File**.
>
> **2** Select **Office Outlook Personal Folders File**, and click **OK**.
>
> **3** Type a file name, and click **OK**.
>
> **4** Type a name for the folder, and click **OK**.

249 **To create a Personal Address Book**

> **1** On the **Tools** menu, click **E-mail Accounts**.
>
> **2** Select the **Add a new directory or address book** option, and click **Next**.
>
> **3** Select the **Additional Address Books** option, and click **Next**.
>
> **4** In the **Additional Address Book Types** list, click **Personal Address Book**, and then click **Next**.
>
> **5** Type the address or browse to the location where you want to add the new address book, and click the **Open** button.

249 **To create a personal distribution list**

> **1** On the **Tools** menu, click **Address Book**.
>
> **2** Click the down arrow to the right of the **Show Names from the** box, and click **Personal Address Book**.
>
> **3** On the toolbar, click the **New Entry** button.
>
> **4** In the **Put this entry** area, click the down arrow to the right of the **In the** box, and then click **Personal Address Book**.
>
> **5** In the **Select the entry type** list, click **Personal Distribution List**, and then click **OK**.
>
> **6** Type a name for the new distribution list, and click the **Add/Remove Members** button.

7   In the **Show Names from the** list, click **Personal Address Book.**

8   Hold down the Ctrl key, click the names of the contacts you want to add to the list, and then click the **Members** button.

254   **To encrypt a message**

1   On the message form's toolbar, click the **Options** button.

2   In the **Security** area, click the **Security Settings** button.

3   Select the **Encrypt message contents and attachments** check box.

254   **To digitally sign a message**

1   On the message form's toolbar, click the **Options** button.

2   In the **Security** area, click the **Security Settings** button.

3   Select the **Add digital signature to this message** check box.

254   **To send an e-mail with restricted permissions**

●   On the message form's toolbar, click the **Permission** button.

256   **To change the way Outlook handles external content**

1   On the **Tools** menu, click **Options.**

2   In the **Options** dialog box, on the Security tab, click **Change Automatic Download Settings.**

3   In the **Automatic Picture Download Settings** dialog box, select the check boxes for the options you want.

4   Click **OK** in each of the open dialog boxes to save your settings.

256   **To view the blocked content in an individual e-mail message:**

1   In the message, click the **InfoBar.**

2   On the shortcut menu, click **Show Blocked Content.**

257   **To set advanced e-mail options**

1   On the **Tools** menu, click **Options.**

2   Click the **E-mail Options** button.

3   Click the **Advanced E-mail Options** button.

4   Set the options you want, and then click **OK** in the open dialog boxes.

I

261 **To turn off desktop alerts**

> **1** On the **Tools** menu, click **Options**.
>
> **2** On the **Preferences** tab, click the **E-Mail Options** button.
>
> **3** Click the **Advanced E-mail Options** button.
>
> **4** Clear the **Display a New Mail Desktop Alert** check box.
>
> **5** Click **OK** in the open dialog boxes.

261 **To customize desktop alert settings**

> **1** On the **Tools** menu, click **Options**.
>
> **2** On the **Preferences** tab, click the **E-Mail Options** button.
>
> **3** Click the **Advanced E-mail Options** button.
>
> **4** Click the **Desktop Alert Settings** button.
>
> **5** Change the settings as you want.
>
> **6** Click **OK** in the open dialog boxes.

261 **To flag, delete, or mark a message as read by using a desktop alert**

> **1** In the desktop alert, click the **Options** button.
>
> **2** Click **Flag Item, Delete Item,** or **Mark as Read.**

264 **To manage Windows SharePoint Services alerts**

> **1** On the **Tools** menu, click **Rules and Alerts.**
>
> **2** Click the **Manage Alerts** tab.

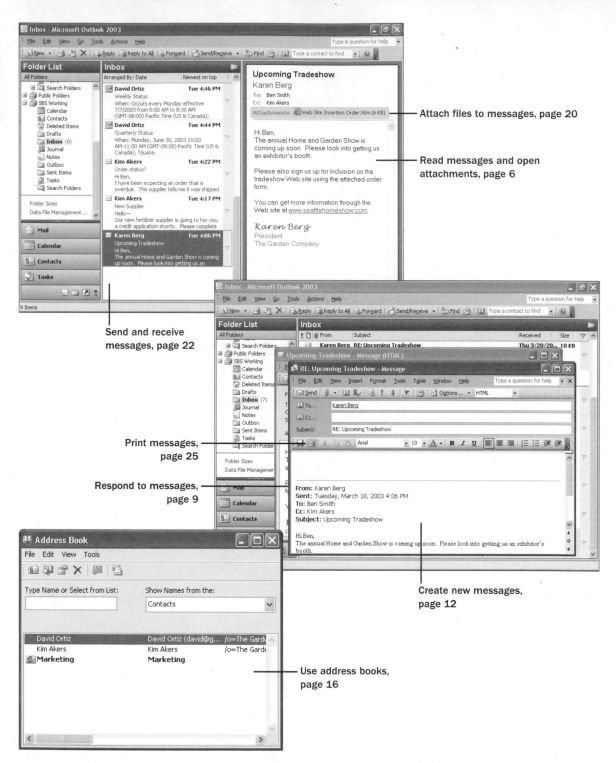

Attach files to messages, page 20

Read messages and open attachments, page 6

Send and receive messages, page 22

Print messages, page 25

Respond to messages, page 9

Create new messages, page 12

Use address books, page 16

Chapter 1 at a Glance

1 Working with Outlook

In this chapter you will learn to:

✔ Start Outlook for the first time.

✔ Read messages and open attachments.

✔ Respond to messages.

✔ Create new messages.

✔ Use address books.

✔ Attach files to messages.

✔ Send and receive messages.

✔ Print messages.

✔ Create and send instant messages.

Microsoft Office Outlook 2003 is a personal information management program that helps you manage your time and information more effectively and enables you to share information and collaborate with others more easily.

Electronic mail, or *e-mail*, is an essential form of communication in today's workplace. In Outlook, you will find all the tools you need to use e-mail effectively and manage your electronic messages. With Outlook, you can:

■ Send and receive e-mail messages.

■ Attach files to your messages.

■ Create and manage an address book.

■ Organize and archive your messages.

■ Personalize your messages.

You can also use Outlook to send *instant messages* to your online contacts.

This chapter first discusses the ways Outlook can be set up and what to expect when you initially start the program. Then you'll learn how to create, read, respond to, and print messages; attach files to messages and open attachments; and create and use an address book. Finally, you will learn how to create and send instant messages from within Outlook.

See Also   Do you need only a quick refresher on the topics in this chapter? See the Quick Reference entries on pages xxvii–xxix.

Important Before you can use the practice files in this chapter, you need to install them from the book's companion CD to their default location. See "Using the Book's CD-ROM" on page xiii for more information.

Starting Outlook for the First Time

Outlook 2003 supports e-mail accounts that work with a computer running *Microsoft Exchange Server* or a computer set up as an *Internet mail* server. This topic discusses these two types of accounts and explains what you might expect to see the first time you start Outlook.

If you are connected to a *local area network (LAN)* that includes a computer running Microsoft Exchange Server, you send and receive e-mail both internally (within your organization) and externally (over the Internet) using that server. Your network or system administrator will supply the information you need to set up an Exchange e-mail account. With Outlook 2003, you can connect to your Exchange Server from anywhere you can connect to the Internet.

If you are working on a stand-alone computer or on a network that does not have its own mail server, using Internet mail requires that you have an e-mail account with an *Internet Service Provider (ISP)*. You connect to the ISP using a modem and a phone line, a high-speed connection such as DSL or cable, or through a LAN, as follows:

- If you are using a modem, you can manually establish a connection when you need it, or you can set up *dial-up networking* to automatically connect whenever you start Outlook. Your ISP can provide the phone number, modem settings, and any other special information you need for both types of connection.

- If you are connected to a LAN, it must be configured to provide access to your ISP from your computer. Your network or system administrator can provide you with the appropriate information to gain access to Internet mail through the LAN.

Regardless of how you connect to your ISP, to send and receive Internet mail, you will need to know the names of your incoming and outgoing e-mail servers, your account name, and your password.

Different Types of Internet Mail Accounts

Outlook 2003 supports three types of Internet mail accounts—POP3, IMAP, and HTTP.

- *Post Office Protocol 3 (POP3)* is a type of e-mail account commonly provided by ISPs. With a POP3 account, you connect to an e-mail server, and download your messages to your local computer.

- *Internet Message Access Protocol (IMAP)* is similar to POP3 except that your messages are stored on the e-mail server. You connect to the server to read the message headers, and select which messages you want to download to your local computer.

- *Hypertext Transfer Protocol (HTTP)* is used whenever you access Web pages from the Internet. When HTTP is used as an e-mail protocol, messages are stored, retrieved, and displayed as individual Web pages. Hotmail is an example of an HTTP e-mail account.

When you start Outlook 2003 for the first time, what you see depends on whether you have upgraded to Outlook 2003 from a previous version or are using it on your computer for the first time:

- Upgrading to Outlook 2003. If you have used a previous version of Outlook on your computer, you already have an Outlook *profile*. This profile is a collection of all the data necessary to access one or more e-mail accounts and address books. In this case, Outlook 2003 picks up your existing profile settings, and you don't have to re-set them.

- Using Outlook for the first time. If this is the first time you are using Outlook on your computer, you will be asked to create a profile. To complete this step, you will need specific information about your e-mail account, including your account name, your password, and the names of the incoming and outgoing e-mail servers that handle your account. Your system administrator or ISP can provide you with this information.

If you are using Outlook for the first time on your computer, follow these steps to set up your Outlook profile.

BE SURE TO install and activate Microsoft Office Outlook 2003 before beginning this exercise.

1 Click the **Start** button, point to **All Programs**, then **Microsoft Office**, and then click **Microsoft Office Outlook 2003**.

Outlook starts and displays the Outlook 2003 Startup Wizard.

2 Click **Next**.

The Account Configuration dialog box appears with the Yes option selected.

3 Click **Next**.

The Server Type dialog box appears.

4 Select the option that corresponds to your e-mail account, and click **Next**.

An account settings dialog box appears. The content of this dialog box is determined by the type of e-mail account you selected in the Server Type dialog box.

5 Complete the wizard by entering the information provided by your system administrator or ISP.

When you finish the wizard, the Outlook program window appears.

6 If this is the first time you've started a Microsoft Office program on your computer, you are prompted to enter your full name and initials in the **User Name** dialog box. This information is used to identify and track changes that you make within Office documents. Enter the requested information, and click **OK**.

Important If you upgraded to Outlook 2003 from an earlier version, any custom settings you made for your old version of the program carry over to the new version. As a result, as you work your way through the exercises in this book, some of the instructions might not work quite the same way for you, and your screen might not look the same as the book's graphics. The instructions and graphics are based on a default installation of Outlook on a networked computer with an Exchange e-mail account. If you are not working on a network or you have changed the default settings, don't worry. You will still be able to follow along with the exercises, but you might occasionally have to reverse a setting or skip a step. (For example, if AutoPreview is already active on your screen, you would skip the step to turn on AutoPreview.)

The Navigation Pane

New In
Office 2003
Navigation
Pane

The new Navigation Pane replaces the Outlook Bar from previous versions of Outlook. The Navigation Pane provides quick access to Outlook's components and folders. It can display the Mail, Calendar, Contacts, Tasks, Notes, Journal or Shortcuts pane or the Folder List, which includes Search Folders and Public Folders. The Calendar, Contacts, Tasks, Notes, and Journal panes include easy-to-use links to share your folders or open other Outlooks users' shared folders.

To hide or show the Navigation Pane:

■   On the **View** menu, click **Navigation Pane**.

To make the Navigation Pane taller or shorter:

■   Point to the top of the Navigation Pane so that the cursor becomes a double-headed arrow and drag up or down.

Navigation Pane items are displayed in order, as large buttons in the upper rows of the pane, and then as small buttons on the bottom row. Any buttons the Navigation Pane is not big enough to display are available on the "Configure buttons" button's shortcut menu.

To change which buttons the Navigation Pane displays and their order:

1   Click the **Configure buttons** button, and on the shortcut menu, click **Navigation Pane Options**.

2   To add or remove a button, select or clear its check box.

3   To change the position of a button, click its name and then click the **Move Up** or **Move Down** button until the buttons are in the order you want.

See Also   For more information about customizing navigation in Outlook, see Chapter 9, "Customizing and Configuring Outlook."

Reading Messages and Opening Attachments

Microsoft Office Specialist

When you start Outlook, any new messages on your *e-mail server* are displayed in your Inbox. With Outlook, you can view and read your messages in several ways:

- You can scan for your most important messages by using *AutoPreview*, which displays the first three lines of each message in your Inbox.

- You can read a message without opening it by viewing it in the *Reading Pane*.

- You can open the message in its own window for easier reading by double-clicking the message in the Inbox.

E-mail messages can contain many types of files as *attachments*. For example, a colleague might send a Microsoft Word document to you by attaching it to an e-mail message. You can open these files from the Reading Pane or from an open message.

The examples in this book center around a fictitious plant and garden accessories store called The Garden Company. The practice files used in this book are the messages and other items of Ben Smith, the administrative assistant for the Garden Company. In this exercise, you will preview a message, open a message, and open an attachment.

USE the *SBSWorking* data file in the practice file folder for this topic. This practice file is located in the *My Documents\Microsoft Press\Outlook 2003 SBS\Working* folder and can also be accessed by clicking *Start/All Programs/Microsoft Press/Outlook 2003 Step by Step*.
BE SURE TO start Outlook before beginning this exercise.
OPEN the *SBSWorking* data file from within Outlook.

Maximize

1   If the Outlook window does not fill your screen, click the **Maximize** button in the upper-right corner of the program window so you can see its contents.

Folder List

2   In the **Navigation Pane** on the left side of the window, click the **Folder List** icon.

Expand

3   In the **Folder List** click the **Expand** button next to the *SBS Working* folder and then click the Inbox in the *SBS Working* folder.

Expand buttons

Navigation Pane

Toolbar

Reading Pane

You now see the initial practice files for this course.

4   If necessary, move the vertical divider between the center and right panes so you can see the contents as shown in the graphic above.

5   On the **View** menu, click **AutoPreview**.

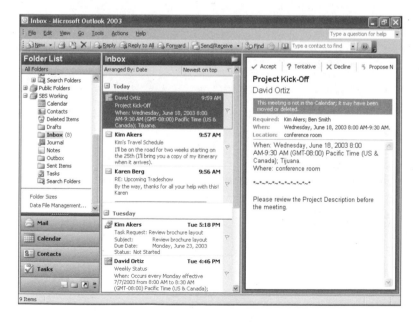

You can now see up to three lines of each of each message in your Inbox.

6 In the SBS Working Inbox, locate the original **Upcoming Tradeshow** message (not the later reply) from Karen Berg, the owner of The Garden Company. Then click the message to display it in the Reading Pane.

Message header

Attached file

New in
Office 2003
Reading Pane

Using the scroll bar if necessary, you can see the full content of the message in the Reading Pane. Note that the Reading Pane shows the full *message header* (the information that appears at the top of the e-mail message, including the subject, sender, and recipients) and the names of any attached files.

7 In the message header, double-click **Web Site Insertion Order.htm** to open the attachment.

8 If you see a message warning you about opening attachments, click the **Open** button.

The Web Site Insertion Order form appears in your default Web browser.

9 Click the **Inbox** taskbar button to return to that folder without closing the e-mail message.

10 On the **View** menu, point to **Reading Pane** and then click **Bottom**.

The Reading Pane now appears at the bottom of the Outlook window rather than on the right side.

11 On the **View** menu, point to **Reading Pane** and then click **Off** to close the Reading Pane entirely.

You can now see more of the messages in the folder at a glance.

12 Double-click the **Upcoming Tradeshow** message to open it.

The message appears in its own Message window.

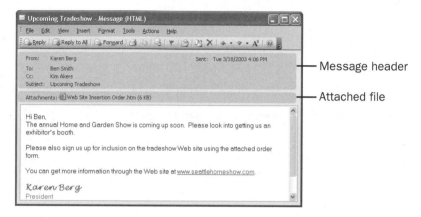

— Message header

— Attached file

Note the message header and the attached file at the top.

Restore Down

Don't worry if your window is not the same size as this one. As with other windows, you can size Outlook windows to suit the way you work by using the Maximize and Restore Down buttons, or by dragging the window's frame.

Close

13 Click the **Close** button to close the Upcoming Tradeshow message window.

Responding to Messages

Microsoft Office Specialist

You can respond to e-mail messages in different ways. You can reply only to the person who sent the message, or you can reply to the person who sent the message and all the people to whom the original message was addressed. Whether you reply to only the sender or to everyone, your reply does not include any files that were attached to the original message.

You can forward a message you have received to anyone, not just the person who originally sent the message or any of the other recipients. A forwarded message includes any files that were attached to the original message.

In this exercise, you will reply to and forward messages.

USE the *SBSWorking* data file in the practice file folder for this topic. This practice file is located in the *My Documents\Microsoft Press\Outlook 2003 SBS\Working* folder and can also be accessed by clicking *Start/All Programs/Microsoft Press/Outlook 2003 Step by Step*.
BE SURE TO start Outlook and open the *SBSWorking* data file before beginning this exercise.
OPEN the *Upcoming Tradeshow* message in the *SBS Working* Inbox.

1 Look at the header information at the top of the Message window.

Note that this message was sent to Ben Smith, and was copied to Kim Akers, the head buyer for The Garden Company. The message also includes an attachment.

2 On the Message window Standard toolbar, click the **Reply** button.

The Reply Message *form* is displayed on your screen.

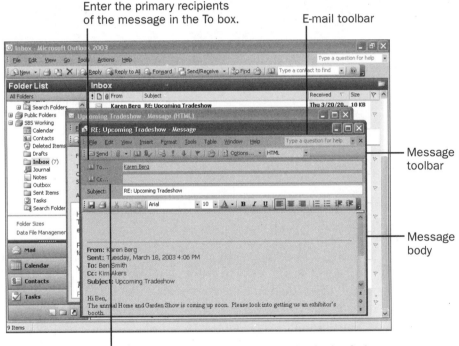

Enter the primary recipients of the message in the To box.

E-mail toolbar

Message toolbar

Message body

Enter the recipients of courtesy copies in the Cc box.

Note that the reply will be sent only to Karen Berg and that the attachment is not included. Note also that a prefix, *RE:*, has been added to the subject line. This prefix indicates that this is a response to an earlier message.

New in
Office 2003
Word as your
e-mail editor
simplifications

Tip   If Microsoft Word is your default e-mail editor, the Reply form displays Word's new E-mail toolbar in addition to Outlook's Standard toolbar. The E-mail toolbar groups the e-mail-related buttons from the Standard and Formatting toolbars, so you have more room to work.

See Also   For more information, see "Customizing Menus and Toolbars" in Chapter 9, "Customizing and Configuring Outlook."

---

3   With the insertion point in the body of the message, type **What size booth would you like?**

4   Click the **Send** button.

The reply is sent to Karen Berg.

Important   Because the e-mail addresses in these exercises are fictitious, any messages you send to these addresses will be returned to you as undeliverable. Simply delete any returned message by clicking it and then clicking the Delete button.

5   If the original message closes, reopen it from the practice file Inbox.

Tip   You can instruct Outlook to close an open message when you respond to it. On the Tools menu, click Options. On the Preferences tab, click the E-mail Options button. In the E-mail Options dialog box, select the "Close original message on reply or forward" check box, and then click OK in each dialog box to close it.

6   On the toolbar, click the **Reply to All** button.

The Reply Message form appears. You can see from the message header that this reply will be sent to both Karen Berg and Kim Akers. Again, the attachment is not included.

7   Type **I faxed the form to the show organizers.**

8   Click the **Send** button.

The reply is sent to Karen Berg and Kim Akers.

9   Reopen the original e-mail if necessary.

10   On the toolbar, click the **Forward** button.

The Forward Message form appears.

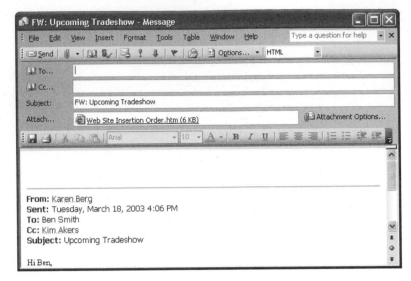

Note that the address lines are blank and that the attachment is included. Note also that a prefix, *FW:*, has been added to the subject line. This prefix indicates that this is a forwarded message.

11 In the **To** box, type your own e-mail address.

12 Press the Tab key until you get to the message body, type You might be interested in this!, and then click the **Send** button.

New in
Office 2003
Desktop Alerts

The message is forwarded to you. When you receive the message, a small transparent notification called a *desktop alert* pops up in the lower-right corner of your screen. You can hold the mouse over the desktop alert to solidify the box and read the first few lines of the message, click the alert to open the message, or click one of the buttons in the box to flag the message for follow-up, delete it, or mark it as read.

13 When the message arrives in your Inbox, open it and examine the message header.

Note how the subject line and attachment appear.

Close

14 If necessary, close the open Message window by clicking its **Close** button.

See Also You can send instant replies to meeting requests and messages with voting buttons. For more information see "Changing Message Settings and Delivery Options" in Chapter 2, "Managing E-Mail Messages" and "Responding to Meeting Requests" in Chapter 5, "Scheduling and Managing Meetings."

Creating New Messages

Microsoft
Office
Specialist

With Outlook, communicating by e-mail is quick and easy. You can send messages to people in your office and at other locations. You can personalize your messages using

Outlook's many formatting options; you can also embed hyperlinks in and attach files to your messages.

If you have installed Microsoft Office Word 2003, Outlook can use Word as its default e-mail editor. Many of Word's powerful text-editing capabilities, including styles, tables, and themes, are available to you as you create messages in Outlook. Word will check your spelling as you type, correcting many errors automatically. You can also have Word check the spelling of your message when you send it.

Important   The exercises in this book assume that you are using Word as your default e-mail editor.

Tip   If Word is not your default e-mail editor and you would like it to be, on the Tools menu, click Options. Click the Mail Format tab, and select the "Use Microsoft Word to edit e-mail messages" check box. To turn off Word as your default e-mail editor, make sure the check box is cleared.

In this exercise, you will compose and send a new e-mail message. You can complete this exercise from the practice file Inbox or your own.

OPEN the Inbox.

New Mail
Message

1   On the toolbar, click the **New Mail Message** button.

An Untitled Message form appears. Take a few minutes to investigate the Message window menus and commands. If you are familiar with Word, you will recognize many of them.

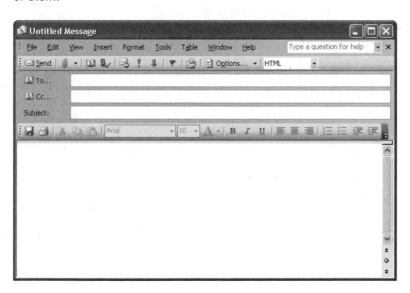

Tip By clicking the down arrow to the right of the New Mail Message button, you can choose to create other types of Outlook items such as appointments, contacts, tasks, notes, or faxes, as well as organizational items such as folders and data files.

2 In the **To** box, type Karen@gardenco.msn.com. Then type ; (a semi-colon), and type Kim@gardenco.msn.com.

Tip By default, Outlook requires that you separate multiple e-mail addresses with semicolons. If you prefer, you can instruct Outlook to accept both semicolons and commas. To do this, on the Tools menu, click Options. On the Preferences tab, click the E-mail Options button, and then click the Advanced E-mail Options button. Select the "Allow comma as address separator" check box, and then click OK to close each window.

If your recipient's address is in your *address book* or you've typed it in a message header before, Outlook automatically completes the address for you, and pressing the ⌨Tab key inserts the entry. If there are multiple matches, Outlook presents a list of items that match what you've typed so far. Use the arrow keys to select the item you want, and press the Enter key.

Tip If you are working on a network that uses Exchange Server, when you send messages to other people on your network, you can type just the part of the address that is to the left of the @ sign. The remaining part of the address identifies the server that handles the e-mail account, so within an organization, the server name is not needed.

3 Press ⌨Tab, and in the **Cc** box, type your own e-mail address.

Tip If you want to send a copy of a message to a person without the other recipients being aware of it, you can send a "blind" copy. Display the Bcc box by clicking the arrow to the right of the Options button, and then clicking Bcc. Then type the person's e-mail address in the Bcc box.

4 Press the ⌨Tab key to move to the **Subject** box, and type **Today's schedule**.

5 Press ⌨Tab again, and type **Here are the people who will be working today.** Then press ⌨Enter twice.

Important After your message has been open for a period of time, Outlook saves a *draft* of it in the Drafts folder so that any work you have done is saved if you are somehow disconnected from Outlook before you send the message. If you close a message without sending it, Outlook asks you if you want to save the message in the Drafts folder. To find these messages later, click the Drafts folder under your name in the All Mail Folders list. If the All Mail Folders list is not visible, click the Mail icon on the Navigation Pane to display it.

6   On the **Table** menu, point to **Insert**, and then click **Table**.

Word's Insert Table dialog box appears.

7   Change the number of columns to **4**, and click **OK**.

A table appears in your message.

8   Fill in the cells of the table as shown here, pressing [Tab] to move from cell to cell.

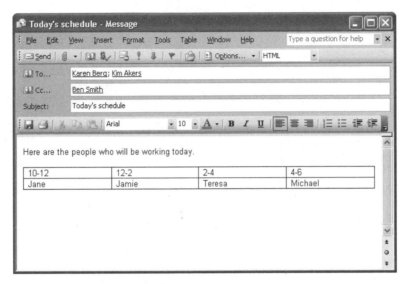

9   Click the **Send** button.

The Message form closes, and the message is sent on its way.

Recalling Messages

If you are connected to a network that uses Microsoft Exchange Server, you can recall messages you've sent. For example, if you discover errors in a message you've sent, you can recall the message so that you can correct the error and resend the message.

To recall a message:

1   In the *Sent Items* folder, open the message you want to recall.

2   On the **Actions** menu, click **Recall This Message**.

3   Select whether you want to delete unread copies of the message or delete unread copies and replace them with a new message, and then click **OK**.

You can recall or replace a message only if its recipient is logged on, using Microsoft Outlook, and has not yet read the message or moved it from the Inbox.

Using Address Books

You can store e-mail addresses along with other contact information in the Outlook address book so you don't have to type them each time you send a message. Instead, you simply click the To button in the Message form, and then select recipients by name.

If you are using Outlook with Exchange Server, an Exchange address book called the *Global Address List* might already be available to you. This resource contains the e-mail addresses of all the people on your network. If a Global Address List is available, Outlook will use this as your default address book. Because the Global Address List is maintained by your system administrator, you cannot add to it; you must use another address book to create any entries not included in that list. By default, entries you create are stored in your *Contacts* folder, which is a type of address book.

Address book entries can be for an individual contact or for a *distribution list*— a group of individual addresses stored as a single entity. For example, to facilitate communication with a team, you might create a distribution list including the addresses for all the people working on a particular project.

Tip   With or without an address book, you can address messages by typing the full address into the To, Cc, or Bcc boxes in the Message form.

In this exercise, you will create address book entries, create a distribution list, and address a message from the address book.

1   On the **Tools** menu, click **Address Book**.

The Address Book window appears. If you are working on a network, the "Show Names from the" setting is *Global Address List*. Otherwise, it is *Contacts*.

2   Click the down arrow to the right of the **Show Names from the** box, and click **Contacts** (not **All Contacts**) in the drop-down list.

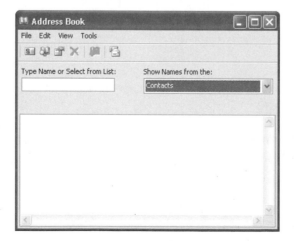

New Entry

3   On the toolbar, click the **New Entry** button.

The New Entry dialog box appears.

4   In the **Select the entry type** box, click **New Contact**, and then click **OK**.

A new Contact form appears.

5   In the **Full Name** box, type **David Ortiz**.

6   In the **E-mail** box, type **David@gardenco.msn.com**.

7   Click the **Save and Close** button.

The Contact form closes, and the contact appears in the Address Book window.

8   Now you'll add another entry. Click the **New Entry** button, click **New Contact**, and then click **OK**.

The Contact form appears.

9   In the **Full Name** box, type **Kim Akers**.

10   In the **E-mail** box, type **Kim@gardenco.msn.com**.

11   Press the ⌨Tab key, and in the **Display as** box, delete the e-mail address and parentheses so that the box contains only the name *Kim Akers*.

12   Click the **Save and Close** button.

The Contact form closes, and the contact appears in the Address Book window.

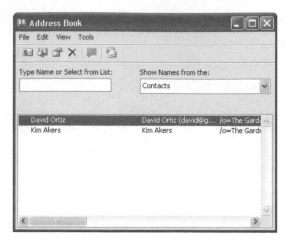

13 Now you'll create a distribution list. Click the **New Entry** button, click **New Distribution List**, and then click **OK**.

The Distribution List form appears.

Maximize

Tip If a form window is too small to work with easily, you can click the Maximize button or size it by dragging its frame.

14 In the **Name** box, type **Marketing**, and then click the **Select Members** button.

The Select Members dialog box appears.

15 If necessary, click the down arrow to the right of the **Show Names from the** box, and click **Contacts** in the drop-down list.

16 With David Ortiz selected in the **Name** list, click the **Members** button.

David Ortiz is added to the distribution list.

17 In the **Name** list, click **Kim Akers**, and click the **Members** button.

Kim Akers is added to the distribution list.

Tip To add multiple names to the distribution list simultaneously, click a name in the Name list, hold down the Ctrl key, click any additional names you want to add, and then click the Members button.

18 Click **OK** to close the **Select Members** dialog box.

You return to the Distribution List form.

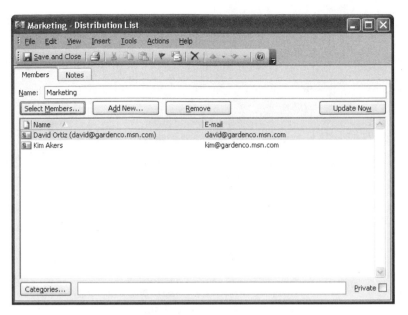

19 Click the **Save and Close** button.

The Distribution List form closes, and the Address Book window appears with the contacts and distribution list shown.

Close

20 Click the **Close** button.

The Address Book window closes.

New Mail
Message

21 On the toolbar, click the **New Mail Message** button.

A new, blank Message form opens.

22 Click the **To** button in the message header.

The Select Names dialog box appears.

23 If necessary, change the **Show Names from the** setting to **Contacts**.

24 In the **Name** list, click **Kim Akers,** and then click the **To** button.

Kim's name is added to the list of recipients in the To box.

25 In the **Name** list, click **Marketing,** and then click the **Cc** button.

The distribution list's name is added to the list of recipients in the Cc box.

Tip   You can type distribution list names in the To and Cc boxes just like any other e-mail address. Outlook will then match what you type with the name in your address book and will display the name as bold and underlined, which indicates that the name represents a distribution list rather than an individual address.

26 Click **OK**.

The Select Names dialog box closes, and the recipient names are added to the To and Cc boxes on the Message form.

27 Close the message without sending it. When prompted to save it, click **No**.

Attaching Files to Messages

Microsoft Office Specialist

A convenient way to distribute files such as Word documents or Excel spreadsheets to other people or groups of people is to attach them to an e-mail message. Outlook makes it easy to attach files to your messages.

Important   You can attach any type of file to an e-mail message, but when sending attachments, be sure that your recipients have the software required to open your file. For example, if you are attaching a Word document, your recipients must have Word installed on their computers to open your attachment.

In this exercise, you will attach a Word document to an e-mail message.

USE the *Attachment* document in the practice file folder for this topic. This practice file is located in the *My Documents\Microsoft Press\Outlook 2003 SBS\Working\Attach* folder and can also be accessed by clicking *Start/All Programs/Microsoft Press/Outlook 2003 Step by Step*.

New Mail
Message

1 On the toolbar, click the **New Mail Message** button.

A new, blank Message form appears.

2 In the **To** box, type your own e-mail address.

3 Click in the **Subject** box, and type First Draft.

4 Press the ⌷Tab⌷ key, and then type Here is a document for your review.

5 Press ⌷Enter⌷ to move to the next line.

Insert File

6 On the Message form's toolbar, click the **Insert File** button (not the down arrow to the right of the button).

The Insert File dialog box appears.

Tip You can embed a hyperlink to a Web site in an e-mail message simply by including the site's *uniform resource locator (URL)*. To embed a hyperlink, simply type the URL (for example, *www.microsoft.com*) followed by a space. Outlook formats the URL to appear as a link. Your recipients can simply click the link in the message to open the Web page.

7 Browse to the practice file folder, click the **Attachment** document, and then click the **Insert** button.

The document appears in the Attach box in the message header.

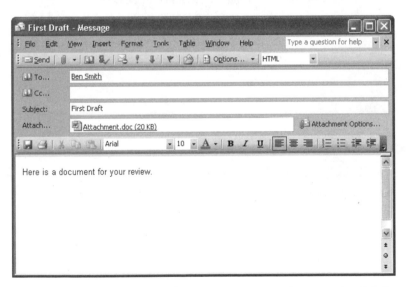

8 Close the message without sending it. If prompted to save it, click **No**.

Sending Attachments for Shared Review

New In
Office 2003
Live
Attachments

When you send an e-mail attachment with the default options, it is sent as an independent file that each recipient can edit separately. If your team is running Microsoft Windows SharePoint Services, you have the option of sending Microsoft Office System documents as *shared attachments* (also known as *live attachments*). Shared attachments are saved on the SharePoint Document Workspace Web site, which is a team Web site where your group can collaborate to work on files and discuss a project. When working on shared files in a Document Workspace, multiple people can work on a single version of a file rather than sending the document back and forth for editing.

To send a shared attachment:

1   Create and address a message and attach an Office document to it.

2   In the message header, click the **Attachment Options** button.

     The Attachment Options task pane opens.

3   In the **Attachments Options** task pane, select the **Shared attachments** option.

4   In the **Create Document Workspace at** box, type the URL for the Document Workspace server. You must have appropriate permissions to access this server.

     If a Document Workspace site does not already exist at the specified URL, it will be created for you.

5   Send the message.

Sending and Receiving Messages

Depending on your e-mail account and network configuration, messages you send could go out instantaneously or be kept in your Outbox until you choose to send them. If you are connected to the Internet, your messages will usually go out instantaneously. If you are not connected to the Internet (for example, if you use a dial-up connection), your messages will typically be kept in your Outbox until you connect.

How you receive messages also depends on your type of e-mail account and your Outlook configuration. Outlook might check for new messages periodically and download them automatically. Or, you might need to manually check for new messages.

Copies of messages you send are kept in the Sent Items folder by default. To see these messages, click the Sent Items folders in your mailbox in the Mail pane or Folder List.

Tip   If you do not want to keep copies of your sent messages, on the Tools menu, click Options, click the E-mail Options button, clear the "Save copies of messages in Sent Items folder" check box, and click OK.

In this exercise, you will send a message, check for new messages, and delete a message.

BE SURE TO start this exercise in your own Inbox.

New Mail
Message

1   On the toolbar, click the **New Mail Message** button.

A new Message form appears.

2   In the **To** box, type your own e-mail address.

3   Click in the **Subject** box, and type **Sending and Receiving Test**.

4   Press the Tab key, and in the message body, type **This is a test.** Then click the **Send** button.

The message closes.

Mail

5   If the **Mail** pane is not open, click the **Mail** icon on the Navigation Pane.

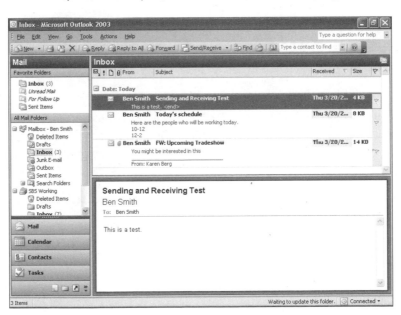

6 In the **All Mail Folders** list, click the **Outbox** folder under your own mailbox.

The contents of the Outbox are displayed. If the message you sent appears in the Outbox, you must send the message manually. If the Outbox is empty, your message was sent automatically.

 7 To send any messages in your Outbox and check for new messages on your e-mail server, click the **Send/Receive** button on the toolbar.

Outlook connects to your e-mail server to send and receive messages. Depending on your setup, it might access your modem and connection line. When your message is sent, it disappears from the Outbox. When new messages are received, they appear in your Inbox.

8 In the Favorite Folders list, click **Inbox** to see your new message(s).

The contents of the Inbox are displayed.

Multiple E-Mail Accounts

With Outlook, you can get all your e-mail in one place by configuring more than one account in your profile. To add an e-mail account to your profile:

1 On the **Tools** menu, click **E-mail Accounts** to start the E-mail Accounts Wizard.

2 Select the **Add a new e-mail account** option, and then click **Next**.

3 Select the appropriate e-mail server type option, and then click **Next**.

4 Enter the required server and account settings, and then click **Next**.

5 Click **Finish** to close the E-mail Accounts Wizard.

If you have more than one e-mail account in your profile, you can send your mail from any of your accounts. On the E-mail toolbar in the Message form, click the down arrow to the right of the Accounts button, and then click the account you want in the drop-down list. The Accounts button is only visible when multiple accounts are configured.

Printing Messages

Microsoft Office Specialist

There might be occasions when you need a hard copy, or printout, of an e-mail message. For example, you might need to print the directions to an afternoon appointment or distribute copies of a message at a meeting. With Outlook, you can print your e-mail messages in much the same way you would any other document.

Depending on the format (*HTML*, *Rich Text*, or *Plain Text*) of the message you want to print, you can set a number of page setup options, including paper size, margins, and orientation. You can also use Print Preview to see how a message will appear when printed. (Print Preview is not available for messages in HTML format.)

See Also   For more information about Outlook e-mail message formats, see "Formatting Messages" in Chapter 2, "Managing E-Mail Messages."

In this exercise, you will change the page setup for a message and then print it.

USE the *SBSWorking* data file in the practice file folder for this topic. This practice file is located in the *My Documents\Microsoft Press\Outlook 2003 SBS\Working* folder and can also be accessed by clicking *Start/All Programs/Microsoft Press/Outlook 2003 Step by Step*.
BE SURE TO start Outlook, open the *SBSWorking* data file, and install a printer before beginning this exercise.
OPEN the *Upcoming Tradeshow* message in the *SBS Working* Inbox.

1   On the message window's **File** menu, point to **Page Setup**, and click **Memo Style**.

The Page Setup dialog box appears.

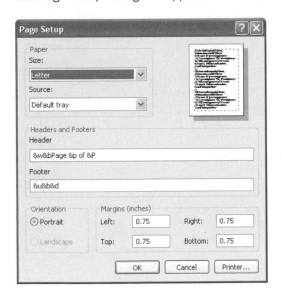

2   In the **Left** box, type **1.0** to set the left margin to 1 inch, and click **OK**.

The Page Setup dialog box closes, and your new settings are now in effect for this message.

3   On the **File** menu, click **Print**.

The message is printed with the default print options.

CLOSE the *Upcoming Tradeshow* message.

Troubleshooting   If the Save As dialog appears, you do not have a printer installed. If you are working on a network, your administrator can provide the information you need to install a printer. If you are working on a stand-alone computer, click the Start button, and then click "Printers and Faxes." Then under "Printer tasks" click "Add a printer," and follow the wizard's instructions.

Tip   You can change print options in the Print dialog box. To display the Print dialog box, on the File menu, click Print.

Creating and Sending Instant Messages

Microsoft Office Specialist

You can communicate with your contacts in real time with *instant messages*. Instant messaging is a private online chat method. After you establish a connection with someone who is online and using instant messaging, messages you send to that person appear on his or her screen instantly. Likewise, you see responses from that person instantly on your screen. Instant messaging is especially useful for brief exchanges and can be much more immediate than e-mail. By default, Outlook supports instant messaging using Microsoft MSN Messenger Service or Microsoft Exchange Instant Messaging Service. When Outlook starts, you are automatically logged on to the service you installed.

Before you can use instant messaging, you must obtain the instant messaging addresses of the people you want to communicate with, and add those addresses to the Outlook Contact forms of those people. Then they have to tell their instant messaging programs to accept messages from your address.

After this setup work is done, when you log on to your instant messaging service, you can see whether a contact is online. A contact's online status is displayed in the InfoBar on the Contact form and on any e-mail address associated with the contact. You can choose how your status appears to others. For example, if you need to step away from your desk, you can set your status to *Be Right Back* so that any contacts who are online can see that you are temporarily unavailable.

Important   For this exercise, you will need the assistance of a co-worker or friend who is using MSN Messenger or Exchange Instant Messaging Service. You must have already added that person to your MSN Messenger contacts, and that person must have accepted your request to add him or her. For help with any of these tasks, refer to the MSN Messenger online Help.

In this exercise, you will create and send instant messages.

BE SURE TO have the person to whom you want to send an instant message log on to their IM account before beginning this exercise.

1   On the **Tools** menu, click **Options**.

2   In the **Options** dialog box, click the **Other** tab.

3   Under **Person Names**, select **Enable the Person Names Smart Tag** check box, and then select the **Display Messenger Status in the From field** check box.

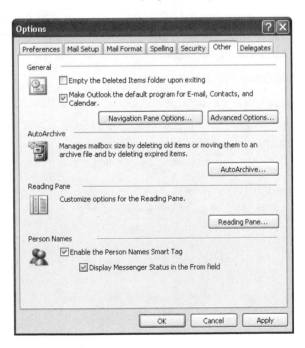

4 Click **OK**.

Tip When smart tags appear next to your contacts' names in messages, the smart tags indicate their Online status.

Contacts icon

5 In the Navigation Pane, click the **Contacts** icon.

The contents of the Contacts folder are displayed.

New Contact

6 If you already have a contact entry for the person who is assisting you with this exercise, double-click that entry. If you do not have a contact entry for that person, click the **New Contact** button.

The Contact form opens.

7 If you are creating a new contact, in the **Full Name** box, type the person's name.

8 Click in the **IM address** box, and type the e-mail address the person uses for instant messaging.

Note that this address might not be the same address used for e-mail correspondence. You'll need to get this information from the person you want to contact using instant messaging.

9 Click the **Save and Close** button.

The contact information is saved.

Person Names
Smart Tag

10 In a message window or the Reading Pane, click the contact's **Person Names Smart Tag** next to their name on the **From**, **To** or **CC** line, and then on the shortcut menu click **Send Instant Message**.

The Instant Message window appears.

11 In the message box, type Hello, and click the **Send** button.

The message is sent. It appears in an Instant Message window on your contact's screen. The status bar indicates when your contact is typing a message. Wait for a reply, and when you receive it, try sending a few more messages.

CLOSE the instant messaging window.
BE SURE TO return Outlook to its default state. Turn AutoPreview off and turn the Reading Pane on, at the right side of the window. Then close the *SBS Working* data file.

Key Points

- Messages to you appear in your Inbox. You can see the first few lines of each message in AutoPreview, open a message in its own window, or preview messages in the Reading Pane.

- You can reply to the sender or to the sender and all other recipients using the Reply and Reply to All buttons. A copy of each e-mail message you send is stored in the Sent Mail folder.

- You can add attachments to your messages using the Insert File button.

- You can store e-mail addresses in an address book so that when you send a message, you can click the To button in the Message form and then select recipients by name.

- You can send instant messages to your contacts who have also added you to their contact list by using the Person Names Smart Tag.

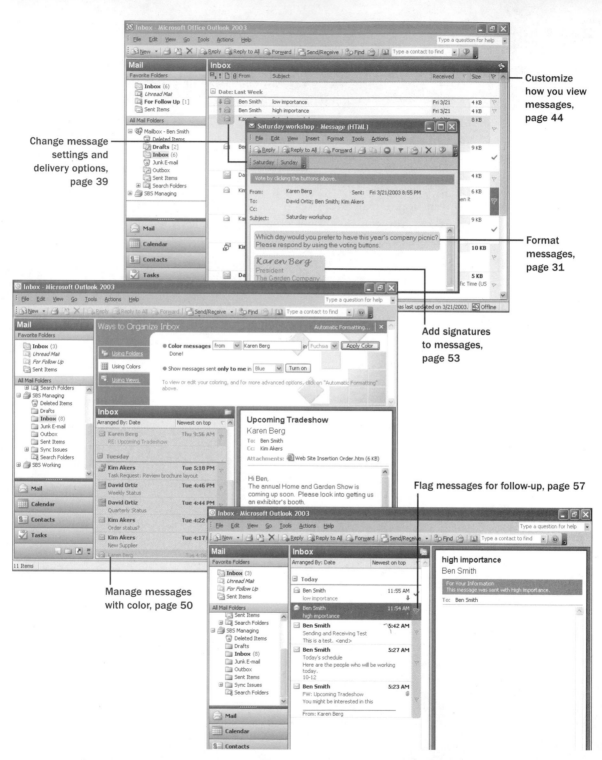

Customize how you view messages, page 44

Change message settings and delivery options, page 39

Format messages, page 31

Add signatures to messages, page 53

Flag messages for follow-up, page 57

Manage messages with color, page 50

Chapter 2 at a Glance

2 Managing E-Mail Messages

In this chapter you will learn to:

✔ Format messages.

✔ Change message settings and delivery options.

✔ Customize how you view messages.

✔ Manage messages with color.

✔ Add signatures to messages.

✔ Flag messages for follow-up.

In today's business world, e-mail is an essential method of communication. But when you use your e-mail regularly and receive a large volume of messages, it can be difficult to manage them all. Microsoft Office Outlook 2003 has many features to help you read, organize, find, and store e-mail messages quickly.

You can choose to view your messages in a way that makes it easier for you to scan, read, and respond to them. You can organize your messages in folders, search for messages by category and other criteria, and archive your messages in Outlook or on your hard disk.

See Also Do you need only a quick refresher on the topics in this chapter? See the Quick Reference entries on pages xxx–xxxii.

Important Before you can use the practice files in this chapter, you need to install them from the book's companion CD to their default location. See "Using the Book's CD-ROM" on page xiii for more information.

Formatting Messages

Microsoft Office Specialist

E-mail messages are sent in one of three formats: HTML, Plain Text, or Outlook Rich Text Format (RTF). Outlook supports all three formats. Other e-mail programs might be able to work with only some of them.

■ *HTML* is the default Outlook message format. HTML supports text formatting, numbering, bullets, pictures and backgrounds in the message body, styles, and stationery. Most popular e-mail programs support HTML messages.

■   *Outlook Rich Text Format* supports a host of formatting options including text formatting, bullets, numbering, background colors, borders, and shading.

■   *Plain Text* is supported by all e-mail programs, but as the name implies, messages in Plain Text do not include any formatting.

For the most part, the HTML message format will meet your needs. When you send an HTML message to someone whose e-mail program doesn't support HTML format, the message is displayed as Plain Text in the recipient's e-mail program. Outlook automatically converts RTF messages you send over the Internet into HTML format. When you reply to or forward a message, Outlook uses the format of the original message by default. However, you can choose the format for any message you send.

When sending messages in HTML format, you can enhance the appearance of your messages using *stationery* and *themes*. When you use stationery, you can specify the background, fonts, bullets, images, and other elements you want to use in outgoing e-mail messages. You can choose from a collection of predefined stationery that comes with Outlook, customize one of the patterns, create new stationery, or download new patterns from the Web. If you use Microsoft Office Word as your e-mail editor, you can choose from additional patterns available as Word themes.

Important   The exercises in this book assume that you are using Word as your default e-mail editor. If Word is not your default e-mail editor and you would like it to be, on the Tools menu, click Options. Click the Mail Format tab, and select the "Use Microsoft Word to edit e-mail messages" check box. To turn off Word as your default e-mail editor, clear the check box.

In this exercise, you will format messages in HTML, Rich Text, and Plain Text formats, and then you will compose messages using stationery and themes.

BE SURE TO start Outlook before beginning this exercise.
OPEN your Inbox folder.

New Mail
Message

1   On the toolbar, click the **New Mail Message** button.

A blank Message form appears.

2   Click in the body of the message, and type **Wow! Have you seen the new roses?**

By default, the text is formatted in 10-point Arial (the Normal style).

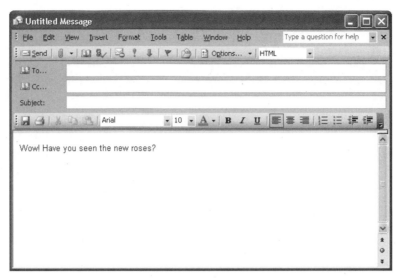

Font Size

3 Select the word *Wow!* (including the exclamation point), click the down arrow to the right of the **Font Size** box, and then click **16**.

A

Font Color

4 Click the down arrow to the right of the **Font Color** button, and then click the red square.

HTML

Message
Format

5 Click the down arrow to the right of the **Message format** box, and then click **Plain Text**.

A message box appears, indicating that Plain Text format does not support some of the formatting in the message.

Tip   If you want to bypass this warning in the future, select the "Don't show this dialog box again" check box before continuing.

6   Click the **Continue** button.

The text is formatted in 10-point Courier New (the Plain Text style), and the formatting buttons on the E-mail toolbar become unavailable.

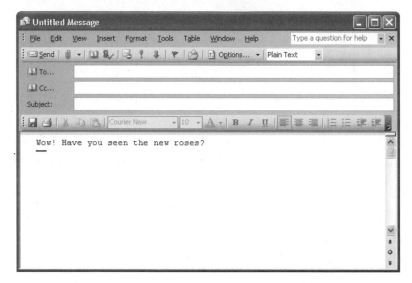

7   Click the down arrow to the right of the **Message format** box, and then click **Rich Text**.

The text formatting does not change, but the formatting buttons become available.

Close

8   Click the Message form's **Close** button, and when asked if you want to keep a draft of the message, click **No**.

The Message form closes.

9   On the **Tools** menu, click **Options**.

The Options dialog box appears.

10   Click the **Mail Format** tab.

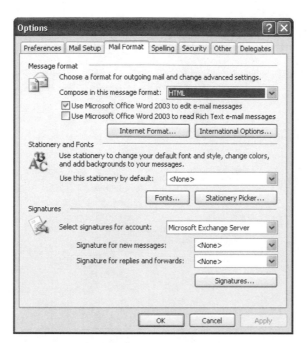

11 In the **Message format** area, click the down arrow to the right of the **Compose in this message format** box, click **Plain Text**, and then click **OK**.

The Options dialog box closes. The default message format for new messages is now set to Plain Text.

12 On the toolbar, click the **New Mail Message** button.

The Message form appears, with Plain Text format selected in the Message Format box.

13 Close the Message form.

14 On the **Tools** menu, click **Options**, and then click the **Mail Format** tab.

15 In the **Message format** area, click the down arrow to the right of the **Compose in this message format** box, and then click **HTML**.

16 In the **Stationery and Fonts** area, click the down arrow to the right of the **Use this stationery by default** box, click **Ivy**, and then click **OK**.

The Options dialog box closes. New messages will now be formatted in HTML format using the Ivy stationery.

17 On the toolbar, click the **New Mail Message** button.

The Message form appears, using the Ivy stationery.

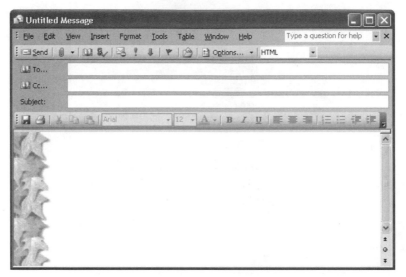

18 Click in the body of the message, and type Bring your family and come to.

By default, the text is formatted in green, 12-point Arial (the Normal style for this stationery).

Tip   You can customize message stationery. On the Mail Format tab of the Options dialog box, click the Stationery Picker button. To edit existing stationery, click the stationery design you want, click the Edit button, apply the font, background, and color formatting you want, and then click OK. To create new stationery, click the New button in the Stationery Picker dialog box, and follow the directions in the wizard that appears.

19 On the **Format** menu, click **Theme**.

The Theme dialog box appears, with an extensive list of available formats.

20 In the **Choose a Theme** list, click **Compass**.

A preview of the Compass theme appears in the Theme dialog box.

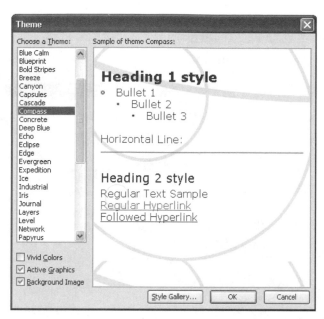

21 Scroll down the **Choose a Theme** list, click **Papyrus**, and then click **OK**.

The Theme dialog box closes, and the Sandstone theme is applied to the message, replacing the Ivy stationery.

22 In the body of the message, press the ⌈Enter⌋ key, type The Garden Company Summer Picnic, press the ⌈Enter⌋ key, type June 24th from 11:00 A.M. to 5:00 P.M., and then press the ⌈Enter⌋ key again.

Center

23 Click in the first line of text, and on the E-mail toolbar, click the **Center** button.

The line is now centered in the body of the message.

24 Click in the second line of text, and on the **Format** menu, click **Styles and Formatting**.

The Styles and Formatting pane appears at the right side of the message window.

Maximize

25 Click the **Maximize** button so you can see all the choices.

26 In the **Pick formatting to apply** area of the **Styles and Formatting** pane, click **Heading 1**.

The event title is now formatted with the Heading 1 style.

27 Click the third line of text, and in the **Pick formatting to apply** area of the **Styles and Formatting** pane, click **Heading 3**.

The time and date are now formatted with the Heading 3 style.

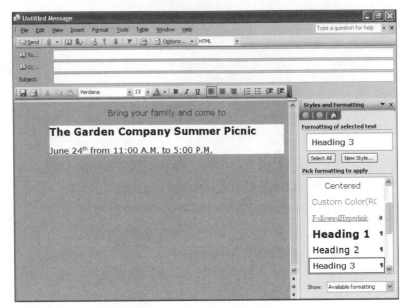

28 On the Message form, click the **Close** button, and when asked if you want to keep a draft of the message, click **No**.

The Message form closes, discarding the draft.

29 On the **Tools** menu, click **Options**, and then click the **Mail Format** tab.

30 In the **Stationery and Fonts** area, click the down arrow to the right of the **Use this stationery by default** box, click **<None>** at the top of the drop-down list, and then click **OK**.

The Options dialog box closes. New messages will now be formatted in HTML with no stationery applied.

BE SURE TO open a new message window, click the Restore Down button, and then close the window to restore the default size.

Changing Message Settings and Delivery Options

Microsoft Office Specialist

To help you manage your e-mail and convey the meaning of your messages more effectively, you can set the importance, sensitivity, and a number of delivery options for e-mail messages.

You can set a message to High, Normal, or Low *importance*. Messages sent with High importance are indicated by a red exclamation point. Messages sent with Normal importance have no special indicator. Messages sent with Low importance are indicated by a blue downward-pointing arrow. These indicators show up in the Importance column in the Inbox.

You can also set message *sensitivity* to Normal, Personal, Private, or Confidential. Messages marked as Private cannot be modified after they are sent.

To help you manage messages you receive, you can choose to have people's replies to your messages sent to another e-mail address. For example, you might have replies sent to a new e-mail address as you transition from one to another. To help you manage messages you send, you can choose whether to save copies of your sent messages and in which folder they should be saved. You can also specify when a message will be delivered and make a message unavailable after a certain date.

If your *e-mail server* is a Microsoft Exchange Server, you can use voting buttons to let e-mail recipients quickly respond to a question.

In this exercise, you will use voting buttons to respond to a message, set the importance of a message, and modify the delivery options for a message.

BE SURE TO start Outlook and display the Reading Pane before beginning this exercise.
USE the *SBSManaging* data file in the practice file folder for this topic. This practice file is located in the *My Documents\Microsoft Press\Outlook 2003 SBS\Managing* folder and can also be accessed by clicking *Start/All Programs/Microsoft Press/Outlook 2003 Step by Step*.
OPEN the *SBSManaging* data file from within Outlook.

1   In the practice file Inbox, click the **Saturday workshop** message from Karen Berg.

The message appears in the Reading Pane. At the top of the message is an Infobar with instructions for voting.

2   Click the **Infobar**, and then click **Vote: Saturday.**

Tip   If you open the message, you will see buttons corresponding to each of the voting options. In an open message, click the buttons rather than the Infobar to cast your vote.

A dialog box appears, giving you the options to send the response immediately or edit it first.

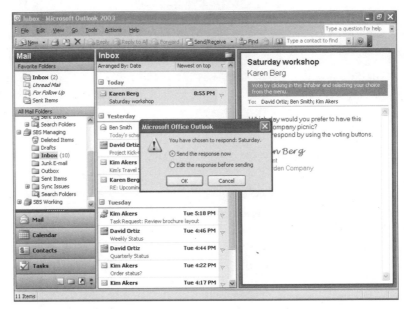

3 Leave the **Send the response now** option selected, and click **OK**.

The Infobar now shows that you have responded.

New Mail Message

4 Click the **New Mail Message** button.

A new, blank e-mail message opens in its own window. If Word is your e-mail editor, Word's e-mail toolbar is displayed at the top of the window.

5 On the Message form's toolbar, click the **Options** button.

The Message Options dialog box appears.

6 In the **Message settings** area, click the down arrow to the right of the **Importance** box, and click **High** in the drop-down list.

7 In the **Delivery options** area, select the **Have replies sent to** check box, delete the text that appears in the adjacent box, and type te$t@gardenco.msn.com.

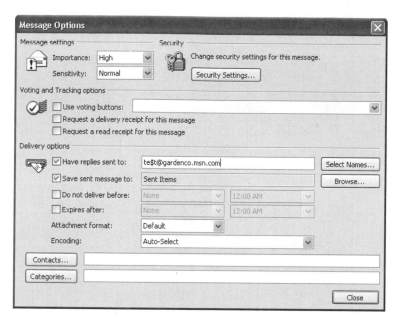

8 Click **Close**.

The Message Options dialog box closes, and you return to the Message form. The "Importance: High" button is selected.

9 In the **To** box, type your own e-mail address.

10 Click in the **Subject** box, type **high importance**, and then click the **Send** button.

The Message form closes, and the message is sent.

11 Click the **New Mail Message** button, and then click the **Options** button.

12 In the **Delivery options** area, click the **Browse** button.

The Select Folder dialog box appears.

13 In the **Folders** list, locate your own mailbox, click the *Drafts* folder underneath it, and then click **OK**.

When you send this message, a copy will be saved in your Drafts folder.

Tip Saving frequently sent messages to your Drafts folder makes it easy for you to create and send new versions without entering the recipients and text every time.

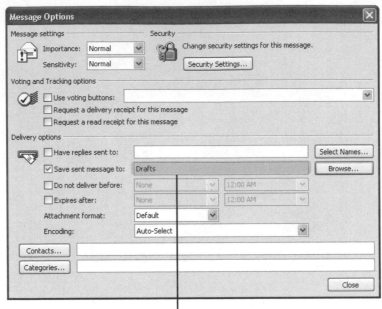

"Save sent message to" box

14 Click **Close**.

The Message Options dialog box closes, and you return to the Message form.

15 In the Message form, click the **Importance: Low** button.

Importance:
Low

16 In the **To** box, type your own e-mail address.

17 Click in the **Subject** box, type **low importance**, and click the **Send** button.

The Message form closes, and the message is sent.

18 Open your own Inbox.

Send/Receive

19 If the messages have not yet arrived in your Inbox, click the **Send/Receive** button.

When the messages arrive, the *high importance* message is marked with a red exclamation point and the *low importance* message is marked with a downward-pointing blue arrow. A corresponding message is displayed in the message header that is visible in the Reading Pane.

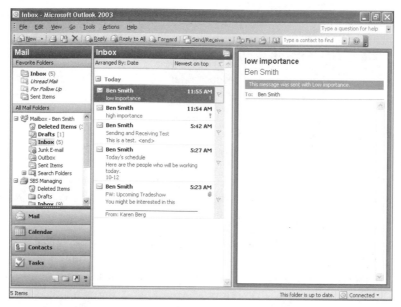

 20 Click the *high importance* message, and then click the **Reply** button.

The Reply form appears. The To box contains the e-mail address you entered earlier, te$t@gardenco.msn.com.

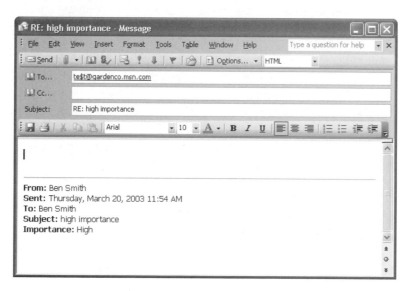

Close

21 Close the Reply form without saving the message, and then close the original message.

22 In the **Folder List**, click your *Drafts* folder.

The contents of the Drafts folder are displayed, including the copy of the message you sent with Low importance.

Customizing How You View Messages

Microsoft Office Specialist

As your Inbox gathers messages, it can be challenging to prioritize them. You can use Outlook to customize how you view, group, and sort messages. You can then quickly determine which are the most important, decide which can be deleted, and locate any messages that need an immediate response.

New In Office 2003

Arrangements

In addition to the Reading Pane and AutoPreview view options, you can choose to view only messages received in the last seven days, only unread messages, only messages sent to a certain person or distribution list, or a timeline of all your received messages. Outlook 2003 offers 13 pre-defined arrangements so you can see your messages the way you want. To experiment with the view options, on the View menu, point to Arrange By, point to Current View, and then click the view option you want.

See Also For more information about viewing messages in the Reading Pane or by using the AutoPreview feature, see "Reading Messages and Opening Attachments" in Chapter 1, "Working with Outlook."

Regardless of the *view* you choose, you can group and sort your messages by any column simply by clicking the column heading. By default, messages in your Inbox are grouped by the received date in descending order—the most recent messages appear at the top of the list. Messages you received this week are grouped by day. Earlier messages are grouped by weeks or longer periods. But you can sort columns in either ascending or descending order. You can also group your messages by the contents of any column—by the sender of the message, for instance, or by the subject.

New in Office 2003

Arrange by Conversation

A new feature in Outlook 2003 is the ability to arrange messages by conversation. This is a grouped view similar to sorting messages by subject, but the conversations are displayed in order by date. For conversations with multiple messages, the unread or flagged messages are displayed by default. Additional messages are indicated by a small down arrow to the left of the conversation title. Click the down arrow to display all the messages in the conversation.

In this exercise, you will sort and group messages, select a defined message view, and customize your message view.

BE SURE TO start Outlook, open the *SBSManaging* data file, and turn the Reading Pane off before beginning this exercise.

USE the *SBSManaging* data file in the practice file folder for this topic. This practice file is located in the *My Documents\Microsoft Press\Outlook 2003 SBS\Managing* folder and can also be accessed by clicking *Start/All Programs/Microsoft Press/Outlook 2003 Step by Step*.

OPEN the practice file Inbox folder.

1   In the practice file *Inbox* folder, note the downward-pointing arrow in the **Received** column heading.

This indicates that the messages are currently sorted in descending order by receipt date.

2   Click the **From** column heading.

Outlook groups the messages in alphabetical order by sender. Within each group, the messages are still sorted by date received.

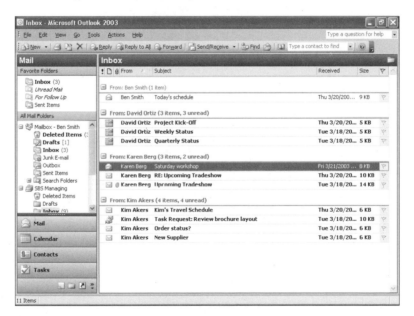

3   Click the **From** column heading again.

Outlook groups the messages in reverse alphabetical order.

4   Click the **Size** column heading.

Outlook groups the messages by size.

5   On the **View** menu, point to **Arrange By**, and then click **Subject**.

Outlook organizes the listed messages into message threads.

Note that the total number of items and the number of unread items in each group is indicated in parentheses following the conversation subject.

6 Scroll down, and click the minus sign to the left of the *Upcoming Tradeshow* subject line.

The two messages with this subject are hidden, and the minus sign changes to a plus sign.

Messages indicator

7 On the **View** menu, point to **Arrange By**, and then click **Show in Groups** to turn this feature off.

Messages are no longer grouped; they are simply listed by subject.

Tip Unread items are distinguished from read items by their bold type and closed-envelope icons. For the purposes of this exercise, if you do not have any unread messages in the practice file Inbox, right-click a message, and click Mark as Unread on the shortcut menu. The message header in the Inbox will then change to bold, and its message icon will change from an open to a closed envelope.

8 On the **View** menu, point to **Arrange By**, point to **Current View**, and then click **Unread Messages in This Folder**.

Outlook filters the messages to show only unread messages.

Folder banner

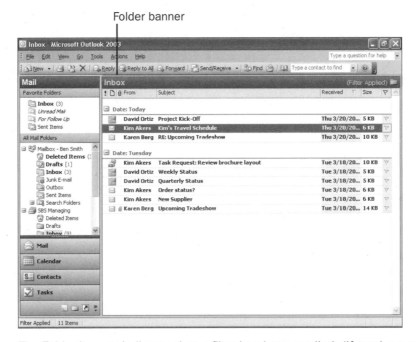

The Folder banner indicates that a filter has been applied. (If you have no unread messages in your Inbox, it will appear to be empty.)

9 On the **View** menu, point to **Arrange By**, point to **Current View**, and then click **Messages**.

The messages are no longer filtered.

Tip You can also use the Ways to Organize pane to select a view for your messages. On the Tools menu, click Organize to open the pane. Then click Using Views, and click a view in the list.

10 On the **View** menu, point to **Arrange By**, point to **Current View**, and click **Customize Current View**.

The Customize View: Messages dialog box appears.

11 Click the **Fields** button.

The Show Fields dialog box appears.

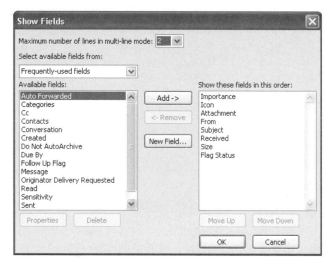

12 In the **Available fields** list, click **Sensitivity**, and then click the **Add** button.

The Sensitivity field is added to the list of columns to be shown in this view.

13 In the **Show these fields in this order** list, drag **Sensitivity** to appear just after **Importance**, and then click **OK**.

The Show Fields dialog box closes, and you return to the Customize View: Messages dialog box.

Tip To change the order of columns in any view, simply drag the column headings to the locations you prefer. While you are dragging a column heading, red arrows indicate where the column will appear when you release the mouse button.

14 Click the **Other Settings** button.

The Other Settings dialog box appears.

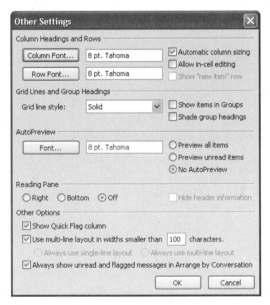

15 Click the down arrow to the right of the **Grid line style** box, click **Small dots**, and then click **OK**.

The Other Settings dialog box closes, and you return to the Customize View: Messages dialog box.

16 In the **Customize View: Messages** dialog box, click **OK**.

The Inbox is displayed with the new view settings.

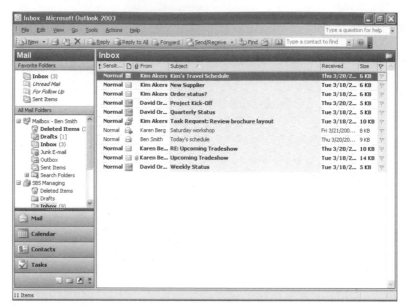

17 Drag the **Sensitivity** column heading downward, and release the mouse button when a large black X appears over the heading.

The Sensitivity column is removed from the view.

18 On the **View** menu, point to **Arrange By**, point to **Current View**, and then click **Define Views**.

The Define Views dialog box appears.

19 Click the **Reset** button, click **OK**, and then click **Close**.

The practice file Inbox display is restored to the default view settings.

Managing Messages with Color

Microsoft Office Specialist

Color-coding messages can help you easily distinguish messages received from certain people. For example, you might show all messages from your boss in red, and all messages from the finance department in green. You can also choose to have messages that were sent directly to you displayed in a different color than messages sent to a distribution list.

In this exercise, you will color-code messages.

BE SURE TO start Outlook and open the *SBSManaging* data file before beginning this exercise.
USE the *SBSManaging* data file in the practice file folder for this topic. This practice file is located in the
My Documents\Microsoft Press\Outlook 2003 SBS\Managing folder and can also be accessed by clicking
Start/All Programs/Microsoft Press/Outlook 2003 Step by Step.
OPEN the practice file Inbox folder.

1 On the **Tools** menu, click **Organize**.

The Ways to Organize pane appears.

2 In the **Ways to Organize** pane, click **Using Colors**.

The Using Colors tab is displayed with the sender of the currently selected message
filled in.

3 Scroll to the bottom of the *Inbox* folder, and click the **Upcoming Tradeshow** message
from Karen Berg.

4 In the **Color Messages** area, make sure *from* is selected in the first box, and *Karen
Berg* appears in the second box.

5 In the third box, click **Fuchsia** in the drop-down list, and click the **Apply Color** button.

Messages from Karen Berg are now displayed in the selected color.

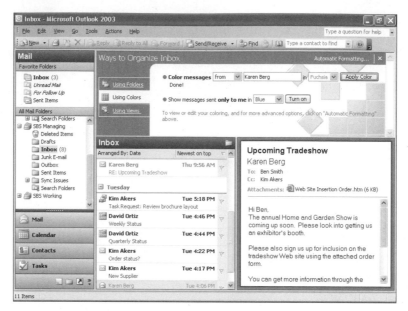

6 In the upper-right corner of the **Ways to Organize** pane, click **Automatic Formatting**.

The Automatic Formatting dialog box appears.

7 In the **Rules for this view** list, clear the **Mail received from Karen Berg** check box.

8 Click the **Delete** button.

The *Mail received from Karen Berg* rule is deleted.

9 In the **Automatic Formatting** dialog box, click **OK**.

The dialog box closes and the Inbox messages return to their normal color.

CLOSE the *Ways to Organize* pane and the *SBSManaging* data file.

Adding Signatures to Messages

Microsoft
Office
Specialist

By using a *signature*, you can personalize your messages and save time. A signature is a predefined block of text that can be inserted, manually or automatically, at the end of your messages. Signatures can include any text you like, but they typically include your name, title, and company name. Signatures can be formatted in the same ways that message text can be formatted.

**New in
Office 2003**
Unique
signature
per account

In Outlook 2003, you can create a variety of signatures and assign a different signature to each of your Outlook accounts. If you like, you can create multiple signatures for different uses, such as formal business e-mail, casual business e-mail, and personal e-mail.

In this exercise, you will create a signature, and then instruct Outlook to insert the signature in all the new messages you create.

OPEN the practice file Inbox folder or your own Inbox.

1   On the **Tools** menu, click **Options**.

The Options dialog box appears.

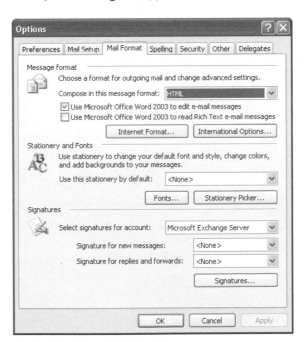

2   Click the **Mail Format** tab, and then click the **Signatures** button.

The Create Signature dialog box appears.

3   Click the **New** button.

The Create New Signature dialog box appears.

4 Type **Professional** as the name of your signature, and then click the **Next** button.

The Edit Signature dialog box appears.

5 In the **Signature text** box, type **Regards** and a comma, press the Enter key, and then type your name.

6 Select your name, and then click the **Font** button.

The Font dialog box appears.

7 Change the font to **Arial Narrow**, the style to **Bold Italic**, and the size to **14**.

The text shown in the Sample area reflects your changes.

8 Click **OK**.

9 Select both lines of text, and click the **Paragraph** button.

The Paragraph dialog box appears.

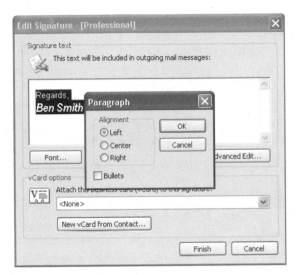

10 Click **Center**, and then click **OK**.

11 Make any other changes you want, and then click **Finish**.

Your newly created signature is now available in the Create Signature dialog box.

12   Click **OK**.

The Options dialog box appears. Note that the signature you just created is selected in the "Signature for new messages" list, and your default account is selected in the "Select signatures for account" list. Outlook will insert your signature into all new e-mail messages you send from this account.

Tip   If you have more than one e-mail account set up in Outlook, you can use a different signature with each account. Follow the steps to create a new signature; then on the Mail Format tab of the Options dialog box, select the alternate account in the "Select signatures for account" list, select the signature you want to use with that account in the "Signature for new messages" list, and click Apply.

13   Click **OK**.

The Options dialog box closes.

New Mail
Message

14   On the toolbar, click the **New Mail Message** button.

A new message, containing your new signature, appears in the Message form.

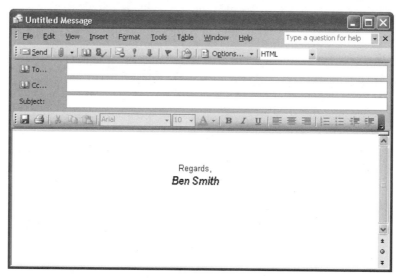

15   Close the message.

Tip   To automatically insert your signature into forwarded messages and replies, on the Tools menu, click Options, and then click the Mail Format tab. Select the account in the "Select signatures for account" list, click the signature you want in the "Signature for replies and forwards" list, and click OK.

16 On the **Tools** menu, click **Options**, and then click the **Mail Format** tab.

17 In the **Signature for new messages** list, click **<None>**, and then click **OK**.

New messages will now appear without a signature.

BE SURE TO delete the *Professional* signature file if you don't want to keep it.

Flagging Messages for Follow-Up

Microsoft Office Specialist

You can't answer every message as soon as you read it, but you can mark messages that require response or action by attaching a *follow-up flag*. Flags come in six colors; you can use the different colors to indicate different types of follow-up, and you can set a *reminder* to pop up when the follow-up is due. You can quickly view your flagged messages by using the For Follow-up *search folder*.

Each message in your Inbox has a shaded Flag Status icon that indicates whether a message is flagged or completed. You can flag messages in any folder but the Flag Status icon appears only in active Inbox folders.

New in Office 2003
Quick Flags

FrontPage 2003 features Quick Flags, an easy way to flag a message. Simply click the shaded Flag Status icon to the right of a message, once to flag it for follow up, and again to mark it as completed. To change the current flag color, right-click the flag and click the color you want on the shortcut menu. To change the default flag color, right-click the flag, point to Set Default Flag, and then click the color you want. To remove a flag, right-click the flag and then click Clear Flag. You can also add a reminder to any flagged item.

Important Because the Flag Status column does not appear in the practice file folders, this exercise is conducted in your own Inbox. The messages shown in your Inbox will vary from those shown here.

In this exercise, you will flag received messages, update flags, view messages by flag status, and flag a new outgoing message to bring it to the recipient's attention.

OPEN your own Inbox.

Flag Status

1 In your Inbox, click the **Flag Status** icon next to any message.

The icon and the flag turn red.

2 Click the **Flag Status** icon again.

The icon turns white and the flag changes to a check mark to indicate that the task is completed.

3   Right-click the **Flag Status** icon of another message (not a task or appointment), and then click **Add Reminder** on the shortcut menu.

The Flag for Follow Up dialog box appears.

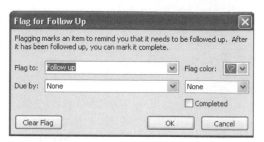

4   In the **Flag to** list, click **For Your Information**, in the **Flag color** list, click **Blue Flag**, and then click **OK**.

The message's Flag Status icon turns blue.

5   Click the message to display it in the Reading Pane.

The label *For Your Information* appears at the top of the message.

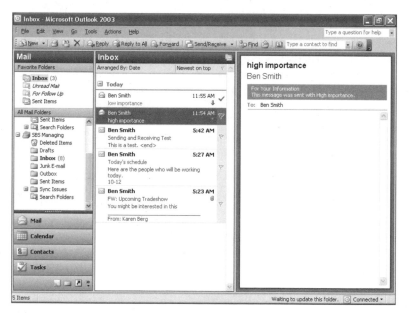

6   Open a different message.

7   On the message window's Standard toolbar click the **Follow Up** button.

The Flag for Follow Up dialog box appears.

Follow Up

8 Select the **Completed** check box, and then click **OK**.

The label at the top of the message shows the completed status.

9 Close the message.

In the Inbox, the Flag Status column now displays a check mark.

10 In the **Favorite Folders** list, click **For Follow Up.**

The message you flagged for follow up is displayed. If you have flagged multiple messages they are grouped by flag color.

New Mail
Message

11 Click the **New Mail Message** button.

A new message window appears.

12 On the message window's Standard toolbar, click the **Follow Up** button.

Tip If Outlook alerts you that it is unable to open the For Follow Up folder, in the Navigation Pane, click the plus sign next to Search Folders, and then click the For Follow Up Search Folder.

The Flag for Follow Up dialog box appears.

13 In the **Flag to** box, type a custom label.

14 In the **Due By** list, click a date, and then click **OK**.

Your label text and deadline appear at the top of the message.

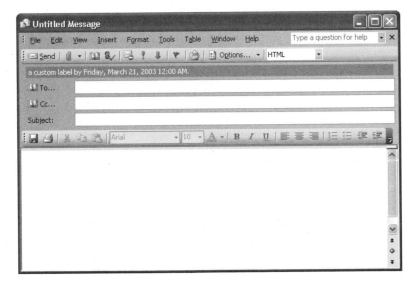

15 Close the message without saving it.

16 In the **Favorite Folders** list, click **Inbox**.

17 Right-click the **Flag Status** icon of each of the messages you flagged in this exercise, and then click **Clear Flag** to remove the flag.

Key Points

■ You can send messages in various formats. HTML messages support the most formatting, including stationary and themes.

■ You can create a signature for Outlook to add to new messages and/or forwarded messages and replies you send.

■ Messages can be grouped and sorted by sender, time, subject, size, or other fields.

■ You can create rules to display messages in particular colors depending on the sender, subject, contents, time, who else they were sent to, or almost any other criteria.

■ You can flag new and received messages for follow up at a later time. All your flagged messages appear in your For Follow Up folder, and Outlook can send you a reminder when the follow-up is due.

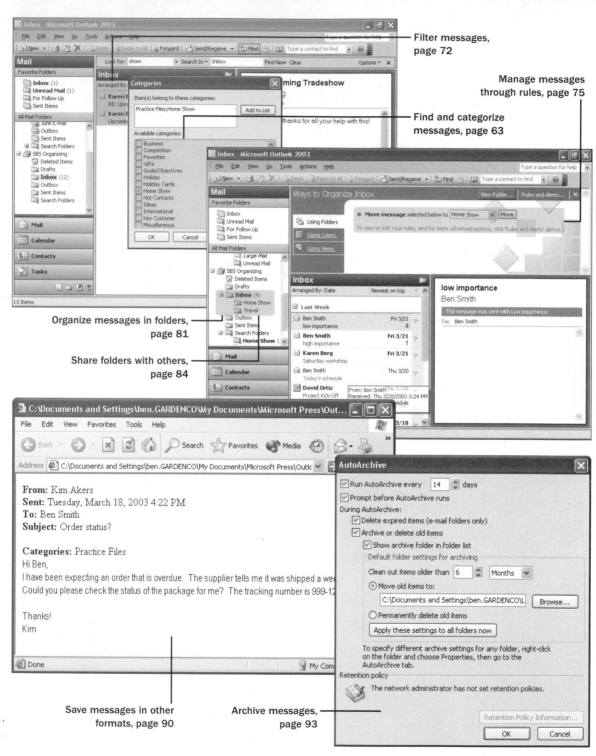

Filter messages, page 72

Manage messages through rules, page 75

Find and categorize messages, page 63

Organize messages in folders, page 81

Share folders with others, page 84

Save messages in other formats, page 90

Archive messages, page 93

Chapter 3 at a Glance

3 Finding and Organizing E-Mail Messages

In this chapter you will learn to:

✔ Find and categorize messages.

✔ Use Search Folders.

✔ Filter messages.

✔ Manage messages through rules.

✔ Organize messages in folders.

✔ Share folders with others.

✔ Save messages in other formats.

✔ Archive messages.

As you learn the fundamentals of sending, receiving, and managing *e-mail* messages, you will see how using e-mail can help you work more efficiently. Because you can customize the format of your messages, select from a number of message and delivery options, filter messages, and set up *personal folders* and *address books*, you can configure Microsoft Office Outlook 2003 to be as convenient and useful as possible. For example, if your company is working on a number of projects at the same time, you might ask each project team to use a particular phrase or keyword in the subject line of messages related to each project. Then when you need to focus on a particular project, you can filter messages to display only those items related to it.

See Also   Do you need only a quick refresher on the topics in this chapter? See the Quick Reference entries on pages xxxiii–xxxvi.

Important   Before you can use the practice files in this chapter, you need to install them from the book's companion CD to their default location. See "Using the Book's CD-ROM" on page xiii for more information.

Finding and Categorizing Messages

Microsoft Office Specialist

If you are having trouble locating a particular message in your *Inbox* or another message folder, you can search for it using Outlook's Find or Advanced Find features. You can look for messages in a single folder, a group of folders you select, or all your folders. You can instruct Outlook to search through the text of every message or only the Subject field.

To make finding messages easier, you can create *categories* and assign messages to them. With categories, you group messages by a common characteristic. Outlook includes a set of predefined categories, and you can create your own. For example, you might assign all messages about invoices and payments to the Finance category, or you might create a Payroll category for all messages related to timesheets and paychecks.

In this exercise, you will find a message using the Find feature, create a category, assign messages to it, and then find messages using the Advanced Find feature.

USE the *SBSOrganizing* data file in the practice file folder for this topic. This practice file is located in the *My Documents\Microsoft Press\Outlook 2003 SBS\Organizing* folder and can also be accessed by clicking *Start/All Programs/Microsoft Press/Outlook 2003 Step by Step*.
BE SURE TO start Outlook before beginning this exercise.
OPEN the *SBSOrganizing* data file from within Outlook, and then open the practice Inbox.

 1 On the toolbar, click the **Find** button.

The Find pane appears above the practice Inbox.

2 In the **Look for** box in the **Find** pane, type **show**, a word that you know is contained within a message in your Inbox. Then click the **Find Now** button.

Outlook searches your messages and displays only those that contain the word you typed.

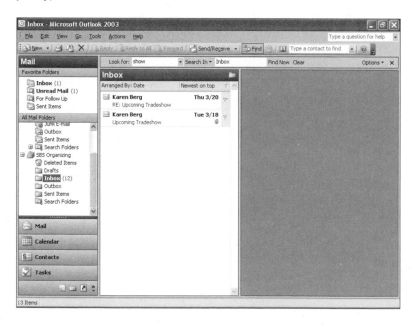

3 Press Ctrl+A to select both the found messages.

4 Right-click the selected messages, and click **Categories** on the shortcut menu.

The Categories dialog box appears.

Tip The messages in the practice file Inbox are categorized so they can easily be removed from your computer when you are finished with this course.

5 In the **Item(s) belong to these categories** box, after *Practice Files*, type ;**Home Show** to add a new category, and then click the **Add to List** button.

The category is added to the list and automatically selected for the messages.

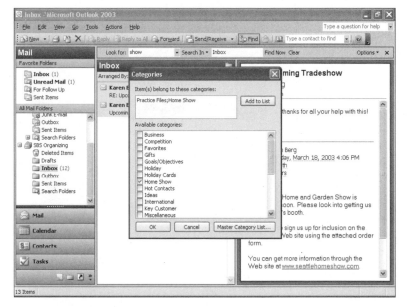

6 In the **Categories** dialog box, click **OK**.

7 To redisplay all the messages, click the **Clear** button.

All your messages are displayed.

8 In the Inbox, click the **Today's schedule** message from Ben Smith once to select it.

9 On the **Edit** menu, click **Categories**.

10 In the **Available categories** list, select the **Home Show** check box, and then click **OK**.

The message is assigned to the category.

11 In the **Find** pane, click the **Options** button, and then click **Advanced Find** in the **Options** drop-down list.

The Advanced Find window appears.

12 In the **Advanced Find** window, click the **More Choices** tab, and then click the **Categories** button.

The Categories dialog box appears.

13 In the **Available categories** list, select the **Home Show** check box, and then click **OK**.

The Categories dialog box closes, and you return to the Advanced Find window. Your category appears in the Categories box.

14 Click the **Find Now** button.

Outlook searches your messages and displays the matching items in a list at the bottom of the Advanced Find window.

CLOSE the Advanced Find window and the Find pane.

Using Search Folders

Microsoft Office Specialist

Search Folders, like Outlook's Find feature, show all the files that match a set of search criteria, and can show files from different folders together in one place. Unlike Find, when you create a Search Folder, it becomes part of your mailbox and is always kept up to date.

New in Office 2003
Search Folders

The default Outlook 2003 installation includes three Search Folders: The For Follow Up folder displays messages flagged for follow-up, the Large Messages folder displays messages larger than 100 kilobytes (KB), and the Unread Mail folder displays messages that are marked as unread.

Search Folders are *virtual folders.* Each message in your mailbox is stored in only one Outlook folder (such as your Inbox), but it might appear in many Search Folders. Changing or deleting a message in a Search Folder changes or deletes the message in the Outlook folder where it is stored.

In this exercise, you will first experiment with the default Search Folders and then create and use a custom Search Folder.

USE the *SBSOrganizing* data file in the practice file folder for this topic. This practice file is located in the *My Documents\Microsoft Press\Outlook 2003 SBS\Organizing* folder and can also be accessed by clicking *Start/All Programs/Microsoft Press/Outlook 2003 Step by Step.*
BE SURE TO start Outlook and open the *SBSOrganizing* data file before beginning this exercise.
OPEN your own Outlook mailbox.

1   In the **All Mail Folders** list, click the plus sign next to *Search Folders* (in your own Outlook mailbox, not the *SBS Organizing* data file), and then click **Large Mail**.

In the content pane, the Large Mail Search Folder displays all your Outlook items that are larger than 100 kilobytes.

Troubleshooting   Depending on your previous use of Outlook, the default Search Folders might be empty.

2   Click the **Unread Mail** Search Folder.

In the content pane, the Unread Mail Search Folder displays the Outlook items that are marked as unread, from all your Outlook folders.

3   In the **All Mail Folders** list, expand the **SBS Organizing** data file.

The Search Folder provided as part of the SBS Organizing practice data file doesn't currently display any saved searches.

4 Right-click the practice *Search Folders* folder, and then click **New Search Folder** on the shortcut menu.

The New Search Folder dialog box appears.

5 In the **Select a Search Folder** list, under **Mail from People and Lists**, click **Mail from and to specific people**.

A browse box appears in the Customize Search Folder area at the bottom of the dialog box.

6 Click the **Choose** button.

The Select Names dialog box appears.

7 In the **Show Names from the** list, click **Contacts**. Then in the **Name** list, double-click **David Ortiz** and then **Kim Akers**, and then click **OK**.

In the New Search Folder dialog box, David Ortiz and Kim Akers are now listed in the "Show mail sent to and received from" box.

8   In the **Search mail in** drop-down list, click **SBS Organizing**. Then click **OK**.

9   If necessary, double-click the *Search Folders* folder to expand it, and then click the *David Ortiz* Search Folder.

The new Search Folder displays all the mail sent to or received from David Ortiz or Kim Akers.

10   Click the first message to display it in the Reading Pane.

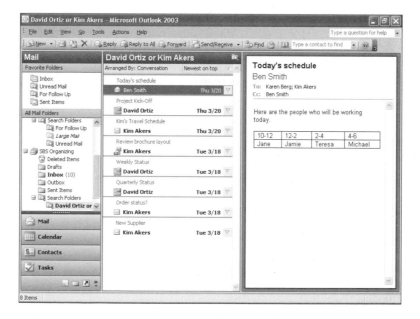

11 Right-click the new Search Folder, and then click **Rename** on the shortcut menu.

The name of the folder is selected for editing.

12 Type **Marketing**, and press the Enter key.

The Search Folder is renamed.

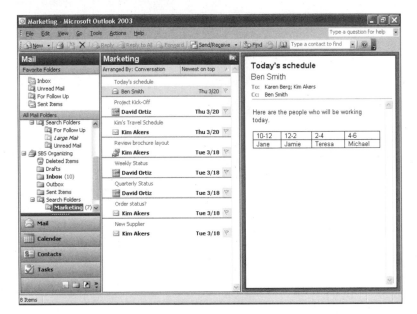

13 On the **File** menu, point to **New**, and then click **Search Folder**.

The New Search Folder dialog box appears.

14 In the **Select a Search Folder** list, scroll to the **Custom** area, click **Create a custom Search Folder**, and then click the **Choose** button.

The Custom Search Folder dialog box appears.

15 In the **Name** box, type **Home Show**, and then click **Criteria**.

The Search Folder Criteria dialog box appears.

16 Click the **More Choices** tab, and then click the **Categories** button.

The Categories dialog box appears.

17 In the **Available Categories** list, select the **Home Show** check box, and then click **OK**.

In the Search Folder Criteria dialog box, *Home Show* appears in the text box to the right of the Categories button.

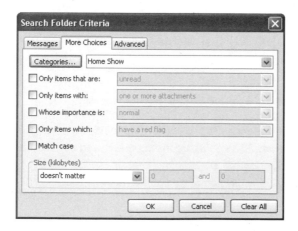

18 Click **OK** in each of the three open dialog boxes.

The new *Home Show* Search Folder appears in the Navigation Pane, and the content pane displays the items that are categorized as Home Show-related.

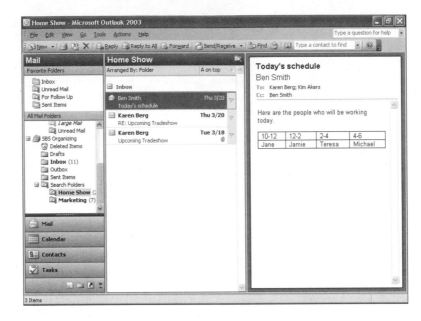

See Also For more information about creating categories and assigning Outlook items to categories, see "Finding and Categorizing Messages" earlier in this chapter.

Filtering Messages

Microsoft Office Specialist

As messages accumulate in your Inbox, it can be a challenge to find specific messages or groups of messages. To help meet this challenge, you can *filter* your messages to display only those messages that meet common criteria, helping you identify a specific collection of messages.

In this exercise, you will define a view to filter messages.

USE the *SBSOrganizing* data file in the practice file folder for this topic. This practice file is located in the *My Documents\Microsoft Press\Outlook 2003 SBS\Organizing* folder and can also be accessed by clicking *Start/All Programs/Microsoft Press/Outlook 2003 Step by Step.*
BE SURE TO open the *SBSOrganizing* data file before beginning this exercise.
OPEN the practice file Inbox.

1 On the **View** menu, point to **Arrange By**, point to **Current View**, and then click **Define Views**.

The Custom View Organizer dialog box appears.

2 Click the **Copy** button.

The Copy View dialog box appears.

3 In the **Name of new view** box, type **Filtered for Show**, and click **OK**.

The Copy View dialog box closes, and the Customize View dialog box appears, showing the settings from the view you copied.

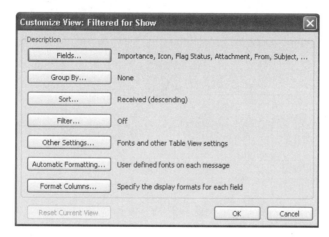

4 Click the **Filter** button.

The Filter dialog box appears.

5 In the **Search for the word(s)** box, type show, and click **OK**.

The Filter dialog box closes, and the Customize View dialog box shows the new filter settings.

6 In the **Customize View** dialog box, click **OK**.

The View Summary dialog box closes, and you are returned to the Custom View Organizer dialog box, which shows the new view in the View Name list.

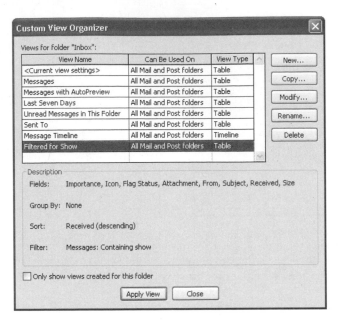

7 With **Filtered for Show** highlighted in the **View Name** list, click the **Apply View** button.

The Define Views for "Inbox" dialog box closes, and the Inbox is displayed, containing only the messages with the word *show* in the subject. The Folder banner indicates that a filter is applied.

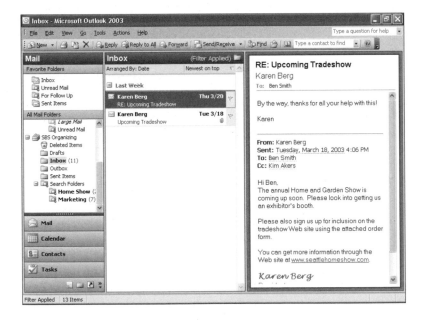

8 On the **View** menu, point to **Arrange By**, and then **Current View**.

The list of available views that appears includes the new *Filtered for Show* view.

9 On the **Current View** shortcut menu, click **Messages**.

The filter is removed, and the Inbox displays all the messages.

Managing Messages through Rules

*Microsoft
Office
Specialist*

You can instruct Outlook to evaluate your e-mail messages in the same way that you would evaluate them, and to make corresponding decisions about what to do with them. These instructions are called *rules*. You can create rules that process messages as they arrive or as you send them; checking for names, words, attachments, categories, or other message conditions on which you might base processing decisions. After the messages are evaluated, Outlook can automatically move, copy, delete, forward, redirect, reply to, or otherwise process messages that meet the criteria you set.

*New In
Office 2003*
New icon rules

In Outlook 2003, you can choose from a collection of standard rule or create your own by using the Outlook Rules Wizard. All your rules are summarized in a list, and differentiated by icons that indicate what they do.

Rules that are applied to messages as they are received or processed by the Exchange server are called *server rules*. Rules that are applied to messages stored on your computer are called *client rules*.

In this exercise, you will create a rule to manage messages that meet specific criteria.

USE the *SBSOrganizing* data file in the practice file folder for this topic. This practice file is located in the *My Documents\Microsoft Press\Outlook 2003 SBS\Organizing* folder and can also be accessed by clicking *Start/All Programs/Microsoft Press/Outlook 2003 Step by Step.*
BE SURE TO open the *SBSOrganizing* data file before beginning this exercise.
OPEN the practice file Inbox.

1 On the **Tools** menu, click **Rules and Alerts**.

The Rules and Alerts dialog box appears.

Troubleshooting You can set Outlook rules only when you are online.

Tip You cannot use Outlook rules to filter messages to an HTTP e-mail account.

New Rule... **2** Click the **New Rule** button.

The first page of the Rules Wizard appears, with the "Start creating a rule from a template" option selected. Take a moment to look over the types of rules you can create from a template.

3   In the **Select a template** list, click **Move messages from someone to a folder**, and then click the **Next** button.

4   In the **Select condition(s)** list, clear the **from people or distribution list** check box, and select the **with specific words in the subject** check box.

The "Edit the rule description" box is updated to reflect the change. The underlined words in the description are values that you must specify to complete the rule.

5   In the **Edit the rule description** box, click the underlined words **specific words**.

The Search Text dialog box appears.

6   In the **Specify words or phrases to search for in the subject** box, type Travel, click the **Add** button, and then click **OK**.

The "Rule description" box is updated to reflect the change.

7   In the **Edit the rule description** box, click the underlined word **specified**.

The Rules and Alerts dialog box appears, showing a list of folders for you to choose from.

8   Click the **New** button.

The Create New Folder dialog box appears.

9   In the **Name** box, type Travel.

10   In the **Select where to place the folder** list, scroll to and expand the SBS Organizing folder, and then click the **Inbox** folder.

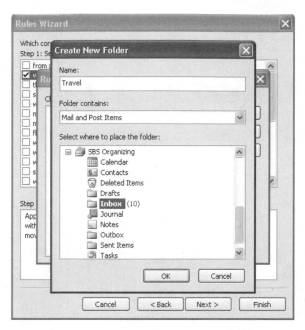

11 Click **OK**.

A new Travel folder appears as a subfolder of the practice Inbox.

12 In the **Rules and Alerts** dialog box, click **OK**.

The dialog box closes, and the "Rule description" box is updated to reflect your folder selection.

13 Click the **Next** button.

14 Review the possible actions you can take through Outlook rules, and then click the **Next** button.

The next page of the Rules Wizard is displayed.

15 In the **Select exception(s)** list, select the **except if it is flagged for action** check box, then in the **Edit the rule description** box, click the underlined word **action**.

The Flagged Message dialog box appears.

16 Click the down arrow to the right of the **Flag** box to see the available options, click **Any**, and click **OK**.

The "Edit the rule description" box is updated to reflect your selection.

17 Click the **Next** button.

The final page of the Rules Wizard is displayed, summarizing the parameters you have set for the Travel rule.

18 Select the **Run this rule now on messages already** in "**Inbox**" check box, and then click the **Finish** button.

Because this rule is created in an Outlook data file that is stored on your computer rather than on the server, Outlook warns you that this is a client-only rule.

19 In the warning box, click **OK**.

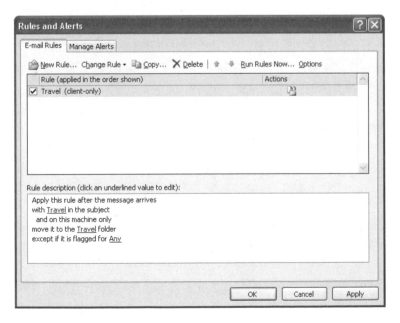

The rule is saved and is now listed in the Rules and Alerts dialog box.

20 Click **OK**.

The rule is now active, and Outlook applies it to the messages in the Inbox.

21 In the **All Mail Folders** list, expand the Inbox if necessary, and then click the **Travel** folder.

The contents of the Travel folder are displayed; in this case, the Kim's Travel Schedule message.

Tip If you are using *Microsoft Exchange Server*, you can filter messages even when you are away from the office by using the *Out of Office Assistant*. You can explore this feature by clicking Out of Office Assistant on the Tools menu.

Filtering Junk E-Mail Messages

Outlook offers several options for managing junk e-mail messages (also called *spam*)— the unsolicited advertisements that can swamp your Inbox if your e-mail address finds its way into the hands of unscrupulous mailing list vendors. When enabled, the Junk E-mail filter will move messages that appear to be junk e-mail to a special folder, or it will delete them. You can specify a list of e-mail addresses or domains whose messages should always be treated as junk; you can also specify those that should never be treated as junk.

To filter junk e-mail:

1 On the **Actions** menu, point to **Junk E-mail**, and then click **Junk E-mail Options**.

The Junk E-mail Options dialog box appears.

2 On the **Options** tab, select a level of protection.

3 If you want Outlook to automatically delete suspected junk e-mail, select the **Permanently delete suspected Junk E-mail instead of moving it to the Junk E-mail folder** check box.

Do not select this check box if you set the protection level to High or Trusted Lists Only.

4 To specify an e-mail address or domain for inclusion in this filter, click the **Safe Senders**, **Safe Recipients**, or **Blocked Senders** tab, click **Add**, type the domain or e-mail address, and click **OK**.

To add the sender or recipient of a message to one of your Junk E-mail lists from your Inbox or other mail folder, right-click the message, point to Junk E-mail, and then click Add Sender to Junk Senders list, Add Sender to Trusted Senders list, or Add to Trusted Recipients list.

Organizing Messages in Folders

After you've read and responded to messages, you might want to keep some for future reference. With Outlook, you can organize your messages in a variety of ways.

Creating folders to organize your messages helps you avoid an accumulation of unrelated messages in your Inbox. For example, you can create a folder for each project you're working on and store all messages regarding a particular project in its own folder. Or you can create a folder to store all messages from your boss. You can move messages to the folders manually or have Outlook move them for you.

See Also For more information about automatically moving messages, see "Managing Messages through Rules" earlier in this chapter.

Tip If you are using a Microsoft Exchange Server account, the Out of Office Assistant can help you manage messages while you are away from the office. You can explore this feature by clicking Out of Office Assistant on the Tools menu.

In this exercise, you will organize messages by moving them to a new folder.

USE the *SBSOrganizing* data file in the practice file folder for this topic. This practice file is located in the *My Documents\Microsoft Press\Outlook 2003 SBS\Organizing* folder and can also be accessed by clicking *Start/All Programs/Microsoft Press/Outlook 2003 Step by Step.*
BE SURE TO open the *SBSOrganizing* data file before beginning this exercise.
OPEN the practice file **Inbox**.

1 On the **Tools** menu, click **Organize**.

The Ways to Organize pane appears.

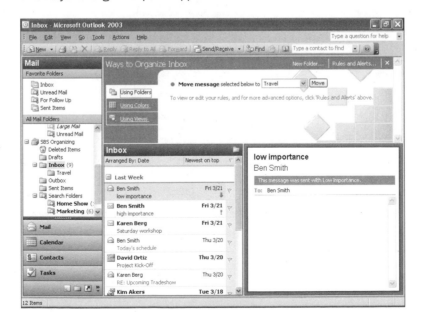

See Also   For information about organizing messages with color, see "Managing Messages with Color" in Chapter 2, "Managing E-Mail Messages."

---

2   At the top of the **Ways to Organize** pane, click the **New Folder** button.

The Create New Folder dialog box appears.

Troubleshooting   If your default data store is a personal folder on your hard disk, the first item in the "Select where to place the folder" box is Personal Folders.

3   In the **Name** box, type **Home Show** as the name of your new folder.

4   In the **Select where to place the folder** list, click the SBS Organizing data file's **Inbox**, and then click **OK**.

The Create New Folder dialog box closes. The new Home Show folder appears as a subfolder of the Inbox folder. (You can scroll down the Navigation Pane to see the folder.)

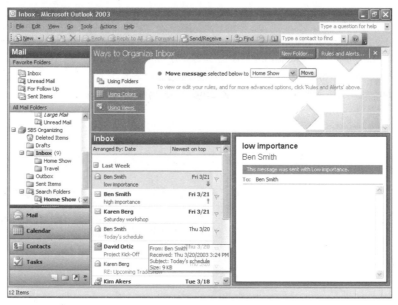

5   In the Inbox, click the **Upcoming Tradeshow** message from Karen Berg, and in the **Ways to Organize Inbox** pane, click the **Move** button.

The message is moved to the new folder.

6   Repeat step 5 to move the **RE: Upcoming Tradeshow** and **Today's schedule** messages to the new folder.

Tip You can automatically move messages to another folder by creating a rule. To create a simple rule, such as moving all messages received from your boss to a separate folder, use the Using Folders tab of the Ways to Organize pane. For more complex rules, click the Rules Wizard button in the top right corner of the Ways to Organize pane.

7 In the **Navigation Pane**, click the **Home Show** folder.

The contents of the new folder are displayed.

8 In the **Navigation Pane**, drag the **Home Show** folder to the *SBS Organizing* folder.

The new folder is now listed at the same level in the folder structure as the Inbox and in alphabetical order with the other items at this level.

9 In the **Folder List**, right-click the **Home Show** folder, and then click **Rename** on the shortcut menu.

The folder name changes to an editable text box.

10 Type Garden Show, and press ⌷Enter⌷.

The folder name changes.

11 In the **Folder List**, click the **Garden Show** folder to display its contents.

Move to Folder

12 Right-click the **Upcoming Tradeshow** message, and then click **Move to Folder** on the shortcut menu.

The Move Items dialog box appears.

13 Click the practice **Inbox**, and then click **OK**.

The message is moved to the Inbox.

Delete

14 Click the **RE: Upcoming Tradeshow** message, and then click the **Delete** button.

The message is deleted.

15 Drag the Today's schedule message to the practice Inbox in the **Navigation Pane**.

The message is moved to the Inbox, and the folder is now empty.

16 In the **Folder List**, click the **Garden Show** folder, and then press [Del].

17 When Outlook asks if you are sure you want to delete the folder, click **Yes**.

The folder is deleted. When you delete a folder, any messages contained within that folder are also deleted. (In this case, the folder is empty.)

CLOSE the Folder List.

Important When you delete any item in Outlook, it is moved to the Deleted Items folder. You can view your deleted items by clicking that folder in the Folder List. You can tell Outlook to empty the Deleted Items folder every time you close the program by setting that option in the Options dialog box. On the Tools menu, click Options, click the Other tab, select the "Empty the Deleted Items folder upon exiting" check box, and then click OK. You can empty the Deleted Items folder at any time by right-clicking the folder in the Folder List and clicking Empty "Deleted Items" Folder on the shortcut menu.

Sharing Folders with Others

When you use Outlook, your messages, contacts, appointments, and other items are stored in folders. By default, the standard Outlook folders (Calendar, Contacts, Deleted Items, Drafts, Inbox, Journal, Junk E-mail, Notes, Outbox, Sent Items, Sync Issues, Tasks, and Search Folders) and the folders you create are private, meaning that only you can access them. However, if you are working on a network that uses Microsoft Exchange Server, you can choose to share private folders, allowing others to access them.

You can share folders with others in two ways. First you can give someone permission to access a folder. For example, you might have a collection of messages you want to share with a co-worker on a project. You can store those messages in a folder and give your co-worker access to that folder. You can select from a number of permission levels ranging from Owner (full access) to Reviewer (read-only access). When you select a permission level, Outlook indicates which actions will be allowed.

For example, you might grant Author access to your assistant who will help you manage incoming e-mail. As an author, your assistant can read items, create items, and edit and delete items that he or she creates, but those with Author permission level cannot create subfolders. Because permissions are defined as properties of an individual folder, you can grant someone Owner access to one folder and Reviewer access to another. You can also give more than one person permission to access a folder and select a different permission level for each person.

The second option for sharing folders is granting Delegate access. When you define someone as a *delegate*, you specify his or her access level to the Calendar, Tasks, Inbox, Contacts, Notes, or Journal as that of Editor, Author, or Reviewer. An editor can read, create, and modify items in the folder. An author can read and create items in the folder. A reviewer can read items in the folder. A delegate can be an editor in one folder and a reviewer in another. As an author or editor, a delegate can also send messages on your behalf. Recipients of messages sent by a delegate see both the manager's and the delegate's names on the message. Regardless of access level, a delegate cannot create subfolders. To allow someone to create subfolders, you must share the folder using permissions.

Important   This exercise requires that you be connected to a Microsoft Exchange Server network.

In this exercise, you will copy a folder to your own mailbox and then practice different ways of sharing the folder.

USE the *SBSOrganizing* data file in the practice file folder for this topic. This practice file is located in the *My Documents\Microsoft Press\Outlook 2003 SBS\Organizing* folder and can also be accessed by clicking *Start/All Programs/Microsoft Press/Outlook 2003 Step by Step*.
BE SURE TO open the *SBSOrganizing* data file before beginning this exercise.

1   In the **Navigation Pane**, drag the button panel down so that all the buttons are minimized and you can see more mail folders.

2   Expand your own mailbox and the SBS Organizing data file so you can see their contents.

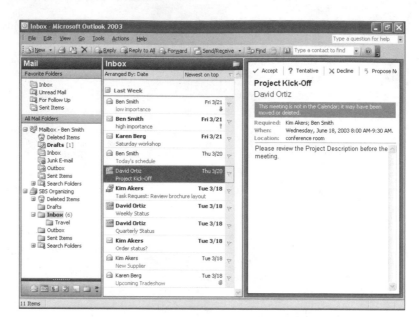

3   Right-click the practice Inbox, and on the shortcut menu, click **Copy**.

The Copy Folder dialog box appears.

4   Scroll to the top of the list and click your own mailbox.

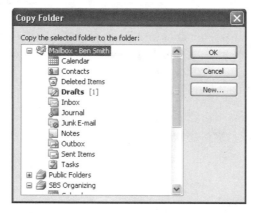

5   Click **OK**.

The practice Inbox folder is copied to your own mailbox as *Inbox1*.

6 In your own mailbox, right-click the **Inbox1** folder, and on the shortcut menu, click **Sharing**.

The Inbox1 Properties dialog box appears, displaying the Permissions tab.

7 Click the **Add** button.

The Add Users dialog box appears.

8 Click the name of the co-worker with whom you want to share this folder, and then click the **Add** button.

The selected name appears in the Add Users box.

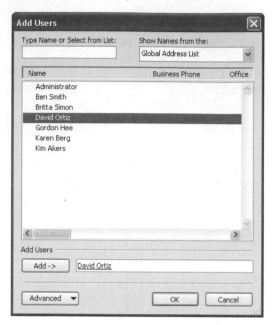

9   Click **OK**.

The Add Users dialog box closes. The Inbox1 Properties dialog box shows the selected co-worker's name in the list.

10   With your co-worker's name selected, in the **Permissions** area, click the down arrow to the right of the **Permission Level** box, and then click **Editor**.

The "Create items" and "Read items" check boxes are selected, and the All option is selected in the "Edit items" and "Delete items" areas.

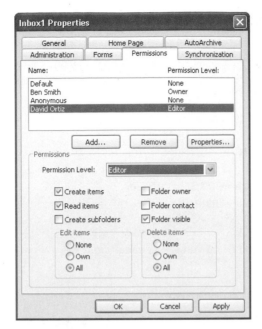

11 Click **OK**.

The new permission settings are applied to the Inbox1 folder. Your co-worker can now view the folder by opening it from within Outlook on his or her computer and can create, edit, and delete items within it.

Tip To open another person's folder, on the File menu, point to Open, and then click Other User's Folder. Click the Name button, click the name of the person sharing the folder with you, and then click OK. In the Folder type drop-down list, click the folder you want to open, and then click OK.

12 If your co-worker is available, ask him or her to open your *Inbox1* folder to verify that the folder is shared as expected.

13 When you are finished, click the **Inbox1** folder, and on the toolbar, click the **Delete** button. When Outlook prompts you to confirm the deletion, click **Yes**.

✕
Delete

The Inbox1 folder is deleted from your mailbox.

BE SURE TO expand the Navigation buttons the way you want them.

Saving Messages in Other Formats

Microsoft Office Specialist

Sometimes a message will contain information that you want to use in another program. You can save a message as a plain text file, which most programs can open or import. Or you might save a message as an HTML document, which would make it easier to post it to a team portal or Web site.

In this exercise, you will save messages to your hard disk in different formats.

USE the *SBSOrganizing* data file in the practice file folder for this topic. This practice file is located in the *My Documents\Microsoft Press\Outlook 2003 SBS\Organizing* folder and can also be accessed by clicking *Start/All Programs/Microsoft Press/Outlook 2003 Step by Step.*
BE SURE TO open the *SBSOrganizing* data file before beginning this exercise.
OPEN the practice file Inbox.

1 In the Inbox, click the **Order status?** message from Kim Akers, and on the **File** menu, click **Save As**.

The Save As dialog box appears.

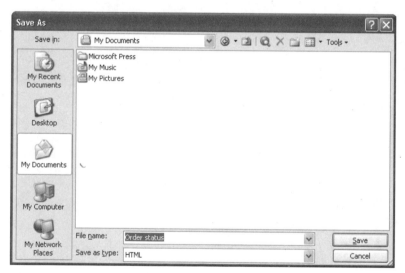

By default, Outlook saves e-mail messages as HTML files.

Tip Your Save As dialog box will show your My Documents folder or the last folder in which you saved an Outlook item. If you have file extensions turned on, the name in the File Name box will be Order status.htm.

2   If the My Documents folder is not displayed in the **Save As** dialog box, click the **My Documents** icon.

3   Double-click *Microsoft Press*, *Outlook 2003 SBS*, *Organizing*, and then click **Save**.

The message is saved in the selected folder as *Order status.htm*.

4   In the Inbox, click the **Today's schedule** message, and on the **File** menu, click **Save As**.

The Save As dialog box appears, already open to the *My Documents\Microsoft Press \Outlook 2003 SBS\Organizing* folder.

5   Click the down arrow to the right of the **Save as type** box, click **Text Only** in the drop-down list, and then click **Save**.

The message is saved in the selected folder as *Saturday workshop.txt*.

6   On the **Start** menu, click **My Documents**. Double-click the *Microsoft Press*, *Outlook 2003 SBS*, and *Organizing* folders.

The folder contains the files you saved, along with the Outlook data file used in this chapter.

Web page

7   Double-click the *Order status* HTML file, which is indicated by a Web page icon.

The message opens in your default *Web browser*.

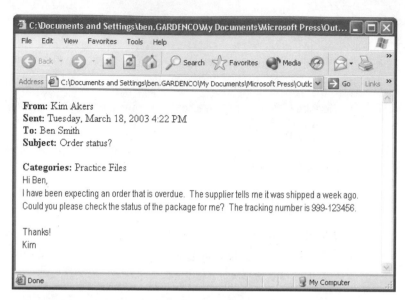

If the message contained any formatting, the HTML format preserves it.

Text page

8 In the *Organizing* folder, double-click the *Today's schedule* text file, which is indicated by a Text page icon.

The message opens in Notepad.

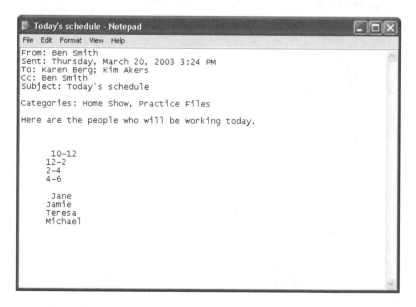

CLOSE the Notepad window, the browser window, and the Organizing folder.

Archiving Messages

*Microsoft
Office
Specialist*

As messages accumulate in your Inbox and other message folders, you might need to consider other ways to store them in order to cut down on the amount of storage space you're using. For example, you might want to *archive* all messages sent or received before a certain date. Archiving messages in a separate Outlook message file helps you manage clutter and the size of your primary message file, while still allowing easy access to archived messages from within Outlook.

You can archive messages manually or automatically. When archived messages are moved to a separate message file, the messages are removed from their original folder. By default, Outlook automatically archives messages in all folders at regular intervals to a location determined by your operating system. You can change the default global settings for the *AutoArchive* function and specify varying archive settings for specific folders. Archive settings selected for a specific folder override the global settings for that folder. If you don't specify AutoArchive settings for a folder, Outlook uses the global settings.

In this exercise, you will investigate your automatic archive options, and then archive messages manually.

USE the *SBSOrganizing* data file in the practice file folder for this topic. This practice file is located in the *My Documents\Microsoft Press\Outlook 2003 SBS\Organizing* folder and can also be accessed by clicking *Start/All Programs/Microsoft Press/Outlook 2003 Step by Step.*
BE SURE TO open the *SBSOrganizing* data file before beginning this exercise.
OPEN the practice file Inbox.

1   On the **Tools** menu, click **Options**.

The Options dialog box appears.

2   Click the **Other** tab, and then click the **AutoArchive** button.

The AutoArchive dialog box appears.

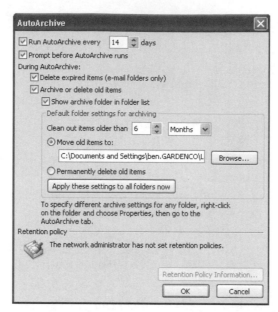

3 Review your AutoArchive default settings—particularly note the interval at which the archive will happen, the age at which items will be archived, and the location in the **Move old items to** box.

4 Click **Cancel** in each of the open dialog boxes.

The dialog boxes close without initiating any changes.

Tip You can use the Mailbox Cleanup feature to see the size of your mailbox, find and delete old items or items that are larger than a certain size, start AutoArchive, or view and empty your Deleted Items folder. To use this feature, on the Tools menu, click Mailbox Cleanup.

Folder List

5 In the **Navigation Pane**, click the **Folder List** icon.

The Folder List appears.

6 In the *SBS Organizing* data file, click the **Inbox** (not the Inbox in your mailbox).

7 On the **File** menu, point to **Folder**, and then click **Properties**.

The Inbox Properties dialog box appears.

8   Click the **AutoArchive** tab.

The AutoArchive options are displayed.

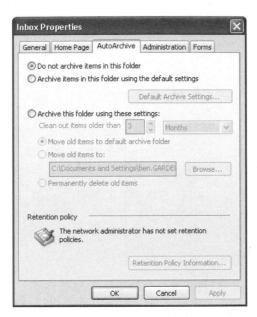

9   Select the **Archive this folder using these settings** option.

10   In the **Clean out items older than** box, select **1** and **Days**.

Important   You would usually stipulate a longer archive period, but for the purposes of this exercise you will archive all the messages in the practice Inbox.

11   Be sure the option to **Move old items to default archive folder** is selected, and click **OK**.

The Inbox Properties dialog box closes. Items in the Inbox will be archived according to the new settings. Items in all other folders will be archived according to the default settings.

12   On the **File** menu, click **Archive**.

The Archive dialog box appears.

13 With the **Archive this folder and all subfolders** option selected, click the **SBS Organizing** folder.

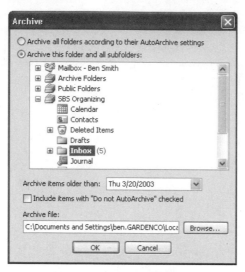

14 In the **Archive items older than** drop-down list, click a date that you know is later than the date of some of the messages in the Inbox, and click **OK**.

Outlook archives the messages in the practice Inbox according to your settings.

15 In the **Folder List**, double-click **Archive Folders** to expand it, and click the **Inbox** folder that appears within that folder.

The contents of the archived Inbox folder are displayed.

BE SURE TO close the *SBS Organizing* data file after completing this chapter.

Checking Addresses

By default, Outlook will check any e-mail address you type against the entries in the Outlook Address Book. If the address book does not contain an entry for a name that you type in the To, Cc, or Bcc boxes of a new message, when you send the message, Outlook will prompt you to select an address book entry or provide a full e-mail address.

To have Outlook check entries from your Personal Address Book:

1   On the **Tools** menu, click **Address Book**.

2   On the Address Book window's **Tools** menu, click **Options**.

3   In the **Addressing** dialog box, click the **Add** button.

4   In the **Add Address List** dialog box, click **Outlook Address Book**, and then click the **Add** button.

5   Click the **Close** button.

6   In the **Addressing** dialog box, click **OK**.

7   In the Address Book window, click the **Close** button.

Key Points

■   You can create folders to organize your mail. You can set up rules to move messages to folders based on the sender, other recipients, words in the subject or body of the message, and other factors.

■   You can use filters and Search Folders to view messages that meet certain search criteria.

■   Outlook can help you manage your mailbox by periodically archiving old items. Different folders can have different archiving schedules.

■   Using Microsoft Exchange Server, you can share folders in your mailbox with other members of your organization.

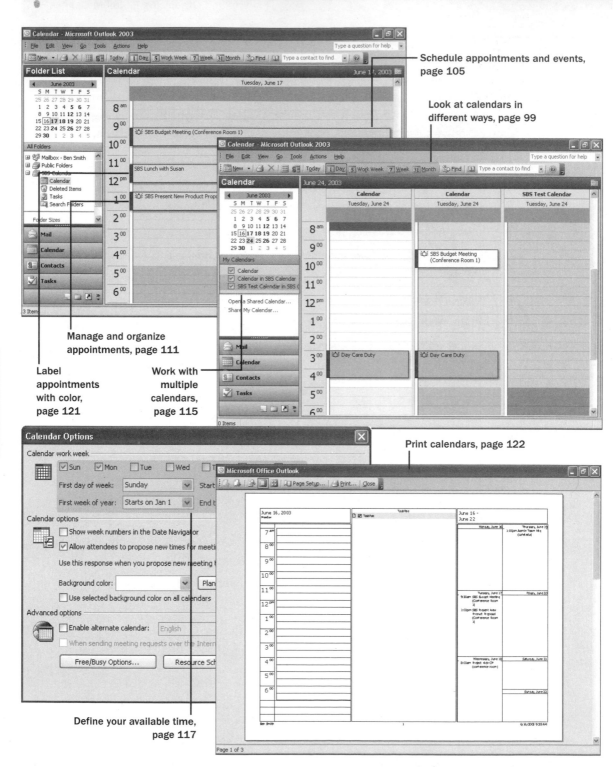

Schedule appointments and events, page 105

Look at calendars in different ways, page 99

Manage and organize appointments, page 111

Label appointments with color, page 121

Work with multiple calendars, page 115

Print calendars, page 122

Define your available time, page 117

Chapter 4 at a Glance

4 Managing Your Calendar

In this chapter you will learn to:
- ✔ Look at calendars in different ways.
- ✔ Schedule appointments and events.
- ✔ Manage and organize appointments.
- ✔ Work with multiple calendars.
- ✔ Define your available time.
- ✔ Label appointments with color.
- ✔ Print calendars.

Managing time effectively is a constant challenge for most people today. The Microsoft Office Outlook *Calendar* makes it easy for you to manage your schedule, including both appointments and events, as well as to view and print your schedule for a day, a week, or a month.

In this chapter, you will experiment with the Outlook Calendar and learn how to use its various features.

See Also   Do you need only a quick refresher on the topics in this chapter? See the Quick Reference entries on pages xxxvi–xxxviii.

Important   Before you can use the practice files in this chapter, you need to install them from the book's companion CD to their default location. See "Using the Book's CD-ROM" on page xiii for more information.

Looking at Calendars in Different Ways

Microsoft Office Specialist

To help you stay on top of your schedule, you can view your Calendar in a variety of ways:

- ■ *Day view* displays one day at a time, separated into half-hour increments.
- ■ *Work Week view* displays your work week in columnar format. By default, the work week is defined as 8:00 A.M. to 5:00 P.M. Monday through Friday. You can define your work week as whatever days and hours you want.

See Also For more information about defining your work week, see "Defining Your Available Time," later in this chapter.

■ *Week view* displays one calendar week at a time.

■ *Month view* displays five weeks at a time.

By default, your Calendar is displayed in Month view. To change the view setting, click the toolbar button for the view you want.

Outlook's default settings break the day into half-hour increments, with the *work week* defined as 8 A.M. to 5 P.M. Monday through Friday. You can change the Calendar's work week to reflect your own working hours, and you can schedule appointments for any time of any day.

The *Date Navigator* serves as a handy month calendar and an easy way to view your schedule for specific dates. To view your schedule for a particular date, simply click that date in the Date Navigator.

About Calendar Views

New in Office 2003

Calendar view

Outlook 2003 offers a streamlined Calendar view that now includes the Date Navigator, a day/time indicator, and the ability to view multiple calendars at once.

Outlook offers a number of ways to view your Calendar. To select the view, on the View menu, point to Arrange By, point to Current View, and then click the view you want.

Click this view	To see
Day/Week/Month	A calendar-like view of appointments, events, and meetings for the period of time you specify. This is the default view, and it includes the Date Navigator.
Day/Week/Month With AutoPreview	The Day/Week/Month view with the addition of the first line of comment text for each Calendar item.
Active Appointments	A list of appointments and meetings scheduled for today and in the future, showing details in columns.
Events	A list of events, showing details in columns.
Annual Events	A list of annual events, showing details in columns.
Recurring Appointments	A list of recurring appointments, showing details in columns.
By Category	A list of all items, grouped by category, showing details in columns.

In this exercise, you will experiment with the different ways to view and move around in your calendar.

Important You can work through this exercise in your own Calendar or in the practice Calendar. If you use your own Calendar and don't already have appointments on it, you will not be able to see all the categories discussed here.

USE the *SBSCalendar* data file in the practice file folder for this topic. This practice file is located in the *My Documents\Microsoft Press\Outlook 2003 SBS\Calendar* folder and can also be accessed by clicking *Start/All Programs/Microsoft Press/Outlook 2003 Step by Step*.
BE SURE TO start Outlook before beginning this exercise.
OPEN the *SBSCalendar* data file from within Outlook.

Folder List

1 In the **Navigation Pane**, click the **Folder List** icon.

2 In the **Folder List**, expand the **SBS Calendar** data file, and then click the subordinate **Calendar**.

By default, the Calendar displays Day view. The current day is shaded in the Date Navigator.

Date Navigator   View buttons

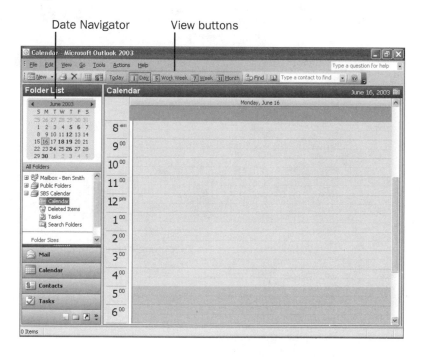

> **Tip** You can increase the size of the Navigation Pane to display two months in the Date Navigator. With your Calendar displayed in Outlook, point to the vertical frame divider between the Navigation Pane and the Calendar. When the pointer changes to a double-headed arrow, drag the frame to the right.

3 In the Date Navigator, click the arrows to scroll to January 2004. Then click **8**.

The Calendar displays the schedule for January 8th, 2004.

4 On the toolbar, click the **Work Week** button.

The Calendar displays the schedule for your currently defined work week. The work week is shaded in the Date Navigator.

The bell indicates that a reminder
will appear before this meeting.

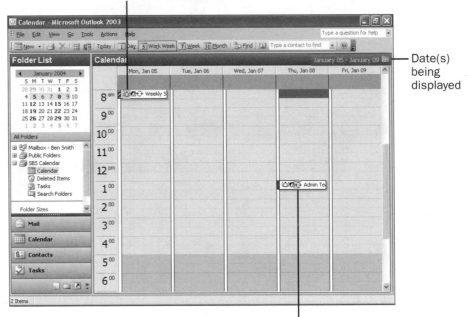

Date(s) being displayed

Circling arrows indicate a recurring appointment.

5 On the toolbar, click the **Week** button.

The Calendar displays the schedule for the seven-day week. The week is shaded in the Date Navigator.

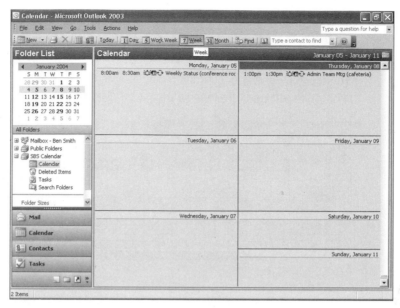

6   In the Date Navigator, click in the margin to the left of the week starting January 11.

The Calendar now shows the schedule for that week.

7   On the toolbar, click the **Month** button.

The Calendar shows the schedule for the current month. The month is shaded in the Date Navigator.

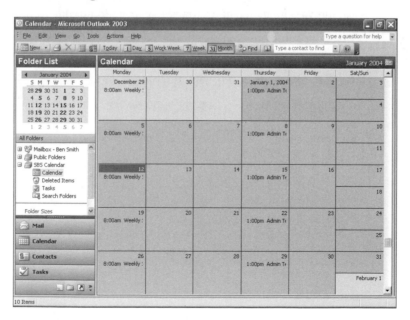

Notice that months are differentiated by alternating colors.

8 On the **View** menu, point to **Arrange By**, point to **Current View**, and then click **Active Appointments**.

The recurring and non-recurring appointments in the practice calendar are displayed. You can sort the appointments by clicking the column headers.

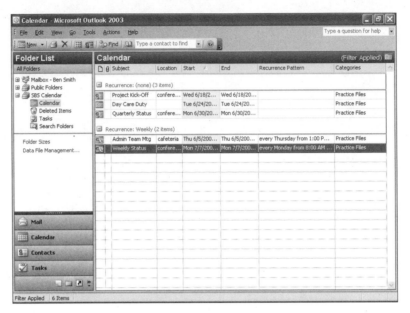

9 On the **View** menu, point to **Arrange By**, point to **Current View**, and click **By Category**.

Calendar items are displayed in a columnar list, grouped by category.

10 Investigate any other views that interest you. When you finish, on the **View** menu, point to **Arrange By**, point to **Current View**, and then click **Day/Week/Month**.

11 On the toolbar, click the **Day** button to display a one-day view.

12 On the toolbar, click the **Go to Today** button to display today's calendar page.

Go to Today

Scheduling Appointments and Events

Microsoft Office Specialist

Adding your time commitments to a calendar can help you manage your daily schedule. You can use Outlook's *Calendar* to schedule *appointments* (which typically last just part of a day) or *events* (which typically last all day long). For example, you might create an appointment in your Outlook Calendar for the time you will spend seeing your doctor, and you might schedule an event for an all-day seminar you plan to attend. Both appointments and events can be *recurring*, meaning they occur repeatedly at regular intervals—for example, daily, weekly, or monthly. You can specify a subject and location for each Calendar item as well as the date and time. You can indicate your availability as available, tentative, busy, or out of the office during the scheduled time, and you can choose to receive a *reminder* of an appointment or event. Reminders are displayed in a small dialog box that appears as the time of the appointment or event approaches. Outlook must be open for you to receive reminders.

In this exercise, you will schedule an appointment, schedule a recurring appointment, and schedule a multi-day event.

Important You can work through this exercise in your own Calendar or in the practice Calendar. If you use your own Calendar, be sure to delete the appointments you create in the exercise. To make it easier to locate and identify the sample appointments, each appointment subject starts with the letters *SBS*.

USE the *SBSCalendar* data file in the practice file folder for this topic. This practice file is located in the *My Documents\Microsoft Press\Outlook 2003 SBS\Calendar* folder and can also be accessed by clicking *Start/All Programs/Microsoft Press/Outlook 2003 Step by Step*.
BE SURE TO start Outlook and open the *SBSCalendar* data file before beginning this exercise.

1   In the **Navigation Pane**, click the **Folder List** icon.

2   In the **Folder List**, expand the **SBS Calendar** data file, and then click the practice **Calendar**.

Calendar

Tip If you want to work through this exercise in your own Calendar, simply click the Calendar icon in the Navigation Pane.

The Calendar appears, showing today's schedule.

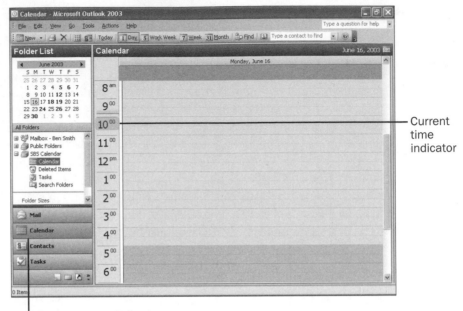

Current time indicator

Link to your own Calendar

Troubleshooting The default Calendar display is Day view. If your Calendar does not look like the one shown in this exercise, click the Day button on the toolbar.

3 In the Date Navigator, click tomorrow's date.

Tomorrow's schedule is displayed.

4 Double-click the 1:00 P.M. time slot.

A new Appointment form appears.

5 In the **Subject** box, type SBS Present New Product Proposal.

6 Press the ⌷Tab⌷ key, and in the **Location** box, type Conference Room 1.

7 Click the down arrow to the right of the second **End time** box (the one that displays the time, not the date), and in the drop-down list, click **2:00 PM** to set the meeting duration to one hour.

8 If necessary, select the **Reminder** check box to indicate that you want Outlook to remind you of this meeting. Click the down arrow to the right of the **Reminder** box, and in the drop-down list, click **30 minutes** to allow time to set up for your presentation.

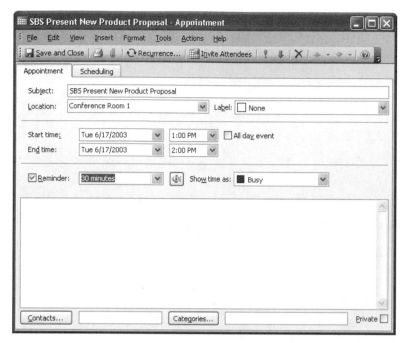

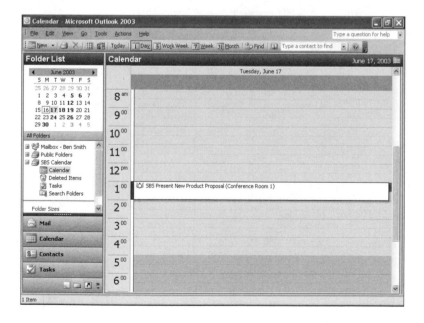

Save and Close   **9**   On the Appointment window toolbar, click the **Save and Close** button. If Outlook warns you that the reminder will not appear, click **Yes**.

The appointment is saved in the Calendar.

Tip You can quickly create an appointment by clicking the appropriate Calendar timeslot and then typing the appointment subject. To create a longer appointment, drag through the timeslots you want, and then type the subject. Appointments created this way use the default reminder setting and don't include a meeting location.

10 In the Date Navigator, click the right arrow to display next month.

11 Click the third Wednesday of the month.

Tip The Date Navigator displays six weeks at a time, including the selected month. The days of the selected month are black; days of the previous and next months are gray, but you can still select them in the Date Navigator.

The schedule for the selected day is displayed.

12 Double-click the 10:00 A.M. time slot.

A new Appointment form appears.

13 In the **Subject** box, type **SBS Status Report**.

14 Press the ⌨Tab key, and in the **Location** box, type **Boss's Office**.

 15 Click the **Recurrence** button.

The Appointment Recurrence dialog box appears.

16 In the **Recurrence pattern** area, select the **Monthly** option, and then select the **The third Wednesday of every 1 month(s)** option.

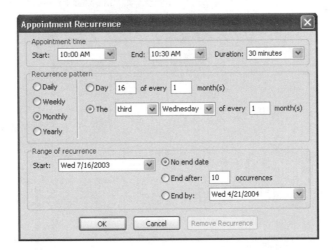

17 Click **OK**.

The recurrence settings are added to the Appointment form.

Create recurring appointments.

18 Click the **Save and Close** button.

The recurring appointment is added to your Calendar. Circling arrows indicate the recurrence.

19 In the Date Navigator, click the right arrow.

The Date Navigator shows the next month, with the third Wednesday appearing bold, indicating that an appointment is scheduled for that day.

20 On the **Go** menu, click **Go to Date**.

The Go To Date dialog box appears.

21 In the **Date** box, type **8/8/04**, and then click **OK**.

The schedule for August 8th, 2004, is displayed.

22 Right-click the 9:00 A.M. time slot, and then click **New All Day Event** on the short-cut menu.

A new Event form appears.

23 In the **Subject** box, type **SBS On Vacation**.

24 Click the down arrow to the right of the **End time** box, and then click the 14th day of August on the drop-down calendar.

25 Clear the **Reminder** check box if it is selected.

26 Click the down arrow to the right of the **Show time as** box, and then click **Out of Office** in the drop-down list.

Tip By default, Outlook adds the typical holidays for your country as Calendar events, but you can add the holidays of other countries. On the Tools menu, click Options. On the Preferences tab, click Calendar Options, and then click the Add Holidays button. Select the check boxes of the countries whose holidays you want to add, and then click OK in each open dialog box.

27 In the lower-right corner of the **Event** form, select the **Private** check box.

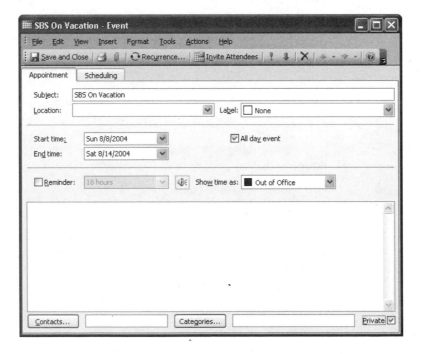

Tip You can easily mark an existing appointment as *private* so that other Outlook users can't see its details. Simply right-click the appointment in the Calendar, and then click Private on the shortcut menu.

28 Click the **Save and Close** button. If Outlook warns you that the reminder will not appear, click **Yes**.

The new event is added to your Calendar. A key icon indicates that the appointment is private.

29 On the toolbar, click the **Go to Today** button.

Today's schedule appears.

Today

Go to Today

BE SURE TO delete the SBS Present New Product Proposal, SBS Status Report, and SBS On Vacation appointments if you worked through this exercise in your own Calendar.

Managing and Organizing Appointments

Microsoft Office Specialist

You can use the Outlook Calendar to manage and organize your appointments in a variety of ways. You can enter details about an appointment to help you remember important information, such as the agenda for a meeting or directions to a client's office. And as with e-mail messages, you can assign meetings to categories and organize them in folders to help you sort your appointments. For example, you might assign a dentist appointment to the Personal category. Outlook includes a selection of useful categories, including Business, Personal, and Miscellaneous, but you can create additional categories to meet your needs. Or you might create a separate Personal calendar folder for your non-work-related appointments. When your schedule changes, you can also move, copy, and delete appointments.

See Also For more information about categories, see "Finding and Categorizing Messages" in Chapter 3, "Finding and Organizing E-Mail Messages."

In this exercise, you will add details to an appointment and assign an appointment to a category. Then you will move, copy, and delete an appointment.

Important You can work through this exercise in your own Calendar or in the practice Calendar. If you use your own Calendar, be sure to delete the appointments you create in the exercise. To make it easier to locate and identify the sample appointments, each appointment subject starts with the letters *SBS*.

USE the *SBSCalendar* data file in the practice file folder for this topic. This practice file is located in the *My Documents\Microsoft Press\Outlook 2003 SBS\Calendar* folder and can also be accessed by clicking *Start/All Programs/Microsoft Press/Outlook 2003 Step by Step*.
BE SURE TO open the *SBSCalendar* data file before beginning this exercise.

1 Click tomorrow's date in the Date Navigator.

Tomorrow's schedule is displayed.

2 Drag through the 9:30 and 10:00 time slots to select them.

3 Type **SBS Budget Meeting**, and press the Enter key.

The appointment is added to the Calendar.

4 With the appointment selected, press Enter again.

The Appointment form appears.

5 Click in the **Location** box, and type **Conference Room 1**.

Tip   Outlook remembers the locations you type in the Location box. Instead of typing the location again, you can click the down arrow to the right of the Location box, and then click the location you want.

6 Be sure the **Reminder** check box is selected, and in the **Reminder** list, click **1 hour**.

7 Click the comments area below the reminder, and type a rough agenda for the meeting.

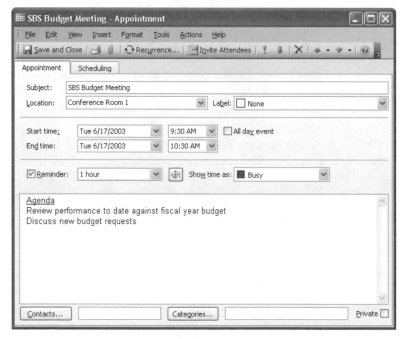

Tip   To format the comment text, select the text to be formatted, click the Format menu, and then click Text or Paragraph.

8 At the bottom of the **Appointment** form, click the **Categories** button.

The Categories dialog box appears.

9 Click in the **Item(s) belong to these categories** box, type Finance, and click the **Add to List** button.

The Finance category is added to the list and is selected.

10 In the **Available categories** list, select the **Business** check box, and then click **OK**.

The selected categories are added to the Categories box in the Appointment form.

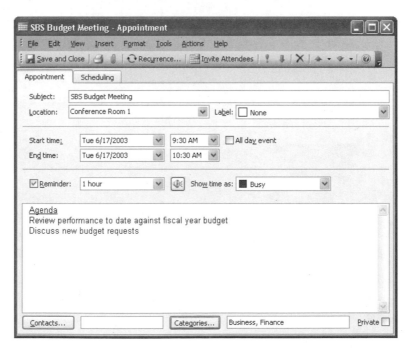

11 Click the **Save and Close** button.

12 If Outlook warns you that the reminder will not appear, click **Yes**.

The Calendar displays the updated appointment.

13 Click the 12:00 P.M. time slot, and type **SBS Lunch with Susan**.

14 Point to the bottom border of the appointment, and when the pointer changes to a vertical double-headed arrow, drag the bottom of the appointment to 1:00 P.M., and then press the [Enter] key.

The Calendar displays the updated appointment. In the Date Navigator, the selected date appears in bold, indicating that appointments are scheduled.

15 Point to the left border of the **SBS Lunch with Susan** appointment.

The pointer becomes a four-headed arrow.

16 Drag the appointment to the 11:30 A.M. time slot.

The lunch appointment is rescheduled for 11:30 A.M.

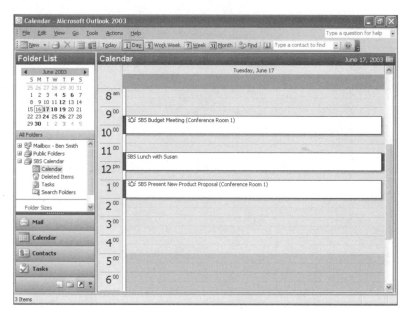

17 Point to the left border of the **SBS Budget Meeting** appointment.

The pointer becomes a four-headed arrow.

18 Using the right mouse button, drag the appointment to the same day of the following week in the Date Navigator.

A shortcut menu appears.

19 On the shortcut menu, click **Copy**.

Outlook displays the schedule for a week from tomorrow, showing the new Budget Meeting appointment.

20 In the Date Navigator, click tomorrow's date.

Tomorrow's schedule is displayed, showing the original Budget Meeting appointment.

✕

Delete

21 Click the **SBS Lunch with Susan** appointment, and on the toolbar, click the **Delete** button.

The appointment is removed from your Calendar.

BE SURE TO delete the SBS Budget Meeting and SBS Budget Team appointments if you worked through this exercise in your own Calendar.

Working with Multiple Calendars

It is often handy to have more than one Calendar. For instance, you might want to maintain one Calendar for yourself, and one for a team project. Or you might want to have separate business and personal calendars. It is easy to create new Calendars.

New in Office 2003
Side-by-side calendars

With Outlook 2003, you can view several Calendars at the same time, and move or copy appointments and events between them. When you view and scroll multiple calendars, they all display the same date or time period.

In this exercise, you will create a new Calendar, and then view all the available Calendars at once.

USE the *SBSCalendar* data file in the practice file folder for this topic. This practice file is located in the *My Documents\Microsoft Press\Outlook 2003 SBS\Calendar* folder and can also be accessed by clicking *Start/All Programs/Microsoft Press/Outlook 2003 Step by Step*.
BE SURE TO open the *SBSCalendar* data file before beginning this exercise.

1 Display the practice Calendar.

New ▾

2 Click the down arrow to the right of the **New** button, and then click **Folder** in the drop-down list.

The Create New Folder dialog box appears.

3 In the **Name** box, type **SBS Test Calendar**.

4 In the **Folder contains** drop-down list, click **Calendar Items**.

5 In the **Select where to place the folder** box, click the **SBS Calendar** folder.

6 Click **OK**.

The new Calendar appears in the SBS Calendar data file.

Calendar

7 In the **Navigation Pane**, click the **Calendar** icon.

The My Calendars list appears in the Navigation Pane, listing the available calendars. The *Calendar in SBS Calendar* check box is selected to indicate the calendar you are viewing.

8 In the **My Calendars** list, select the **Calendar** check box.

Outlook displays your main calendar and the practice calendar side by side.

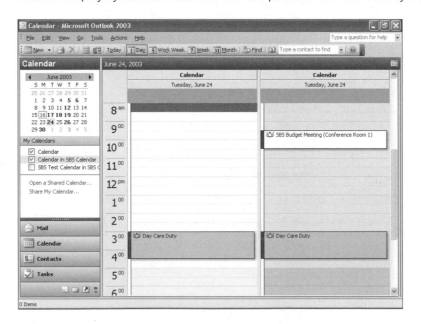

9   In the **My Calendars** list, select the **SBS Test Calendar in SBS Calendars**
check box.

Outlook displays the three calendars side by side. Colored stripes across the
calendar names match the colors on the displayed calendars so you can tell
which is which.

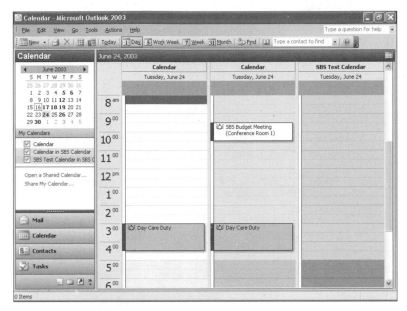

10   In the Date Navigator, click a bold date to find a day with a scheduled meeting
or event.

11   Drag the event from one calendar to the next to move it. Right-click and drag the
event, and then click **Copy** on the shortcut menu.

12   Clear the **Calendar** and **SBS Test Calendar in SBS Calendar** check boxes to display
only the practice calendar.

BE SURE TO move any of your own appointments back to their original dates and times.

Defining Your Available Time

*Microsoft
Office
Specialist*

You can tell Outlook what your work schedule is so that other people can make
appointments with you only during the times that you plan to be available. This
defined time is called your *work week*. The work week is colored differently in your
calendar, and by default is the only time displayed to other people on your network
who look at your calendar.

By default, the work week is defined as Monday through Friday from 8:00 A.M. to 5:00 P.M. You can change this to suit your needs—for instance, if you work a late shift or weekends.

See Also For more information about looking at other people's calendars, see "Viewing Other Users' Calendars" in Chapter 5, "Scheduling and Managing Meetings."

In this exercise, you will view and change your work week.

OPEN your own Calendar.

1 On the toolbar, click the **Work Week** button.

The calendar displays your current work week.

Troubleshooting If your work week does not match the default days and times described here, work through this exercise using your own settings.

2 Scroll the calendar page so you can see the beginning and end of the work day.

Notice that the working hours are shaded differently from the rest of the day.

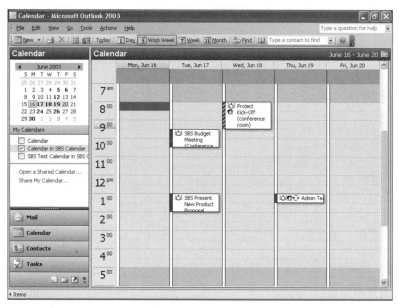

3 On the **Tools** menu, click **Options**.

The Options dialog box appears.

4 In the **Calendar** area of the **Preferences** tab, click **Calendar Options**.

The Calendar Options dialog box appears.

5 In the **Calendar work week** area, select the **Sun** and **Sat** check boxes, and clear the **Tue**, **Wed**, and **Thu** check boxes.

The work week is now set to Friday through Monday.

6 Click the down arrow to the right of the **Start time** box, and click **3:00 PM**. Then click the down arrow to the right of the **End time** box, and click **11:00 PM**.

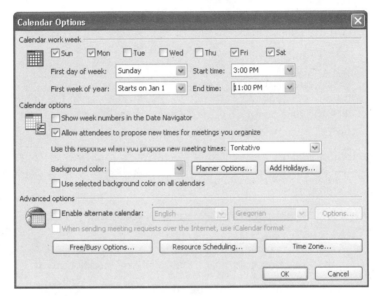

7 Click **OK**, and in the **Options** dialog box, click **OK** again.

Troubleshooting   Outlook doesn't allow you to define a workday that crosses midnight, or to define different start and end times for different days.

The Calendar displays your new default work week.

8 On the **Tools** menu, click **Options**, and then click the **Calendar Options** button.

9 Select the check boxes for your actual work days.

10 Set your actual start and end times.

11 Click **OK** to close each of the dialog boxes and set your default work week.

BE SURE TO set your default work week the way you want.

Working with Multiple Time Zones

If you frequently work with people from other countries or regularly travel internationally, you might want to change the time zone displayed in your Calendar or simultaneously view two time zones.

Each time zone is measured in reference to Greenwich Mean Time (GMT) or Universal Time (UTC). GMT is defined as the time at the Greenwich Observatory in England.

To change your current time zone:

1 On the **Tools** menu, click **Options**.

2 On the **Preferences** tab, click the **Calendar Options** button.

3 In the **Calendar Options** dialog box, click the **Time Zone** button.

4 In the **Time Zone** dialog box, click the down arrow to the right of the **Time zone** box, click the time zone you want, and then click **OK** three times to close all the dialog boxes.

Note that changing your time zone in Outlook is equivalent to changing your time zone in Control Panel. It affects the time displayed on the Windows taskbar and in any other Windows programs.

To simultaneously display two time zones in your Calendar:

1 On the **Tools** menu, click **Options**.

2 On the **Preferences** tab, click the **Calendar Options** button.

3 In the **Calendar Options** dialog box, click the **Time Zone** button.

4 In the **Time Zone** dialog box, select the **Show an additional time zone** check box.

5 In both areas of the dialog box, click in the **Label** box, and type the label you want for the time zone. (For example, *home* or *office*.)

6 Click the down arrow to the right of the second **Time zone** box, click the second time zone you want to display, and click **OK** three times to close all the dialog boxes and return to your Calendar.

You can use the Swap Time Zones button in the Time Zone dialog box to replace the current time zone with the second one. Swapping time zones changes all time-related fields, such as when messages are received or the time of appointments, to the new time zone.

Labeling Appointments with Color

To make important appointments stand out in your Calendar, you can color-code appointments and events, choosing from one of ten preset *labels* such as Important, Business, Personal, Vacation, Travel Required, and Phone Call, or editing the options to suit your needs. You can also mark an appointment as *private*. Private appointments appear in your Calendar, but the details are hidden from others.

In this exercise, you will change an appointment label and then learn how to change the preset labels.

USE the *SBSCalendar* data file in the practice file folder for this topic. This practice file is located in the *My Documents\Microsoft Press\Outlook 2003 SBS\Calendar* folder and can also be accessed by clicking *Start/All Programs/Microsoft Press/Outlook 2003 Step by Step*.
BE SURE TO open the *SBSCalendar* data file before beginning this exercise.

1 In the practice calendar, navigate to June 24, 2003.

Notice that the Day Care Duty appointment is colored green.

2 Double-click the *Day Care Duty* appointment.

The Appointment form appears. Notice that *Personal* is selected in the Label box.

3 Click the down arrow to the right of the **Label** box.

Note the preset options.

4 In the drop-down list, click **Must Attend**.

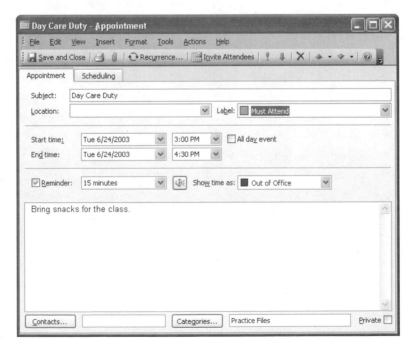

5 Click the **Save and Close** button. If Outlook warns you that the reminder will not appear, click **Yes**.

The updated appointment is saved in your Calendar and the color changes to orange, to indicate that this is a very important appointment.

 **6** On the toolbar, click the **Calendar Coloring** button, and then click **Edit Labels**.

Calendar Coloring

The Edit Calendar Labels dialog box opens.

7 Review the preset options, and then click **Cancel** to close the dialog box without making any changes.

Printing Calendars

Microsoft Office Specialist

When your schedule is full and you find yourself running from one appointment to the next, you might not always be able to check your Outlook Calendar. By printing your Calendar, you can take your schedule with you. You can print your Calendar in a variety of formats, called *print styles*. You can select from the following pre-defined print styles:

- *Daily Style* prints the selected date range with one day per page. Printed elements include the date, day, TaskPad and reference month calendars, along with an area for notes.

- *Weekly Style* prints the selected date range with one calendar week per page, including reference calendars for the selected and following months.

- *Monthly Style* prints a page for each month in the selected date range. Each page includes the six-week range surrounding the month, along with reference calendars for the selected and following months.

- *Tri-fold Style* prints a page for each day in the selected date range. Each page includes the daily schedule, weekly schedule, and TaskPad.

- *Calendar Details Style* lists your appointments for the selected date range, as well as the accompanying appointment details.

You select the date or range of dates to be printed each time you print.

In this exercise, you will print your Calendar in the Daily, Tri-fold, and Monthly styles.

Important   To complete this exercise, you must have a printer installed. To install a printer, click the Start button and then click Control Panel. In Control Panel, click Printers and Other Hardware, and then click "Add a printer." If you are working on a network, your administrator can provide the information you need to install a printer.

BE SURE TO install a printer before beginning this exercise.

Go to Today

1   With your Calendar displayed in Outlook, on the toolbar, click the **Go to Today** button.

The Calendar displays your day's schedule.

Print

2   On the toolbar, click the **Print** button.

The Print dialog box appears, with the Daily Style format and today's date automatically selected.

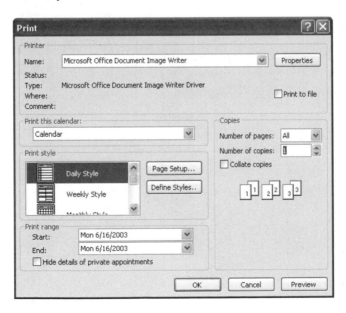

3   Click **OK**.

Outlook prints today's schedule in the Daily Style format, which approximates the Day view.

4   On the toolbar, click the **Print** button again.

The Print dialog box appears, with Daily Style and today's date as the default options.

5   In the **Print style** list, click **Tri-fold Style**.

6   In the **Print range** area, click the down arrow to the right of the **End** box, and click the date two days from today.

7   Click the **Preview** button.

The tri-fold calendar is displayed in Print Preview.

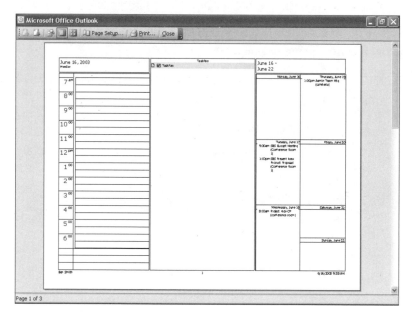

8   On the Print Preview window toolbar, click the **Print** button.

Outlook prints three pages—one page for each day of the selected date range—and closes the Print Preview window.

9 On the toolbar, click the **Print** button again.

Note that Outlook doesn't retain your settings from one print session to the next.

10 In the **Print style** list, click **Monthly Style**.

11 In the **Print range** area, click the down arrow to the right of the **Start** box, and in the drop-down list, click the last day of the current month.

12 Click the down arrow to the right of the **End** box, and in the drop-down list, click the first day of the next month.

13 Click the **Preview** button.

The monthly calendar is displayed in Print Preview.

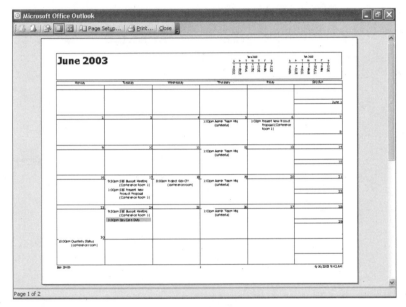

14 On the Print Preview window toolbar, click the **Print** button.

Outlook prints two pages—one page for each month in which the selected date range falls—and closes the Print Preview window.

CLOSE the *SBSCalendar* data file and exit Outlook.

Key Points

- The Calendar tracks and organizes appointments. Appointments can be any length and can recur at any interval. Appointments can have a location and can contain notes.

- You can further organize your appointments by assigning them to categories or folders. You can add color-coded labels to appointments and create rules for Outlook to label appointments for you.

- You can view multiple calendars side by side. Calendars are color-coded for easy reference.

- You can view your calendar by the day, work week, full week, or month. Your calendar can display times for multiple time zones.

- You can print you calendar in predefined Daily, Weekly, or Monthly styles, or create your own print style.

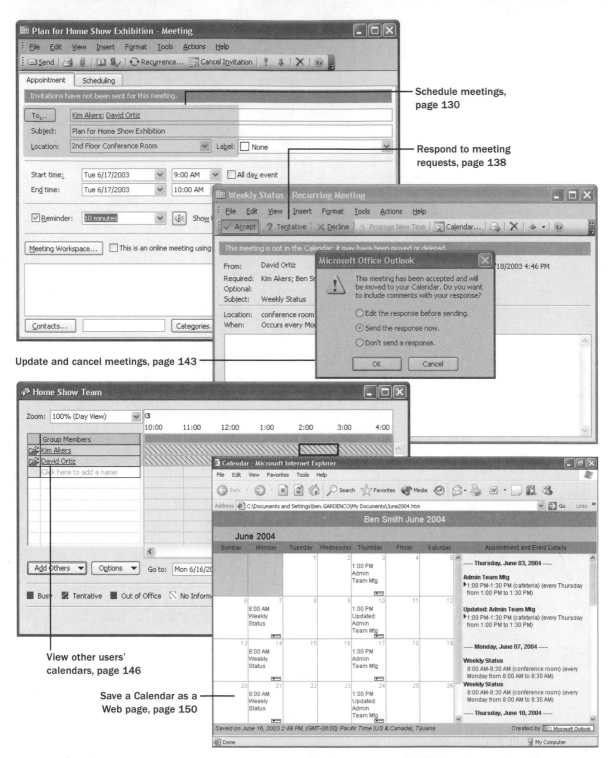

Schedule meetings, page 130

Respond to meeting requests, page 138

Update and cancel meetings, page 143

View other users' calendars, page 146

Save a Calendar as a Web page, page 150

Chapter 5 at a Glance

5 Scheduling and Managing Meetings

In this chapter you will learn to:

✔ Schedule meetings.

✔ Respond to meeting requests.

✔ Update and cancel meetings.

✔ View other users' calendars.

✔ Save a Calendar as a Web page.

Microsoft Office Outlook 2003 can help you with the often onerous task of organizing meetings. You can organize meetings that happen in a particular place and meetings that happen online. You can view other attendees' *calendars* to check their availability. You can send meeting invitations and track attendee responses. And as schedules change, you can update or cancel scheduled meetings.

When another person organizes a meeting, you can respond to the meeting request manually or automatically; if the meeting time doesn't suit you, you can suggest a different time or date, while ensuring that all meeting attendees are kept up-to-date with the changes.

If you need to keep people other people informed of your schedule, you can publish your Outlook Calendar to the Internet and make it available to colleagues, friends, and family members who need the information. If you don't want to share all your calendar details, you can publish only information about when you are available and when you are busy.

See Also Do you need only a quick refresher on the topics in this chapter? See the Quick Reference entries on pages xxxix–xlii.

Important Before you can use the practice files in this chapter, you need to install them from the book's companion CD to their default location. See "Using the Book's CD-ROM" on page xiii for more information.

Scheduling Meetings

Microsoft
Office
Specialist

With Outlook, you can schedule meetings, invite attendees—both those who work for your organization and those who don't—and reserve resources such as conference rooms or equipment. To choose a date and time for your meeting, you can check the availability of attendees and resources by viewing their free/busy information. When inviting attendees from within your organization, you can automatically see their Outlook Calendar information. You can see free/busy information for people outside of your organization only if they make this information available over the Internet.

You also can have Outlook select the meeting time for you. You can indicate whether the attendance of each invitee is required or optional. Outlook uses this information when looking for available meeting times, prioritizing times that work for all required attendees and most optional attendees.

After you have selected a time, you send a *meeting request*—a type of e-mail message —to each invited attendee and requested resource. Responses from attendees and those responsible for scheduling the resources you requested are automatically tracked as you receive them.

In this exercise, you will plan a meeting, invite attendees, and set and then remove a meeting *reminder*.

USE the *SBSMeetings* data file in the practice file folder for this topic. This practice file is located in the *My Documents\Microsoft Press\Outlook 2003 SBS\Meetings* folder and can also be accessed by clicking *Start/All Programs/Microsoft Press/Outlook 2003 Step by Step*.
BE SURE TO start Outlook before beginning this exercise.
OPEN the *SBSMeetings* data file from within Outlook, and then open the practice Contacts in the *SBS Meetings* data file folder.

1   In the **Navigation Pane**, click the **Folder List** icon.

2   In the practice Contacts folder, hold down the ⌨ key and drag the **Kim Akers** contact to your own Contacts folder. Then hold down the ⌨ key and drag the **David Ortiz** contact to your own Contacts folder.

3   In the *SBS Meetings* data file folder, click the practice Calendar.

4   In the Date Navigator, scroll to June 2003, and then click **18**.

The Calendar displays the schedule for June 18, 2003.

5 On the **Actions** menu, click **Plan a Meeting**.

The Plan a Meeting form appears, listing you as the only attendee in the All Attendees list. The icon next to your name indicates that you are the meeting organizer. By default, the first available timeslot is selected for the meeting.

Meeting Organizer icon

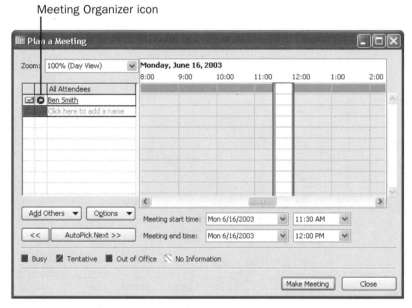

6 Click the **Add Others** button, and in the drop-down list, click **Add from Address Book**.

The Select Attendees and Resources dialog box appears, with your name in the Required box.

Important In this exercise, you have been provided with contact information for fictitious employees of The Garden Company. If you want, you can use the names of your co-workers or other contacts to plan an actual meeting.

7 If you want to complete this exercise using the fictitious contacts, click the down arrow to the right of the **Show Names from the** box, and then click **Contacts**.

8 In the **Name** list, click **Kim Akers**, and then click the **Required** button.

The selected name is added to the Required Attendees box.

9 In the **Name** list, click **David Ortiz**, and then click the **Optional** button.

The selected name is added to the Optional Attendees box.

10 Click **OK**. If prompted to join the *Microsoft Office Internet Free/Busy Service*, click **Cancel**.

The attendees are added to the All Attendees list, with icons that indicate whether their attendance is required or optional.

Optional Attendee icon
Required Attendee icon

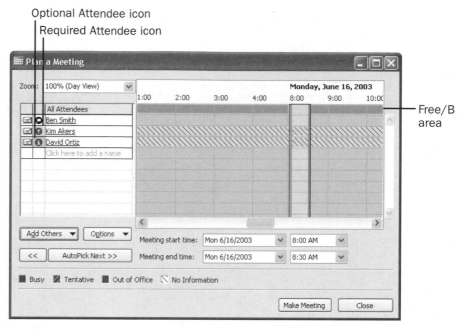

Free/B
area

11 Use the horizontal scroll bar in the Free/Busy area to view attendee availability for Tuesday, June 17, 2003.

This area shows whether attendees are free, tentatively scheduled, busy, or out of the office. Busy time appears in blue, tentatively scheduled time in blue stripes, and time out of the office in purple. (If you are using fictitious names, free/busy information will not be available.)

12 In the Free/Busy area, click the 9:00 A.M. time slot to select that time.

The half-hour time slot you clicked appears as a vertical white bar. The "Meeting start time" and "Meeting end time" boxes change to reflect the date and time you selected.

Tip   To quickly find the next available free time for all attendees and resources, click the AutoPick Next button in the Plan a Meeting dialog box or on the Scheduling tab of the Meeting form.

13 In the Free/Busy area, click the red bar on the right edge of the selected meeting time, and drag it to 10:00 A.M.

The second "Meeting end time" setting reflects the change—the meeting is now scheduled to last for one hour.

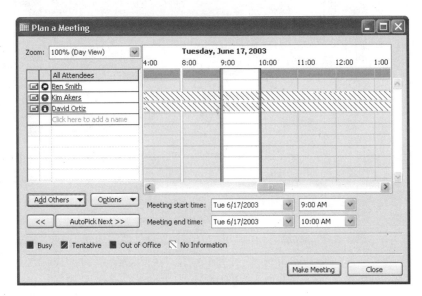

14 Click the **Make Meeting** button.

A new, untitled Meeting form appears with the attendees and meeting time information already set.

15 In the **Subject** box, type **Plan for Home Show Exhibition**, press the ⬚Tab key, and in the **Location** box, type **2nd Floor Conference Room**.

16 Select the **Reminder** check box, click the down arrow to the right of the **Reminder** box, and then click **10 minutes**.

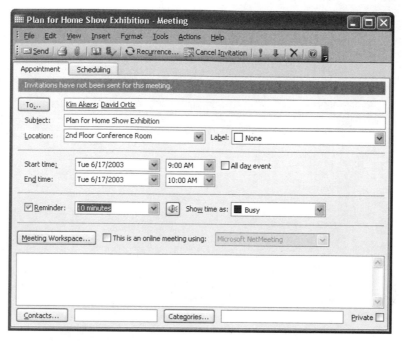

17 On the toolbar, click the **Send** button.

The meeting request is sent.

Important If the attendees you provided are fictitious, e-mail messages you send to them will be returned as undeliverable. You can delete the returned messages at any time.

Close

18 In the **Plan a Meeting** dialog box, click the **Close** button.

The Plan a Meeting form closes.

19 In the Calendar, navigate to June 17, 2003.

The meeting request appears in the 9:00 A.M. – 10:00 A.M. time slot.

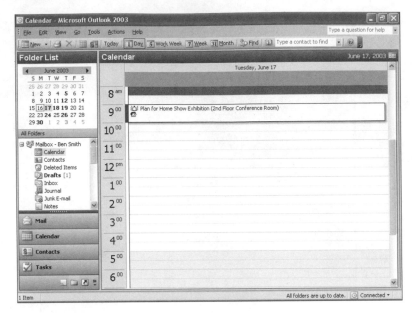

20 Double-click the **Plan for Home Show Exhibition** meeting.

The Meeting form opens.

21 Clear the **Reminder** check box.

22 On the toolbar, click the **Save and Close** button.

The updated meeting is saved. You will not receive a reminder for the meeting, but your meeting attendees will.

Scheduling Meeting Resources

Microsoft Office Specialist

If you are working on a network that uses *Microsoft Exchange Server* and your system administrator has added resources (such as conference rooms, audiovisual equipment, or meeting supplies) to the organization's *Global Address List*, you can reserve those resources for a specific meeting by inviting them to the meeting. Your meeting request is sent to the person designated by your administrator to manage the schedule for the resource. That person responds to your meeting request based on the availability of the resource at the time you requested.

To schedule a resource while creating a meeting request:

1 In the **Meeting** form, click the **Scheduling** tab.

2 Click the **Add Others** button, and then click **Add from Address Book**.

The Select Attendees and Resources dialog box appears.

3 In the **Name** list, select the resource or resources you want to add, click the **Resources** button, and then click **OK**.

4 Send the meeting request as usual.

To schedule a resource for an existing meeting:

1 Open the **Meeting** form.

2 On the **Scheduling** tab, add the resources you want.

3 Click the **Send Update** button.

Scheduling and Hosting Online Meetings

With *NetMeeting*, a program that comes with Microsoft Internet Explorer, you can conduct online meetings over the Internet. You can use NetMeeting to conduct audio and video conferences with one or more other people. NetMeeting conference participants can share applications, collaborate on documents, draw on a shared electronic whiteboard, or transfer files.

To take full advantage of NetMeeting's audio and video capabilities, you need an audio card, video card, speakers, microphone, and camera connected to your computer. Without a camera, you can view other people's video, but they cannot view yours.

To schedule a NetMeeting:

1 Create a new meeting request, including the attendees, subject, and meeting start and end times.

2 Select the **Reminder** check box.

3 Select the **This is an online meeting using** check box, and select **Microsoft NetMeeting** in the adjacent box. You might have to enlarge the window to see its entire contents.

4 Click in the **Directory Server** box, type **logon.netmeeting.microsoft.com** (the name of the Microsoft Internet Directory server).

5 Select the **Automatically start NetMeeting with Reminder** check box.

6 On the toolbar, click the **Send** button.

The meeting request is sent. When the meeting time arrives, NetMeeting starts automatically so that you and the other attendees can connect to the conference.

Your organization might use a *directory server* other than the one named above. Contact your system administrator or ISP for more information.

To host a meeting in NetMeeting, start NetMeeting, and on the Call menu, click Host Meeting. In the Host Meeting dialog box that appears, you can give the meeting a name and password, and set the options for the meeting, including who can place outgoing calls, accept incoming calls, and use NetMeeting features. You can also choose whether or not to require security for the meeting.

Find Someone in a Directory

After the meeting has started, you can place calls to other meeting attendees by clicking New Call on the Call menu. If you don't know an attendee's address, you can find it by clicking the Find Someone in a Directory button and searching for the person's address in the directory.

Tip   For more information on using NetMeeting, start NetMeeting, and on the Help menu, click Help Topics. To start NetMeeting, click the Start button, point to Run, type **conf**, and click OK.

Responding to Meeting Requests

Microsoft Office Specialist

Just as you can send meeting requests, other people can send them to you. When you receive a meeting request, you can respond in one of four ways:

- You can accept the request and inform the requester that you will attend. Meetings that you accept are automatically entered in your Calendar.

- You can tentatively accept a request, indicating that you might be able to attend the meeting. Meetings that you accept tentatively are also entered in your Calendar, but your free/busy information will show you as only tentatively scheduled for that time.

- You can propose a new meeting time, in which case the request is referred to the meeting organizer for confirmation. Your Calendar shows the proposed new meeting time as tentatively scheduled.

- You can decline a meeting, in which case the request is deleted and no entry is made in your Calendar. When you decline a meeting, you can choose whether Outlook notifies the person who sent the request.

In this exercise, you will accept a meeting request, decline a meeting request, and propose a new meeting time in response to a meeting request.

USE the *SBSMeetings* data file in the practice file folder for this topic. This practice file is located in the *My Documents\Microsoft Press\Outlook 2003 SBS\Meetings* folder and can also be accessed by clicking *Start/All Programs/Microsoft Press/Outlook 2003 Step by Step.*
BE SURE TO start Outlook and open the *SBSMeetings* data file before beginning this exercise.
OPEN the practice Inbox in the *SBS Meetings* data file folder.

1 In the practice Inbox, double-click the **Weekly Status** meeting request.

The Meeting form appears.

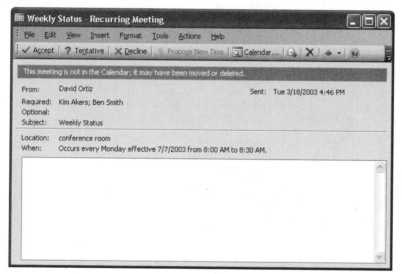

 2 To view the meeting in your Calendar before you respond, click the **Calendar** button on the toolbar.

Your Calendar appears in a new window, displaying the date of the requested meeting. For recurring meetings, the date of the first meeting is displayed. The requested meeting has a blue-striped bar at the left, which means it is tentatively scheduled.

Close

3 In the open Calendar window, click the **Close** button.

The Calendar closes.

4   On the **Meeting** form, click the **Accept** button.

A message box appears, prompting you to choose how you want to respond.

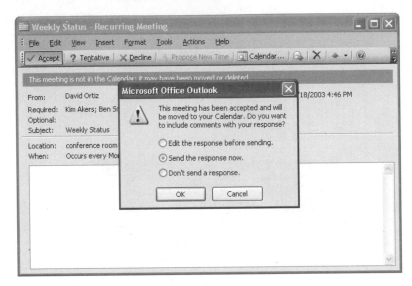

Tip   When accepting or declining a meeting, you can choose to send a standard response, send a response that you compose yourself, or send no response. If you don't send a response to the meeting organizer, your acceptance will not be tallied in the Meeting form. The organizer and other attendees will not know whether you are planning to attend the meeting.

5   With the **Send the response now** option selected, click **OK**.

Your response is sent to the person who requested the meeting, the Meeting form closes, and the meeting is entered in your Calendar.

6   In the Inbox, click the **Project Kick-Off** meeting request; then in the Reading Pane, click the **Decline** button.

A message box appears, prompting you to choose how you want to respond.

7   With the **Edit the response before sending** option selected, click **OK**.

The Meeting Response form appears. The status bar and Subject box indicate that you are declining the Project Kick-Off meeting request.

8   In the message body, type **I will be out of the office on this day**.

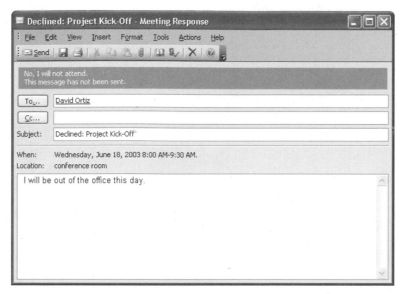

9   On the toolbar, click the **Send** button.

Your response is sent, and the Meeting form closes. The meeting is not added to your Calendar.

10   In the Inbox, right-click the **Quarterly Status** message, and on the shortcut menu, click **Propose New Time**. If prompted to join the Microsoft Office Internet Free/Busy Service, click **Cancel**.

The Propose New Time dialog box appears. The current meeting time is indicated in yellow.

11   In the Free/Busy area, click the **11:00** column, and drag the Meeting Time's right edge to 12:00. Then click the **10:00** column, and drag the Meeting Time's left edge to 11:00.

The meeting start and end times are updated to reflect your changes.

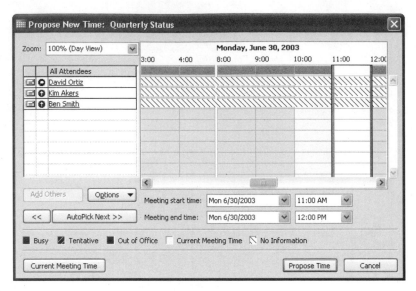

12 Click the **Propose Time** button.

The Propose New Time dialog box closes, and the Meeting Response form appears. The subject of the response indicates that you are proposing a new time for the meeting.

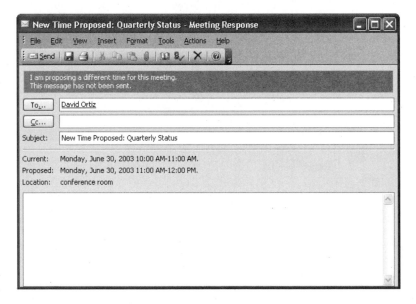

13 In the body of the message, type **I will be out of the office on Monday morning.**, and on the toolbar, click the **Send** button.

Your response is sent, and the Meeting form closes. The meeting is added to your Calendar as tentatively scheduled for the original meeting time.

Automatically Responding to Meeting Requests

You can choose to respond to meeting requests automatically. Outlook will process meeting requests and cancellations as you receive them, responding to requests, adding new meetings to your calendar, and removing cancelled meetings from your calendar. If you choose, Outlook will automatically decline meeting requests that conflict with existing items on your calendar. You can also choose to automatically decline any request for a *recurring* meeting.

To instruct Outlook to automatically respond to meeting requests:

1 On the **Tools** menu, click **Options**.

The Options dialog box appears.

2 On the **Preferences** tab, click the **Calendar Options** button, and then click the **Resource Scheduling** button.

The Resource Scheduling dialog box appears.

3 Select the **Automatically accept meeting requests and process cancellations** check box.

4 Select the **Automatically decline conflicting meeting requests** and/or the **Automatically decline recurring meeting requests** check boxes if you want Outlook to do this.

5 Click **OK** to close each open dialog box.

Updating and Canceling Meetings

Microsoft Office Specialist

People's schedules can shift on a daily basis. Outlook makes it easy to update or cancel meetings as your needs change. For example, an important attendee might be sick or delayed, or have other plans come up that take precedence over your meeting. In this case, you can change the date or time of the meeting or cancel the meeting altogether. You can also add people to or remove people from the list of attendees.

In this exercise, you will create a meeting, reschedule the meeting, change the meeting attendees, and cancel the meeting.

BE SURE TO inform your practice meeting attendees that you are not scheduling a real meeting.
OPEN your Calendar.

Go to Today

1 In your Calendar, click the **Go to Today** button

Your schedule for today is displayed.

New
Appointment

2 On the toolbar, click the **New Appointment** button.

3 In the **Subject** box, type **SBS Practice**.

4 On the **Scheduling** tab, click the **Add Others** button, and then click **Add from Address Book**.

5 Invite two people from your address list to the meeting, and then click **OK**.

6 On the Meeting form toolbar, click the **Send** button.

You now have a meeting with which to work.

7 In the Calendar, double-click the **SBS Practice** meeting.

The Meeting form appears.

8 Click the **Scheduling** tab, and in the Free/Busy area, scroll to the next business day.

9 Click the **11:00 A.M.** time slot, and drag the right edge of the shaded area to **12:00 P.M.** to schedule the meeting to last for one hour.

The start and end times reflect the changes you made to the date and time.

10 In the **All Attendees** list, click the name of one of your invited attendees; press the ⌦ key, and then press ⇥.

The attendee is removed from the list.

11 On the toolbar, click the **Send Update** button.

The updated Meeting form is sent. The removed attendee receives a meeting cancellation.

12 In the Date Navigator, click the next business day, and then double-click the **SBS Practice** meeting.

13 In the **Meeting** form, click the **Tracking** tab.

The Tracking tab displays the response received from each attendee.

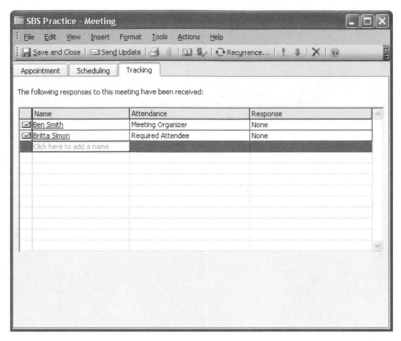

14 On the **Actions** menu, click **Cancel Meeting**.

A message box appears, prompting you to send a cancellation notice to the attendees.

15 With the **Send cancellation and delete meeting** option selected, click **OK**.

16 On the toolbar, click the **Send** button.

The cancellation notice is sent to all remaining attendees, the Meeting form closes, and the meeting is removed from your Calendar.

Tip You can easily send a new e-mail message to all attendees of a particular meeting. Simply open the meeting, and on the Actions menu, click New Message to Attendees. (This method works only on meetings for which attendees have already been invited.)

Viewing Other Users' Calendars

When organizing a meeting, it's helpful to be able to see when attendees are available without having to contact each person individually. With Outlook, you can see when people are free or busy by inviting them to a meeting, adding them to a group schedule, or viewing an Internet or intranet location where they publish their schedules.

A group schedule shows you the combined schedules of a number of people or resources at a glance. For example, you might create a group schedule containing all the people on your project team so you can quickly see when the entire team is available for a discussion.

If you are working on a network that uses Exchange Server, the free/busy information of other network users is available to you by default. In addition, if a person connected to your network has shared his or her Calendar, you can open that person's calendar directly.

In this exercise, you will create a group schedule and then create a meeting from that schedule.

USE the *SBSMeetings* data file in the practice file folder for this topic. This practice file is located in the *My Documents\Microsoft Press\Outlook 2003 SBS\Meetings* folder and can also be accessed by clicking *Start/All Programs/Microsoft Press/Outlook 2003 Step by Step*.
BE SURE TO open the *SBSMeetings* data file before beginning this exercise.
OPEN the practice Calendar in the *SBS Meetings* data file folder.

View Group
Schedules

1 With the Calendar displayed, on the toolbar, click the **View Group Schedules** button.

The Group Schedules dialog box appears.

2 Click the **New** button.

The Create New Group Schedule dialog box appears.

3 In the **Type a name for the new Group Schedule** box, type **Home Show Team**, and then click **OK**.

The Home Show Team group schedule appears, with the current date and time slot selected.

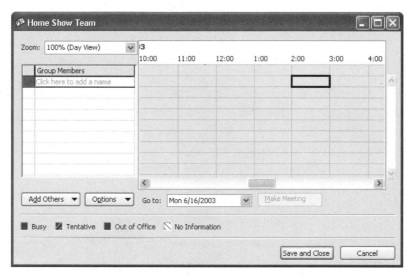

4 Click the **Add Others** button, and then in the drop-down list click **Add from Address Book**.

The Select Members dialog box appears.

5 To complete this exercise using the fictitious employees of The Garden Company, click the down arrow to the right of the **Show Names from the** list, and then click **Contacts**.

Tip You can complete this exercise with your own contacts. Simply select names from your Global Address List in place of the names given here.

6 In the **Name** box, click **Kim Akers**, hold down the ⌃Ctrl key, click **David Ortiz**, and then click the **To** button.

The names are added to the To list.

7 Click **OK**. If prompted to join the Microsoft Office Internet Free/Busy Service, click **Cancel**.

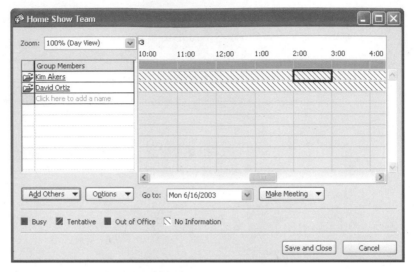

8 To see the most recent schedule information for the group members, click the **Options** button, and then click **Refresh Free/Busy**.

The Free/Busy area is updated. Outlook gathers information from wherever the free/busy information for your group members is stored—your Microsoft Exchange Server, the Microsoft Office Internet Free/Busy Service, or the Internet or Intranet locations selected by group members.

9 Click the down arrow to the right of the **Go to** box, and then click the next Monday.

The Free/Busy area shows the data for the date you selected. However, only half the day is visible.

10 Click the down arrow to the right of the **Zoom** box, and then click **50% (Week View)** on the drop-down list.

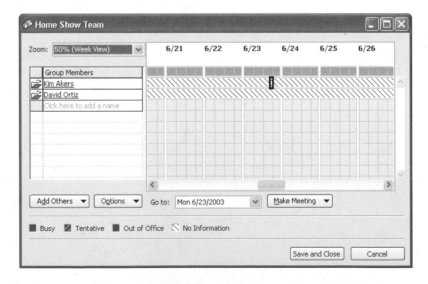

The Free/Busy area displays more of each person's schedule.

11 Click the **Make Meeting** button, and then click **New Meeting with All** in the drop-down list.

A new Meeting form appears, with the group members' names in the To box.

Close

12 Click the **Close** button, and when prompted to save your changes, click **No**.

The Meeting form closes, discarding the meeting request. If prompted to save your changes, click **No**.

13 In the **Home Show Team** group schedule, click the **Cancel** button.

The group schedule closes.

CLOSE the *SBS Meetings* data file and delete the Kim Akers and David Ortiz contacts from your Contacts folder.

Sharing Calendars

You can share your Calendar with other network users just as you would any other folder. To share your Calendar with another network user:

1 In the **Folder List**, right-click the **Calendar**, and then click **Sharing** on the shortcut menu.

2 On the **Permissions** tab of the **Calendar Properties** dialog box, click **Add**.

3 Select the person or people with whom you want to share your Calendar, and then click **OK**.

4 In the **Permissions** area, indicate the permissions you want to give the other network users, and then click **OK**.

If another network user shares his or her Calendar with you, you can open it on your own computer (for instance, to view it side by side with your own). To view a shared Calendar:

1 On the **File** menu, point to **Open**, and click **Other User's Folder**.

The Open Other User's Folder dialog box appears.

2 Click the **Name** button, click the name of a person who has shared his or her Calendar, and then click **OK**.

3 In the **Folder type** box, click **Calendar**, and then click **OK**.

The other user's calendar is displayed.

Saving a Calendar as a Web Page

To help you coordinate your plans with others, you can share your schedule over an intranet or the Internet. Your co-workers and clients can view your schedule even if they aren't using Microsoft Outlook. You can also share your schedule by saving your Calendar as a Web page or by publishing your free and busy times for others to see.

For example, you might post a calendar with important project dates on your company intranet, or you might publish to an Internet location, for your clients to view, the times that you are busy and the times when you are available. When you save your Calendar as a Web page, you can easily post it to any Web site to share it with colleagues, friends, or family members.

Tip When you save your Calendar as a Web page, you can save it to your local computer or a network location. You might have to take additional steps to make that Web page available to others. Your network or ISP administrator can provide the information you need.

In this exercise, you will save your Calendar as a Web page that can be posted on an Internet or intranet site.

OPEN your own Calendar.

1 On the **File** menu, click **Save as Web Page**.

The Save as Web Page dialog box appears.

2 In the **Start date** box, type 6/1/04, press the ⌧ key, and in the **End date** box, type 6/30/04.

3 Click in the **Calendar title** box, delete any existing text, type your name followed by June 2004, and then click the **Browse** button.

The Calendar File Name dialog box appears.

4 On the **Places** bar, click **My Documents**.

5 In the **File name** box, type June2004, and then click the **Select** button.

The Calendar File Name dialog box closes, and the file name and the path to it are inserted into the "File name" box.

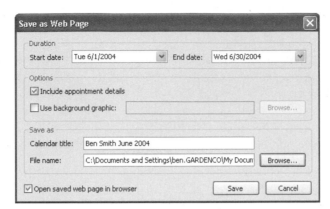

6 Be sure the **Open saved web page in browser** check box is selected, and then click the **Save** button.

The Save as Web Page dialog box closes, and the schedule is displayed in your Web browser. (The browser is loading the file from your computer, not the Internet— you haven't published the schedule to the Internet yet.)

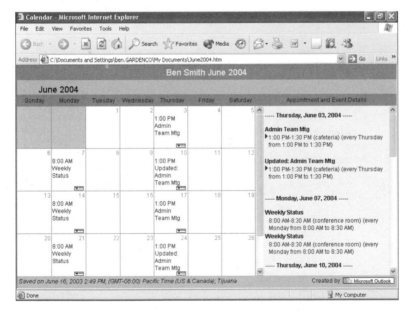

Close

7 Review the Calendar, and then click the browser window's **Close** button.

The Web browser window closes.

Sharing Schedule Information on the Web

Microsoft offers a Web-based service called the Microsoft Office Internet Free/Busy Service that you can use to publish information about your free and busy times to a designated, secure Internet location. If you and your colleagues don't have access to each other's calendars but do have access to the Internet, each of you can join this service and publish your free/busy information for others to view. Easy access to this information can save you a lot of time when you need to coordinate the schedules of a group of busy people.

To make your Calendar information available to other Office users:

1 On the **Tools** menu, click **Options**.

2 In the **Calendar** area, click the **Calendar Options** button, and then in the **Advanced options** area, click the **Free/Busy Options** button.

3 In the **Free/Busy Options** dialog box, select the **Publish and search using Microsoft Office Internet Free/Busy Service** check box.

4 If you want to request that other people make their schedules available through the Microsoft Office Internet Free/Busy Service, select the **Request free/busy information in meeting invitations** check box, and click **OK**.

5 If prompted to install the feature, click **Yes**.

6 When installation is complete, click **OK** to close the open dialog boxes.

You can also choose to publish your free/busy information to an intranet location you specify. Your administrator can provide you with the path to the appropriate location on your organization's intranet.

To publish your free/busy information to an intranet site:

1 In Outlook, on the **Tools** menu, click **Options**.

2 In the **Calendar** area, click the **Calendar Options** button.

3 In the **Advanced options** area, click the **Free/Busy Options** button.

4 In the **Internet Free/Busy** area, select the **Publish at my location** check box, click in the **Publish at my location** box, and type the server location provided by your administrator, followed by the file name you want.

5 Click **OK** to close each of the open dialog boxes.

Your free/busy information is published to the specified location.

6   On the **Tools** menu, point to **Send/Receive**, and then click **Free/Busy Information** to publish your free/busy information to your server.

7   To view your published free/busy information, open your Web browser, and in the **Address** box, type the URL of the file on the server.

Your free/busy information appears as a text file in your browser window.

8   Review the information, and click the browser's **Close** button.

The Web browser window closes.

The contents of the "Publish at my location" box will typically be something like *server**share**username**June2002.vfb*. Include the full path and file name in the "Publish at my location" box.

The retrieval URL might not be the same as the path you entered in the "Publish at my location" box. Your administrator can provide you with the URL.

Key Points

- You can share your Calendar so that other members of your organization can see your appointments and meetings, or share just your free and busy times. You can also publish your Calendar on the Internet or your intranet.

- You can use Outlook to set up meetings, invite participants, and track their responses. If participants share their free and busy information, Outlook can choose a meeting time that best fits their schedules, or you can create a group schedule to show when everyone is free.

- Your organization can add conference rooms, projectors, and other resources to its address book and use Outlook to schedule their use.

- You can use Internet Explorer's NetMeeting feature to hold online meetings.

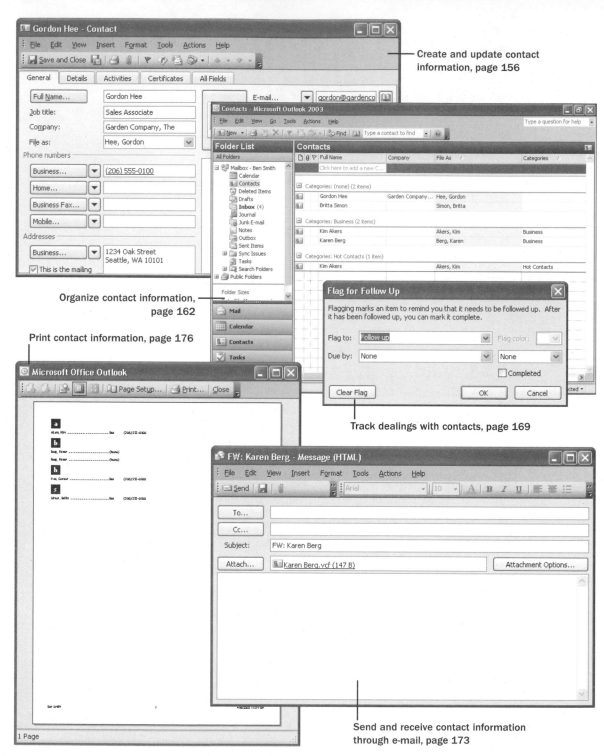

Create and update contact information, page 156

Organize contact information, page 162

Print contact information, page 176

Track dealings with contacts, page 169

Send and receive contact information through e-mail, page 173

Chapter 6 at a Glance

6 Creating and Organizing a List of Contacts

In this chapter you will learn to:

✔ Create and update contact information.

✔ Organize contact information.

✔ Track dealings with contacts.

✔ Send and receive contact information through e-mail.

✔ Print contact information.

Managing the information you have about your *contacts* is crucial for staying organized and connected. To communicate effectively, you must have instant access to current, accurate contact information, including phone numbers, addresses, and *e-mail addresses*. Microsoft Office Outlook 2003 makes it easy to build and maintain your Contacts list. You have many options for viewing, sorting, and printing your contact information, as well as the ability to keep track of your dealings with a particular contact and share contact information with other people through e-mail or with other programs.

Outlook includes several options for storing addresses and other contact information in the *Outlook Address Book*.

■ The *Global Address List* is available if you are working on a network that includes *Microsoft Exchange Server*. It contains all the e-mail addresses and distribution lists in your organization. Your administrator maintains the Global Address List. You can view it, but you cannot change it.

■ The *Contacts list* is created automatically when you configure your Outlook profile. It contains information about the people you have added to your *Contacts folder*.

■ The *Personal Address Book* might also be part of your profile. You can create a Personal Address Book for personal contacts and distribution lists, rather than work-related contacts. The e-mail addresses and distributions lists in this address book are stored in a file with a *.pab* extension.

> **Tip**   If a Personal Address Book is part of your Outlook profile, you can access it in the Address Book dialog box by clicking Personal Address Book in the "Show names from the" drop-down list.

See Also   Do you need only a quick refresher on the topics in this chapter? See the Quick Reference entries on pages xlii–xliii.

 Important   Before you can use the practice files in this chapter, you need to install them from the book's companion CD to their default location. See "Using the Book's CD-ROM" on page xiii for more information.

Creating and Updating Contact Information

Microsoft Office Specialist

Think of your Outlook Contacts list as a powerful electronic Rolodex, where you can store all the information you need to stay in touch with and manage contacts. For each contact, you can store the following types of contact information:

- Name, job title, and company name
- Business, home, and other addresses
- Business, home, fax, mobile, pager, and other phone numbers
- E-mail, Web page, and instant messaging addresses

You can also store the following details for each contact:

- Professional information, including department, office, profession, manager's name and assistant's name
- Personal information, including nickname, spouse's name, birthday, anniversary, and the title and suffix to use in correspondence
- The directory server and e-mail alias to use for online meetings

---

See Also   For information about conducting online meetings using NetMeeting, refer to "Scheduling and Hosting Online Meetings" in Chapter 5, "Scheduling and Managing Meetings."

- The address of the contact's free/busy information server

You can create an entry for a contact with as little as a name, or as much information as you want. You can add general notes, and track all the Outlook activities that are connected with each contact. You can add to or change the information for a contact at any time. To save time, you can create contact entries for people who work for the same company based on an existing contact from that company.

In this exercise, you will create and edit contact entries.

Important   You can work through this exercise in your own Contacts folder or in the practice Contacts folder. If you use your own contacts, substitute them for the names given in the exercise.

USE the *SBSContacts* data file in the practice file folder for this topic. This practice file is located in the *My Documents\Microsoft Press\Outlook 2003 SBS\Contacts* folder and can also be accessed by clicking *Start/All Programs/Microsoft Press/Outlook 2003 Step by Step.*
BE SURE TO start Outlook before beginning this exercise.
OPEN the *SBSContacts* data file from within Outlook.

1   In the **Navigation Pane**, expand the SBS Contacts folder, and click the **Contacts** folder.

The contents of the practice Contacts folder are displayed, showing *address cards* for each of the contacts.

New Contact

2   On the toolbar, click the **New Contact** button.

A new, blank Contact form appears.

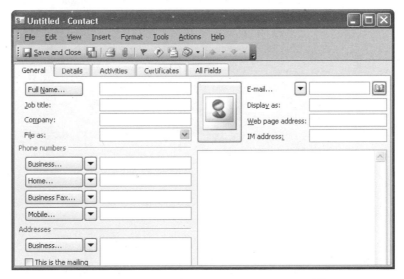

3   In the **Full Name** box, type Gordon Hee, and press the ⎚Tab⎚ key.

Outlook completes the "File as" box, indicating that the contact entry will be filed by the person's last name.

4   In the **Job title** box, type Sales Associate, and press ⎚Tab⎚.

5   In the **Company** box, type The Garden Company, and press ⎚Tab⎚ again.

Outlook formats the name to appear as *Garden Company, The*.

6 In the **Phone numbers** area, click in the **Business** box, type 2065550100, and then press [Tab].

Troubleshooting   The first time you enter a phone number for a contact, Outlook might open a dialog box and prompt you to enter your own country and area code. This information allows Outlook to set up dialing rules. You must enter your area code in the dialog box, and then click OK; you can't close the dialog box without entering the requested information.

Notice that Outlook automatically formats the phone number.

7 In the **Addresses** area, click in the text box, type 1234 Oak Street, press the [Enter] key, and type Seattle, WA 10101.

Tip   Outlook automatically checks addresses for standard elements such as street address, city, state, and zip code. If Outlook cannot identify these elements, the Check Address dialog box appears, prompting you to enter each item in its own box. You can also open the Check Address dialog box by clicking the Address button.

8 Click in the **E-mail** box, type Gordon@gardenco.msn.com, and then press [Tab].

Comments area

Address box

Tip   In a networked organization (for example, if you are connected to a Microsoft Exchange Server), you don't need to type the full e-mail address—you can use the internal e-mail alias for your contact instead. For this contact, that address might be simply *gordon*.

9   Click the **Save and Close** button.

The Contact form closes. Your Contacts folder is displayed, containing the new address card for Gordon Hee.

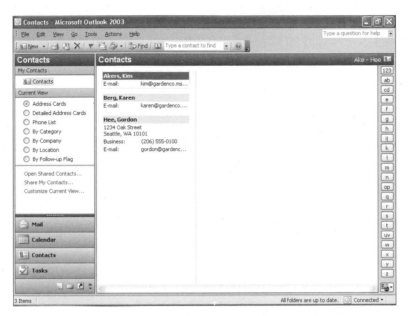

10   In the Contacts folder, double-click the entry for **Kim Akers**.

The Kim Akers – Contact form appears.

11   In the **Business** box, type **206-555-0100** and press Enter.

Notice that Outlook automatically formats the phone number.

12   Click in the **Address** box, type **1234 Oak Street**, press the Enter key, and type **Seattle, WA 10101**.

13   Click the down arrow to the right of the **Business** button, and then click **Home**.

The button label changes to indicate that you are displaying Kim's home address information.

14   Type **111 Magnolia Lane**, press Enter, and type **Seattle, WA 10101**.

15   Click in the **Web page address** box, and type **www.gardenco.msn.com**.

The address is automatically formatted as blue and underlined to show that it is a Web address, or URL.

16   On the **Actions** menu, click **New Contact from Same Company**.

A new Contact form opens, already containing the company name, address, phone number, and Web page address.

17   In the **Full Name** box, type **Britta Simon**, press the [Tab] key, and in the **Job title** box, type **Associate Buyer**.

18   Click in the **E-mail** box, type Britta@gardenco.msn.com.

19   Click the **Save and Close** button in each of the open forms.

The Contact forms close, and the Contacts folder is displayed.

20   In the Contacts folder, double-click the entry for **Karen Berg**.

The Karen Berg – Contact form appears.

21   Click the **Details** tab.

22   Click in the **Spouse's name** box, and type **James**. Then click the down arrow to the right of the **Birthday** box, scroll forward two months, and click **18**.

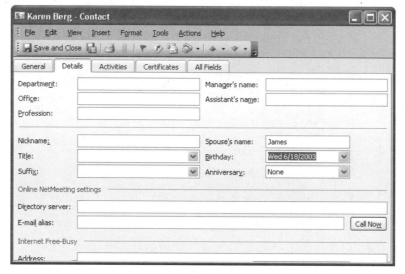

Close

23   Click the **Close** button.

24   Click **Yes** when prompted to save changes, and then click **No** when prompted to create an event in your personal Calendar.

The Contact form closes, saving the updated information, and the Contacts folder is displayed.

Adding a Contact's Picture

New in
Office 2003
Contact Picture

The contact form now includes space for a picture, so you can associate a face with the name and other information in the form.

To add a picture to a contact:

Add Contact
Picture

1   In your **Contacts** folder, open the contact.

2   On the **General** tab, click the **Add Contact Picture** button.

3   Browse to the picture you want to insert, select it, and click **OK**.

The picture is resized to fit the space in the form.

Adding Instant Messaging Contacts

If you use Windows Messenger or MSN Messenger, you can easily add entries from your Outlook Contacts list to your Messenger contact list. Follow these steps:

1   Enter the contact's IM address into his or her Contact form. Save and close the form.

2   In the Contacts folder, right-click the contact entry, and click **New Message to Contact** on the shortcut menu.

3   In the new message window, point to the contact's name in the **To** box.

A Person Names smart tag appears next to the To box.

Person Names
smart tag

4   Click the **Person Names** smart tag, and then click **Add to Messenger Contacts** in the drop-down list.

5   In the **Add a Contact** dialog box, click the **Finish** button and close the message window. If you are prompted to save changes, click **No**.

See Also   For more information about instant messaging and the Person Names smart tag, see "Creating and Sending Instant Messages," in Chapter 1, "Working with Outlook."

Organizing Contact Information

Microsoft Office Specialist

As your collection of contact entries grows, managing and organizing contact information can become a challenge. With Outlook, you can delete contact information you no longer need and restore information that has been inadvertently deleted. You can view and sort your contact information in a number of ways to help you find what you need more quickly.

■ Address Card view displays contact information as it might appear on a business card. Contact entries are displayed in alphabetical order by first or last name, depending on the File as selection.

■ Detailed Address Card view displays contact information in a similar format, but includes details about the contact including the job title and company name. Contact entries are displayed in alphabetical order by first or last name.

■ Phone List view is a columnar list displaying key contact information such as name, company, and contact numbers.

Other columnar views list contacts by category, company, location, and follow-up flag. You can sort these views by any column and customize each view to display the specific information (columns) that you find most useful.

Another way to organize and find contacts is to assign them to categories. For example, you might assign entries for potential new customers to the Hot Contacts category. Then when you are ready to follow up on your initial sales call, you could use this category to find only those entries that require follow up.

In this exercise, you will delete and restore contact entries, view and sort contact entries, and organize contact entries using categories.

Important You can work through this exercise in your own Contacts folder or in the practice Contacts folder. If you use your own contacts, substitute them for the names given in the exercise.

USE the *SBSContacts* data file in the practice file folder for this topic. This practice file is located in the *My Documents\Microsoft Press\Outlook 2003 SBS\Contacts* folder and can also be accessed by clicking *Start/All Programs/Microsoft Press/Outlook 2003 Step by Step*.
BE SURE TO start Outlook and open the *SBSContacts* data file before beginning this exercise.
OPEN the Contacts folder in the *SBS Contacts* data file.

1 Click the contact entry for **Kim Akers**.

2 On the toolbar, click the **Delete** button.

Delete

The entry is removed from the Contacts folder and placed in the Deleted Items folder.

Tip   You can also delete a contact entry using the keyboard. Simply click the entry, and press the ⌈Del⌋ key.

3   In the **Navigation Pane**, click the **Folder List** icon.

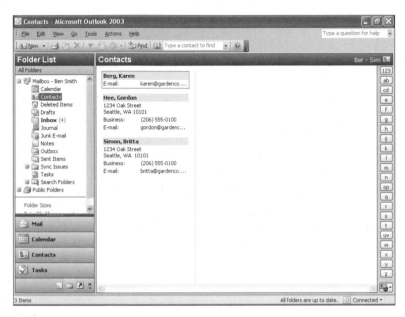

4   Click the **Deleted Items** folder.

5   On the **View** menu, point to **Arrange By** and then click **Subject**.

The contents of the Deleted Items folder are displayed. The contact entry you deleted appears in the folder, with a subject line of *Kim Akers*.

Contacts

6   In the Deleted Items folder, click the contact item for **Kim Akers**, and drag it to the **Contacts** icon at the bottom of the **Navigation Pane**.

The deleted contact is restored to the Contacts folder.

Tip   You can also restore deleted items using the Undo command. Immediately after deleting the item, on the Edit menu, click Undo Delete, or press [Ctrl]+[Z] on the keyboard.

7   In the **Navigation Pane**, click the **Contacts** icon.

The contents of the Contacts folder are displayed, including the restored entry for Kim Akers.

Tip   You can create a new message to a contact at any time by right-clicking the contact entry and clicking New Message to Contact.

8   On the **View** menu, point to **Arrange By**, point to **Current View**, and click **Detailed Address Cards**.

Additional information for each contact is displayed.

9   On the **View** menu, point to **Arrange By**, point to **Current View**, and click **Phone List**.

The contacts are displayed in a grid of columns and rows and are in ascending order based on the *File As* column.

Tip   In the Phone list and other list views, you can quickly add a new contact by using the row at the top of the list. Simply type the information in each cell, press the [Tab] key to move from one column to the next, and press the [Enter] key when you have finished.

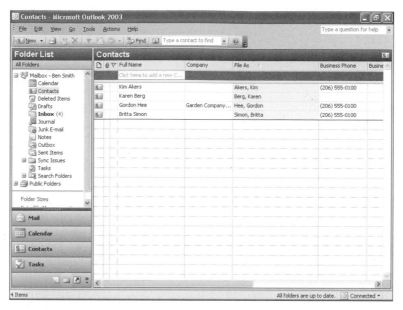

10 Click the **Full Name** column heading.

The contact entries are sorted in ascending order based on the *Full Name* column, as indicated by the up arrow to the right of the column heading.

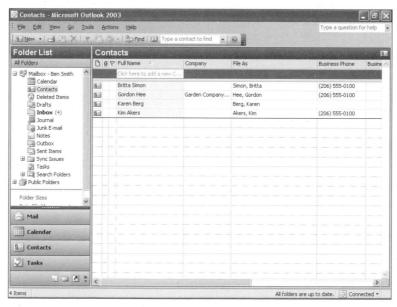

11 Click the **Full Name** column heading again.

The contact entries are sorted in descending order based on the *Full Name* column. The sort arrow now points downward.

12 On the **View** menu, point to **Arrange By**, point to **Current View**, and click **By Company**.

The contact entries are now displayed in a grid that is grouped by company, and sorted by the *File As* column.

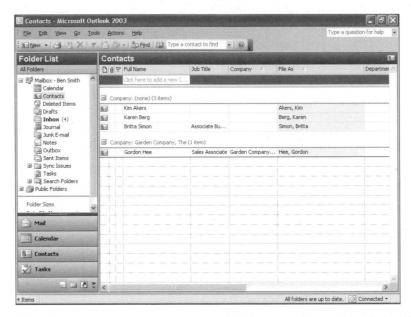

If the company groups are collapsed, click the plus (+) sign to the left of the company name to see the individual contacts for a company.

13 Double-click the contact entry for **Karen Berg**.

The Karen Berg – Contact form appears.

Display Map
of Address

Tip From the Contact form, you can access a contact's Web site. Simply click the link in the "Web page address" box. You can also get a map to the contact's address. On the toolbar, click the Display Map of Address button.

14 Click the **Categories** button.

The Categories dialog box appears.

15 In the **Available categories** area, select the **Business** check box.

16 Click **OK**.

The Categories dialog box closes.

Save and Close **17** On the toolbar of the **Karen Berg – Contact** form, click **Save and Close**.

The Contact form closes, and the contents of the Contacts folder are displayed, including the updated entry for Karen Berg.

18 Double-click the contact entry for **Kim Akers**.

The Kim Akers – Contact form appears.

19 Click the **Categories** button.

The Categories dialog box appears.

20 In the **Available categories** area, select the **Business** check box, and then select the **Hot Contacts** check box.

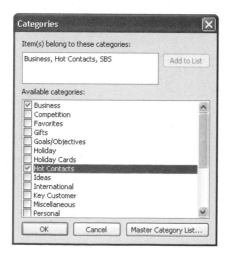

21 Click **OK** to close the **Categories** dialog box.

22 On the toolbar for the **Kim Akers – Contact** form, click the **Save and Close** button.

The Contact form closes, and the contents of the Contacts folder are displayed, including the updated entry for Kim Akers.

23 On the **View** menu, point to **Arrange By**, point to **Current View**, and click **By Category**.

The contact entries are displayed in a grid grouped by category and sorted by the *File As* column.

24 If the **Business** category is not displayed, click the plus (+) sign to its left.

The contact entries in the Business category are displayed.

25 If the **Hot Contacts** category is not displayed, click the plus (+) sign to its left.

The contacts in the Hot Contacts category are displayed. Note that the entry for Kim Akers appears in both categories.

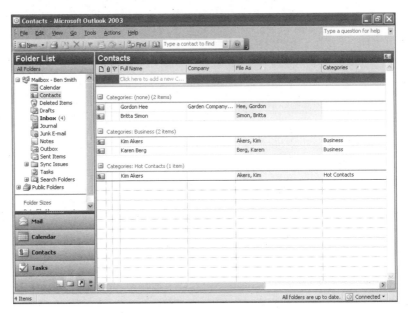

26 On the **View** menu, point to **Arrange By**, point to **Current View**, and click **Address Cards**.

The contact entries are displayed as address cards.

Tip You can customize the existing contact views or define your own new view from scratch. To get started, on the View menu, point to Current View, and click Customize Current View or Define Views.

Tracking Dealings with Contacts

Microsoft
Office
Specialist

Keeping track of what's been done or needs to be done in connection with a particular contact can be challenging. For example, you might have agreed to provide additional information for a sales contact and want to follow up after the material has been received. With Outlook, you can link contacts to other Outlook items including *appointments* or *events*, *Journal entries*, *notes*, and e-mail messages. You can also track all items related to a contact and flag contacts for follow up at a specified time.

You can track items through either the Activities tab of the Contact form, or through the Outlook Journal. The Activities tab is the preferred tracking method; it automatically displays contacts, e-mail messages, journal entries, tasks, and notes associated with the selected contact. You can filter the list to display only items of a certain type.

With the Outlook Journal, you can keep a record of any kind of interaction or activity, even if it is not associated with an item on your computer. You can log phone conversations and meetings with contacts, as well as hard-copy letters you've mailed or received. For example, you might track all interactions with a client to support the hours you bill to that client at the end of the month. Or you might use the Journal to record meeting minutes and document phone conversations related to a particular project so that you can reference them as you work. In addition to tracking items such as e-mail messages and Microsoft Office documents, you can choose which Outlook items will be automatically tracked for the contacts you specify.

In this exercise, you will link items to a contact, track the items linked to a contact, flag a contact for follow up, and resolve the follow-up flag.

Important   You can work through this exercise in your own Contacts folder or in the practice Contacts folder. If you use your own contacts, substitute them for the names given in the exercise.

USE the *SBSContacts* data file in the practice file folder for this topic. This practice file is located in the *My Documents\Microsoft Press\Outlook 2003 SBS\Contacts* folder and can also be accessed by clicking *Start/All Programs/Microsoft Press/Outlook 2003 Step by Step.*

1   In the Inbox, right-click the **Shipped Presentation Materials to Hotel** message, and then click **Options**.

The Message Options form appears.

2   Click the **Contacts** button.

The Select Contacts dialog box appears.

3 In the **Items** list, click **Berg, Karen**, and click **OK**.

The contact is added to the Message Options form, indicating that this message is linked to the contact entry for Karen Berg.

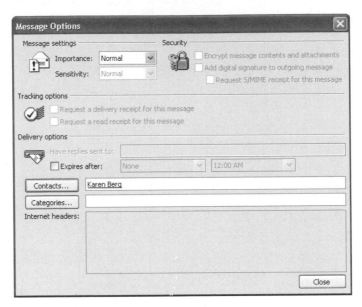

4 Click the **Close** button.

Close

Tip You can link appointments, tasks, and even other contacts to a contact in much the same way. Open the item, and click the Contacts button in the bottom left corner. E-mail messages sent to a contact are automatically linked to the contact.

5 In the **Navigation Pane**, click the **Contacts** icon.

Contacts

The contents of the Contacts folder are displayed.

6 Double-click the contact entry for **Karen Berg**.

The Karen Berg – Contact form appears.

7 Click the **Activities** tab.

The Activities tab is displayed, showing that the Shipped Presentation Materials to Hotel message is linked to this contact.

Important The Activities tab also shows a Calendar item for Karen's birthday. This item was created by Outlook when Karen's birth date was added to the Details tab of the contact entry.

Follow Up

8 With the *Shipped Presentation Materials to Hotel* message selected, on the toolbar, click the **Follow Up** button.

The Flag for Follow Up dialog box appears.

9 Click the down arrow to the right of the **Due by** box, scroll to and click **June 19, 2003**, and click **OK**. (If you are completing this step on a date later than June 19, 2003, click a date that is a few days in the future rather than clicking June 19.)

10 Click the **General** tab.

The Contact form is updated to indicate that a follow-up flag has been set.

11 On the Contact form's toolbar, click the **Save and Close** button.

The Contact form closes. In the Contacts folder, the entry for Karen Berg indicates that a follow-up flag has been set.

12 On the **View** menu, point to **Arrange By**, point to **Current View**, and click **Phone List**.

The contacts are displayed in the Phone List view. A red flag icon to the left of the entry for Karen Berg indicates that a follow-up flag has been set.

13 Double-click the contact entry for **Karen Berg**.

The Karen Berg – Contact form appears.

14 On the toolbar, click the **Follow Up** button.

The Flag for Follow Up dialog box appears.

15 Select the **Completed** check box, and click **OK**.

The Contact form is updated to show that the follow up is complete.

16 On the Contact form's toolbar, click the **Save and Close** button.

The Contact form closes. In the Contacts folder, the flag icon to the left of the entry for Karen Berg has turned into a gray check mark, indicating that follow up is complete.

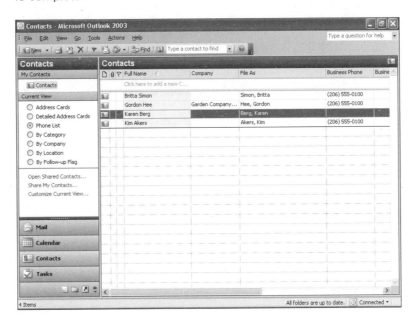

17 On the **View** menu, point to **Arrange By**, point to **Current View**, and then click **Address Cards**.

The contact information is displayed in Address Cards view.

Tip   When viewing contact information in a list, you can quickly mark a follow-up flag as complete by clicking the flag icon and clicking Completed in the drop-down list. If you need to remove a follow up flag, you can clear the flag by displaying the Follow-Up Flag dialog box and clicking the Clear Flag button.

Sending and Receiving Contact Information Through E-Mail

Microsoft Office Specialist

Sharing contact information with your co-workers can save you and your co-workers a considerable amount of time and reduce the possibility of errors because the information is entered only once. With Outlook, you can send and receive contact information through e-mail. If the recipient uses Outlook, you can send contact information as an Outlook address card. Otherwise, you can send the contact information as a *vCard*, the Internet standard for creating and sharing virtual business cards.

In this exercise, you will send contact information through e-mail and save contact information from e-mail to your own Contacts folder.

Important   You can work through this exercise in your own Contacts folder or in the practice Contacts folder. If you use your own contacts, substitute them for the names given in the exercise.

USE the *SBSContacts* data file in the practice file folder for this topic. This practice file is located in the *My Documents\Microsoft Press\Outlook 2003 SBS\Contacts* folder and can also be accessed by clicking *Start/All Programs/Microsoft Press/Outlook 2003 Step by Step.*
OPEN the practice Contacts folder.

1 In the Contacts folder, click the entry for **Karen Berg**.

2 On the **Actions** menu, click **Forward as vCard**.

The Forward Message form appears, with the vCard for Karen Berg added as an attachment.

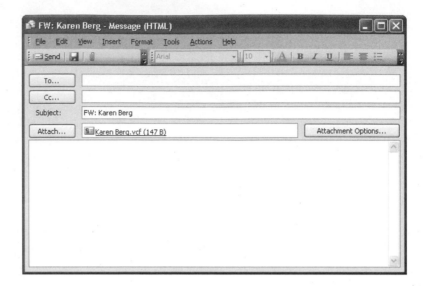

Tip To send information for more than one contact in the same e-mail message, select the contact entries you want to send, and on the Actions menu, click Forward or Forward as vCard. (To select multiple contact entries, hold down the [Ctrl] key, and click each entry in turn.)

Send

3 In the **To** box, type your e-mail address, and click the **Send** button.

The message is sent.

4 In the **Navigation Pane**, click the **Inbox** icon.

The contents of the Inbox are displayed.

Important If your computer is not connected to a network with a mail server, the next step requires that you be connected to the Internet.

5 If the forwarded message has not arrived, on the toolbar, click the **Send/Receive** button.

The forwarded message appears in your Inbox, with a paper clip icon indicating that the message contains an attachment.

6   Double-click the forwarded message.

The Message form appears, showing the vCard in the message.

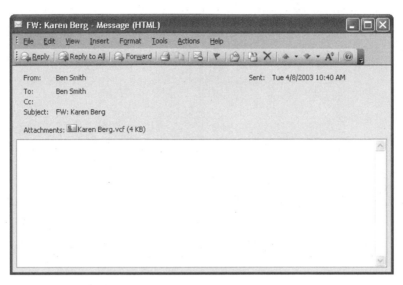

7   Double-click the vCard.

The Opening Mail Attachment dialog box appears.

8   Click the **Open** button.

The Karen Berg – Contact form appears.

Save and Close   **9**   Click the **Save and Close** button.

Because the Contacts folder already contains an entry for Karen Berg, the Duplicate Contact Detected dialog appears.

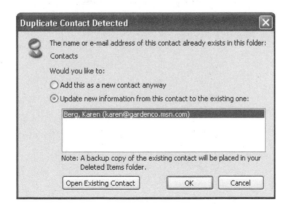

10 Select the **Add this as a new contact anyway** option, and then click OK.

The contact information is saved in your Contacts folder as a second entry named Karen Berg.

11 Close the e-mail message.

12 In the **Navigation Pane**, click the **Contacts** icon.

Contacts

The contents of your Contacts folder are displayed, including the new contact entry for Karen Berg.

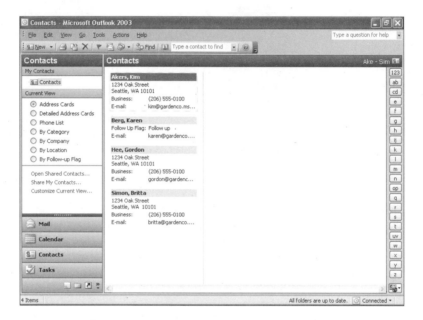

BE SURE TO delete the Karen Berg contact from your own Contacts folder.

Printing Contact Information

Microsoft Office Specialist

To make it easy to take contact information with you while you are away from your computer, you can print your Contacts list. You can print contact information from any of the available views, and for the Address Card views, you can select from a number of print styles. For all views, you can define your own print styles, specifying the layout, the margins, orientation, and more. The print options available to you vary based on the view selected when you chose to print.

In this exercise, you will print a phone list and then print a number of key contact entries as address cards.

Important   To complete this exercise, you must have a printer installed. If you don't have a printer installed, see your administrator or the printer manufacturer's documentation for assistance.

Tip   You can work through this exercise in your own Contacts folder or in the practice Contacts folder.

USE the *SBSContacts* data file in the practice file folder for this topic. This practice file is located in the *My Documents\Microsoft Press\Outlook 2003 SBS\Contacts* folder and can also be accessed by clicking *Start/All Programs/Microsoft Press/Outlook 2003 Step by Step.*
OPEN the practice Contacts folder or your own.

1   On the **View** menu, point to **Arrange By**, point to **Current View**, and click **Phone List**.

The contact entries are displayed in a columnar list.

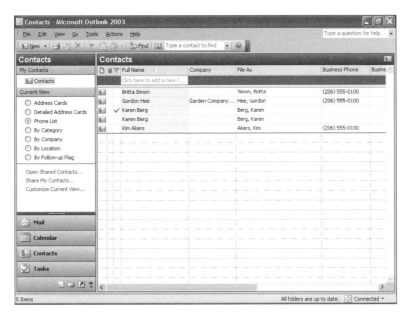

Print

2   On the toolbar, click the **Print** button.

The Print dialog box appears.

3 In the **Print range** box, ensure that the **All rows** option is selected, and click **OK**.

The contact entries are printed in the table style.

4 On the **View** menu, point to **Arrange By**, point to **Current View**, and click **Address Cards**.

The contact entries are displayed as address cards.

5 On the toolbar, click the **Print** button.

The Print dialog box appears.

6 Scroll the **Print style** box, click **Phone Directory Style**, and then click the **Preview** button.

The Print Preview window appears, showing how the contact entries will appear printed in Phone Directory Style format. This style is an alternative to printing the Phone List view.

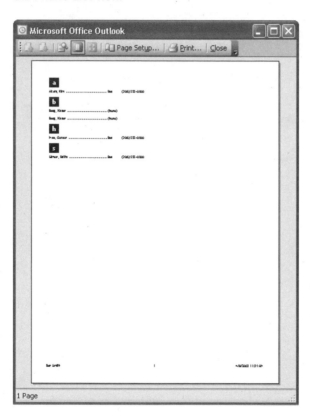

Close

7 On the **Print Preview** window's toolbar, click the **Close** button.

The Print Preview window closes.

8 In the Contacts folder, click the **Britta Simon** contact entry to select it, hold down the Ctrl key, and click the **Karen Berg** contact entry to add it to the selection.

Both the contact entries are selected.

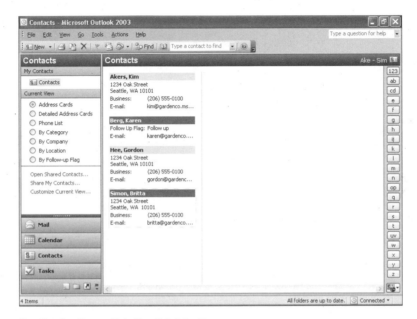

9 On the toolbar, click the **Print** button.

The Print dialog box appears.

10 In the **Print style** box, be sure that **Card Style** is selected.

11 In the **Print range** box, select the **Only selected items** option, and click **OK**.

The contacts you selected are printed in Card Style format.

CLOSE the *SBSContacts* data file. If you are not continuing on to the next chapter, quit Outlook.

Viewing SharePoint Team Services Contacts

New in Office 2003
View SharePoint Team Services contacts

With SharePoint Team Services, you can easily create flexible, simple-to-use team Web sites for collaboration and information sharing. The Contacts page of a team Web site can list contacts' names, companies, phone numbers, e-mail addresses, and the other information stored in Outlook's Contacts list. If you have access to a Windows SharePoint Services team Web site, you can import its contact list to your Outlook contacts folder. Follow these steps:

1 In your Web browser, open the SharePoint contacts list.

2 Click **Link to Outlook**.

   Outlook displays a dialog prompting you to add a SharePoint folder.

3 In the dialog box, click **Yes**.

   Outlook adds a folder named *SharePoint Folders*, if there isn't one already, and creates a list of contacts.

Key Points

- If your network uses Microsoft Exchange Server, the Global Address List contains contact entries for all users. You can create additional contact entries in your Personal Address Book and in the Contacts list in your Outlook profile.

- Contact entries can store names, e-mail and instant messaging addresses, phone numbers, mailing addresses, birthdays, and other information. You can assign categories to contact entries, sort contact entries by category, and create custom categories.

- You can assign follow-up flags to contact entries, and link contact entries to e-mail messages, appointments, tasks, and other Outlook items. You can view all items linked to a contact on the contact form's Activities tab.

- You can import and export contact entries between Outlook, your instant message client, and a SharePoint Services Web site.

- You can right-click a contact entry to send that contact a message or create a message containing their contact information.

- Outlook contains many useful predefined views and print styles for presenting selected information from contact forms.

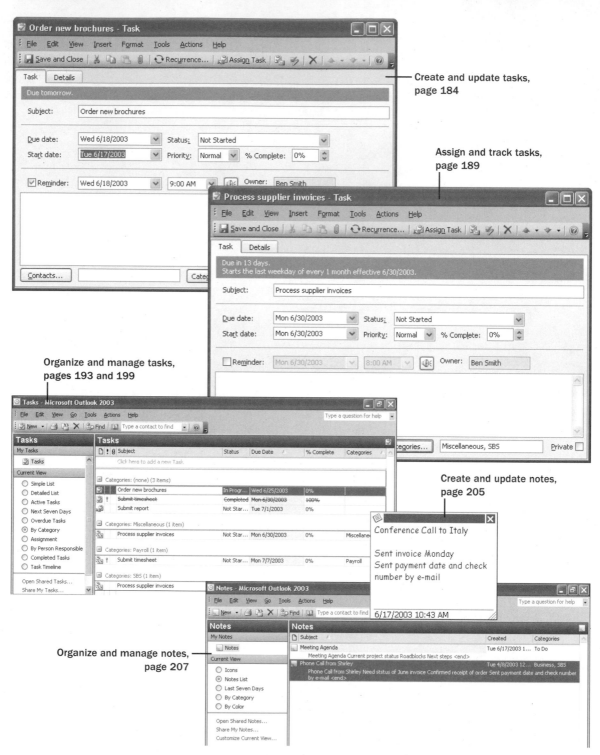

Create and update tasks,
page 184

Assign and track tasks,
page 189

Organize and manage tasks,
pages 193 and 199

Create and update notes,
page 205

Organize and manage notes,
page 207

Chapter 7 at a Glance

7 Keeping Track of Information

In this chapter you will learn to:

✔ Create and update tasks.

✔ Assign and track tasks.

✔ Organize tasks.

✔ Manage tasks.

✔ Create and update notes.

✔ Organize and manage notes.

To-do lists written on scraps of paper or stored in bulky paper planners are often difficult to maintain and easy to lose. With Microsoft Outlook, you can replace these lists with a Tasks list that is easy to maintain, and much more powerful. You can use Outlook to create a list of *tasks*, track the progress of tasks, and assign tasks to others. Plus, Outlook offers ways to organize your tasks to help you manage them more efficiently.

As you work, you might think of ideas, remember small tasks, or jot down messages on notepads or sticky notes. You can use Microsoft Outlook to record these items in the form of electronic *notes* that you can save, edit, and organize.

See Also Do you need only a quick refresher on the topics in this chapter? See the Quick Reference entries on pages xliii–xlvi.

Important Before you can use the practice files in this chapter, you need to install them from the book's companion CD to their default location. See "Using the Book's CD-ROM" on page xiii for more information.

Creating and Updating Tasks

Microsoft Office Specialist

You can create and store a list of tasks for any activity that you want to remember and track to completion. For each task, you can specify a due date and a start date. A task is displayed in your *Tasks list* beginning on the start date. A task that is incomplete past its due date is displayed in red to indicate that it is overdue. You can also set the priority of a task—High for urgent tasks, and Normal and Low for less important tasks. And you can choose to set a *reminder* for a task, much like reminders for *appointments*.

Tasks can recur either at regular intervals or at intervals based on the date on which you mark the task complete. For example, you might create a task to remind yourself to review the status of a project every seven days. If you perform your review on a Friday and mark the task as complete, Outlook creates the next instance of the task as due on the following Friday. If you perform your next review on a Thursday, Outlook creates the next instance of the task as due on the following Thursday. A task that you create to recur at a regular interval will be regenerated at that interval regardless of the status of earlier instances of the task. For example, you might create a task for submitting your employees' expense reports to the finance department on the fifth of each month. When you mark the task as complete, regardless of the day, Outlook creates the next instance of the task and marks it as due on the fifth of the following month.

You can create and modify tasks in the Tasks folder or in the *TaskPad* that appears in the default *Calendar* view.

In this exercise, you'll create a task, create a *recurring* task, set a reminder, update a task, and modify task settings.

BE SURE TO start Outlook before beginning this exercise.

Tasks

1 In the **Navigation Pane**, click the **Tasks** button.

The contents of the Tasks folder are displayed in the default Simple List view.

New Task

2 On the toolbar, click the **New Task** button.

The Task form appears.

3 In the **Subject** box, type Order new brochures.

4 Click the down arrow to the right of the **Due date** box, and then click tomorrow's date.

5 Click the down arrow to the right of the **Start date** box, and then click today's date.

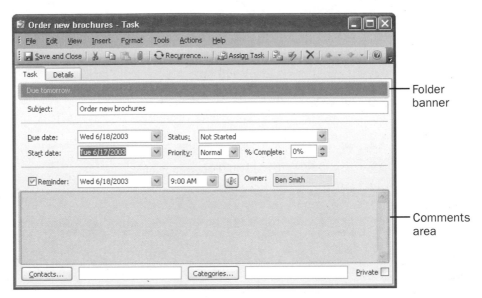

6 Click the **Save and Close** button.

The Task form closes. The new task appears in the Tasks folder.

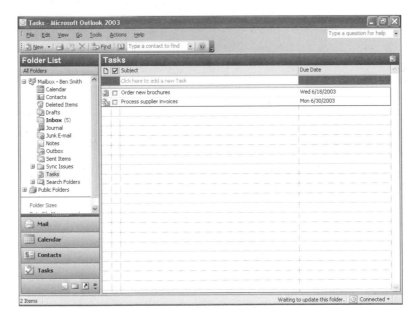

7 On the toolbar, click the **New Task** button.

The Task form appears.

8 In the **Subject** box, type **Submit timesheet**.

9 Click the down arrow to the right of the **Due date** box, and then click the Monday after next.

10 Click the down arrow to the right of the **Start date** box, and then click the next Monday.

11 Click the down arrow to the right of the **Priority** box, and then click **High**.

 12 On the toolbar, click the **Recurrence** button.

The Task Recurrence dialog box appears.

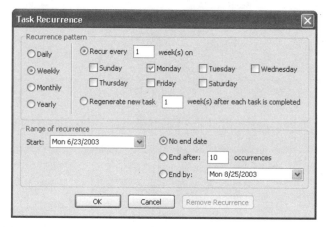

13 In the **Recurrence pattern** area, be sure that the **Weekly** option is selected, and that the **Monday** check box is selected.

As you complete the task each week, the task is regenerated for the next Monday.

14 In the **Range of recurrence** area, select the **End after** option, in the **occurrences** box, type **8**, and then click **OK**.

Outlook will generate eight instances of the task over the next eight weeks.

15 Click the **Save and Close** button.

The Task form closes. The new task appears in the Tasks folder.

Tip   You can quickly create a new task directly in the Tasks folder. Simply click in the "Click here to add a new Task" box. Then type the task subject, press the ⎵Tab⎵ key, type the due date, and press the ⎵Enter⎵ key.

16 Double-click the **Order new brochures** task.

The Task form appears.

17 Click the down arrow to the right of the **Due date** box, and then click the date one week later than the current due date. The current due date is indicated by a yellow box.

18 Click the down arrow to the right of the **Status** box, and then click **In Progress**.

19 Be sure the **Reminder** check box is selected. Then click the down arrow to the right of the first **Reminder** box, and click the date two business days before the new due date.

20 Click the down arrow to the right of the second **Reminder** box, and then click **10:00 AM**.

21 Click in the comments area, type Contact marketing for layout materials, and then click the **Save and Close** button.

The Task form closes. The updated task appears in the Tasks folder.

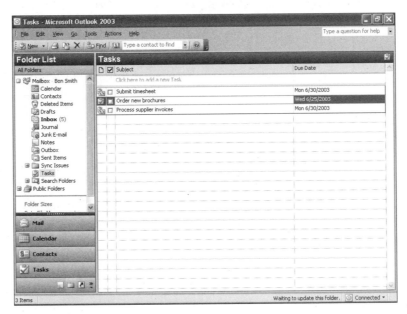

22 On the **Tools** menu, click **Options**.

The Options dialog box appears.

23 In the **Tasks** area, click the down arrow to the right of the **Reminder time** box, and then click **9:00 AM**.

Reminders for all tasks you create will be set for 9 A.M. on the date you choose to be reminded.

24 Click the **Task Options** button.

The Task Options dialog box appears.

25 Click the down arrow to the right of the **Completed task color** box, scroll up, and then click navy blue (the fifth color from the top of the list).

26 Clear the **Send status reports when assigned tasks are completed** check box.

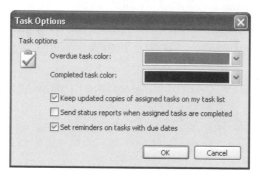

27 Click **OK**, and in the **Options** dialog box, click **OK**.

The Options dialog box closes. The Tasks folder is displayed.

28 To mark the *Submit timesheet* task as complete, select the check box to its left.

The Tasks list is updated to show the completed task in navy blue and crossed out. The Tasks list also displays the next instance of the recurring *Submit timesheet* task.

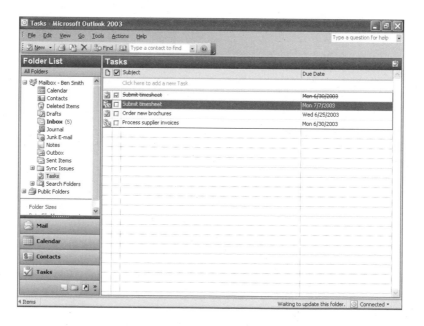

Tip   You can quickly create a task from an e-mail message. Simply drag the message to the Tasks button on the Navigation Pane, and complete the Task form that appears.

Assigning and Tracking Tasks

You can create a task in Outlook but assign it to someone else for completion. You might delegate a task to your assistant, or when your project depends on receiving something from another department, you might assign a task to your *contact* in that department.

Although you can update the tasks you create for yourself, when you assign a task to someone else, only that person can update it. However, you can keep a copy of the task in your Tasks list, and your copy will be updated as the other person updates the tasks. For example, if the other person changes the status or the percent complete, your copy of the task will be updated. You can also specify that you want to receive status reports for the task. Status reports are special e-mail messages that reflect the current status of a task.

In this exercise, you will assign a task to a contact and view and track the task you have assigned.

BE SURE TO start Outlook before beginning this exercise.
OPEN your Outlook *Tasks* folder.

New Task

1   On the toolbar, click the **New Task** button.

The Task form appears.

2   In the **Subject** box, type **Submit report**.

3   Click the down arrow to the right of the **Due date** box, and click the date two weeks from today.

4   Click the down arrow to the right of the **Start date** box, and click the date one week from today.

5   On the toolbar, click the **Assign Task** button.

The Task form is updated to include a To box.

6   In the **To** box, type **kim@gardenco.msn.com**.

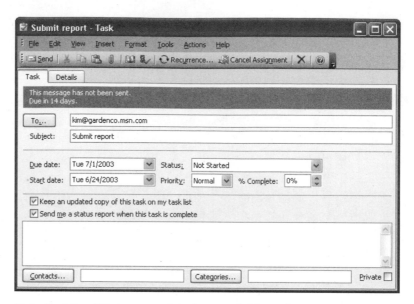

Note that the "Keep an updated copy of this task on my task list" and "Send me a status report when this task is complete" options are selected.

7   Click in the comments area, and type **Inventory report** to describe the type of report you are requesting.

8   On the toolbar, click the **Send** button. If a message appears to notify you that the task reminder has been turned off, click **OK**.

The task request is sent. You will be notified when the assignee accepts or declines the task.

Important   The e-mail addresses used in these exercises are not valid. Any items you send to these addresses will be returned as undeliverable. You can delete the returned messages at any time.

9   On the **View** menu, point to **Arrange By**, point to **Current View**, and then click **Assignment**.

The Tasks folder shows only those tasks that you have assigned to others. For each task, the *Subject*, *Owner*, *Due Date*, and *Status* columns are shown. The Folder banner indicates that the tasks are filtered.

Important   If you assign a task to more than one person, you cannot keep a copy of the task in your Tasks list. To be able to track the progress on tasks assigned to more than one person, create duplicate tasks, and assign each of them to one person.

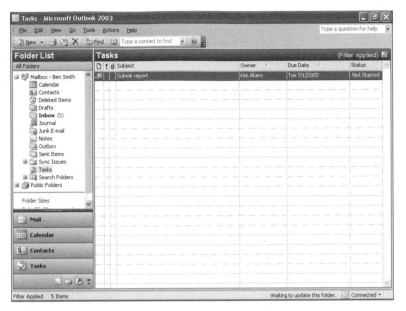

10 In the **Tasks** list, double-click the **Submit report** task.

The Task form appears. As work on the task progresses, its status will be reflected in the header on the Task tab.

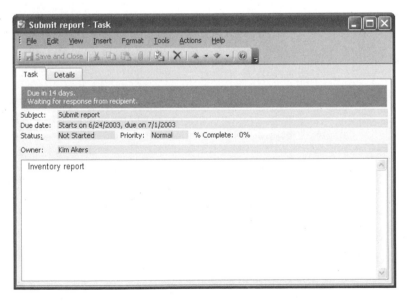

11 Click the **Details** tab.

The Details tab is displayed. As work on the task progresses or the task is completed, any work-related information or the date the task was completed will appear in the header on this tab.

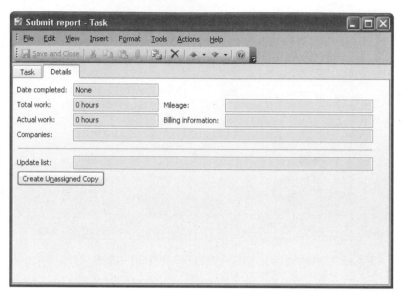

Close

12 Click the **Close** button.

The Task form closes, and you return to the Tasks list.

Tip If you want another person to perform a task but don't need to track the progress of that task, you can send the task as an *attachment* to an e-mail message rather than assigning a task to another person. In the Tasks list, right-click the task, and click Forward on the shortcut menu. Address the message, and then click the Send button. The recipient can then save the attached task to his or her Tasks list. Tasks received in this manner are just like tasks you created for yourself.

13 On the toolbar, click the **New Task** button.

The Task form appears.

14 On the toolbar, click the **Assign Task** button.

The Task form is updated to include a To box.

15 Click the **To** button.

The Select Task Recipient dialog box appears.

16 If **Contacts** is not the active address book, click the down arrow to the right of the **Show Names from the** box, and click **Contacts** in the drop-down list.

17 In the **Name** list, click any contact, click the **To** button, and then click **OK**.

The name and e-mail address of the contact is added to the To box.

18 Click the **Close** button, and when prompted to save the changes, click **No**.

The task is discarded without being saved.

Organizing Tasks

*Microsoft
Office
Specialist*

Staying on top of your tasks can be a challenge as the list grows. To help you organize your tasks, Outlook offers several ways to view and sort them. You can also organize your tasks using folders and *categories*. For example, if you fall behind, you can view only your overdue tasks to get caught up quickly. Or you might assign all tasks related to milestones for a key project to the Goals/Objectives category and then view only the tasks in that category to check the progress of the project.

You can easily organize tasks with folders, categories, and views by using the Ways to Organize Tasks pane. While viewing the Tasks folder, on the Tools menu, click Organize to display this pane.

- To organize tasks in folders, click Using Folders, select the task(s), select the folder, and click the Move button.

- To assign categories to tasks, click Using Categories, select the task(s), select the category, and click the Add button.

- To change the way you view tasks, click Using Views, and select the view you want.

In this exercise, you will change your task *view*, sort your tasks, assign categories to a task, view your tasks by category, and view your tasks in the TaskPad.

USE the *SBSTracking* data file in the practice file folder for this topic. This practice file is located in the *My Documents\Microsoft Press\Outlook 2003 SBS\Tracking* folder and can also be accessed by clicking *Start/All Programs/Microsoft Press/Outlook 2003 Step by Step.*
OPEN the *SBSTracking* data file.

1 With the Tasks folder displayed, on the **View** menu, point to **Arrange By**, point to **Current View**, and then click **Detailed List**.

The details of the tasks, including the status, percent complete, and categories, are displayed.

2 On the **View** menu, point to **Arrange By**, point to **Current View**, and then click **Active Tasks**.

Only tasks that are not complete are shown.

3 Click the **Subject** column heading.

The tasks are sorted in ascending order based on the Subject column.

Tip To manage a list of many tasks, you can organize your tasks in folders. To move a task to a folder, simply drag it from the Tasks list to a Task Items folder in the Folder List. (If you drag the task to a Mail, Calendar, Contact, or Note Items folder, a Message, Meeting, Contact, or Note form opens with the task's subject entered in the form.)

4 On the **View** menu, point to **Arrange By**, point to **Current View**, and then click **Simple List**.

The contents of the Tasks folder are displayed in the default view.

5 Double-click the **Process supplier invoices** task.

The Task form appears. If the date in the "Due date" box is in the past, change it to a date two weeks in the future.

6 Click the **Categories** button.

The Categories dialog box appears.

7 In the **Available categories** list, select the **Miscellaneous** check box.

8 Click **OK**.

The Available Categories dialog box closes. The Miscellaneous category is added to the Task form.

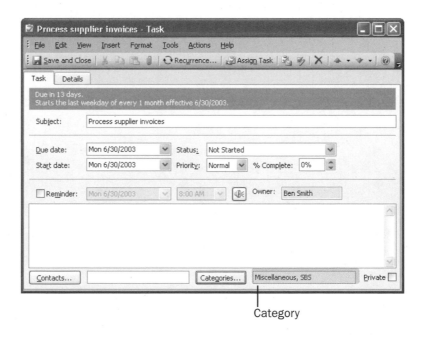

Category

9 Click the **Save and Close** button.

The updated task is saved in the Tasks folder.

10 Double-click the new **Submit timesheet** task.

The Task form appears.

11 Click the **Categories** button.

The Categories dialog box appears.

12 Click in the **Item(s) belong to these categories** box, type Payroll, and then click the **Add to List** button.

The Payroll category is added to the "Available categories" list.

13 In the **Available categories** list, scroll down to see the **Payroll** category.

The check box next to the Payroll category is selected.

14 In the **Categories** dialog box, click **OK**.

The Categories dialog box closes. The Payroll category is added to the Task form.

15 On the Task form's toolbar, click the **Save and Close** button.

The updated task is saved in the Tasks folder.

16 On the **View** menu, point to **Arrange By**, point to **Current View**, and then click **By Category**.

The tasks are displayed, grouped by category.

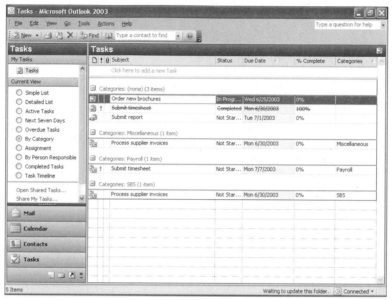

17 If the **Payroll** category is collapsed, click the plus (+) sign to its left.

The task in the Payroll category (Submit timesheet) is displayed.

18 On the **View** menu, point to **Arrange By**, point to **Current View**, and then click **Simple List**.

The contents of the Tasks folder are displayed in the default view.

19 In the **Navigation Pane**, click the **Calendar** button.

Calendar

The Calendar is displayed, and the TaskPad is shown in the bottom right corner of the Outlook window.

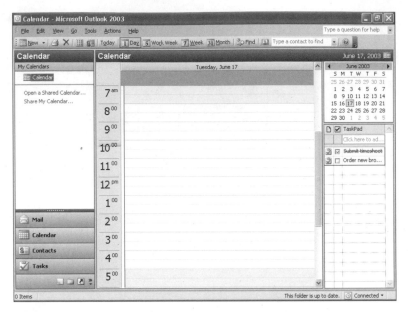

20 If you don't see the **Task Pad** in the bottom right corner of your screen, on the **View** menu, click **TaskPad**.

21 In the **TaskPad**, click the **Click here to add a new Task** box, type Schedule doctor's appointment, and then press the [Enter] key.

The new task is added to the Tasks list in the TaskPad.

22 Double-click the **Schedule doctor's appointment** task.

The Task form appears.

23 Select the **Reminder** check box. Then click the down arrow to the right of the **Reminder** box, and click tomorrow's date.

24 Click the **Save and Close** button.

The Task form closes, and the updated task is saved. You return to the Calendar and the TaskPad.

Managing Tasks

As you complete your tasks, you will want to remove them from your to-do list. You might find that some tasks were not necessary and can be deleted. You might also acquire new tasks that other Outlook users assign to you, asking that you report back on your progress. Outlook makes it easy to manage changes to your tasks and send status reports for tasks requested by others.

Tip If you set reminders for tasks, you will start receiving reminder messages as task due dates approach. When a reminder pops up on your screen, you can respond in one of three ways. Clicking the Dismiss button closes the task—you will receive no further reminders for this task. Clicking the Snooze button sets the reminder to appear again in a specified amount of time. You can also open the item, which closes the reminder.

Accepting and Declining Tasks

When you receive a task request, you must accept or decline the task in the same way that you would accept or decline a meeting.

To accept a task:

1   Double-click the task request to open the Task form.

2   On the toolbar, click the **Accept** button.

3   In the **Accepting Task** dialog box, leave the **Send the response now** option selected, and click **OK**.

The Task form closes, the task request disappears from your Inbox, and the next message in the Inbox appears in the Reading pane. The new task is added to your Tasks list, and a notice of your acceptance is sent to the requester.

To decline a task:

1   Double-click the task request to open the Task form.

2   On the toolbar, click the **Decline** button.

3   In the **Declining Task** dialog box, leave the **Send the response now** option selected, and click **OK**.

The Task form closes, the task request disappears from your Inbox, and the next message in the Inbox appears in the Reading pane. A notice that you have declined the request is sent to the requester.

To track the progress of a task, you can indicate the status and percentage complete. New tasks have the status of *Not Started*. When you begin work on a task, you can mark the task as *In Progress*. You can also enter the percentage of the work that is complete. For example, if you are halfway through a document that you must review, you would mark the task as 50 percent complete. If a task is zero percent complete, the status of the task is set to *Not Started*. When you enter 100 as the percentage complete, the status of the task is set to *Completed*. If the percent complete contains any number between 0 and 100, the task status is *In Progress*. When you have finished the task, you mark the task as *Completed* or enter the percent complete as 100. If work on a task has stalled, you can mark the task as *Deferred* or *Waiting on someone else*.

In this exercise, you will send a status report on a task assigned to you, mark a task as complete, stop a task from recurring, and delete a task.

USE the *SBSTracking* data file in the practice file folder for this topic. This practice file is located in the *My Documents\Microsoft Press\Outlook 2003 SBS\Tracking* folder and can also be accessed by clicking *Start/All Programs/Microsoft Press/Outlook 2003 Step by Step.*
BE SURE TO open the *SBSTracking* data file before beginning this exercise.
OPEN the *Inbox* folder in the *SBS Tracking* data file folder.

Tasks

1 In the **Navigation Pane**, click the **Tasks** button.

The contents of the Tasks folder are displayed.

2 Double-click the **Approve invoice payments** task.

The Task form appears.

3 Click the down arrow to the right of the **Status** box, and click **In Progress.** Then select the contents of the **% Complete** box, and type **50**.

4 Select the **Reminder** check box. Then click the down arrow to the right of the **Reminder** box, and select the last business day before the due date. The due date is indicated by a yellow box.

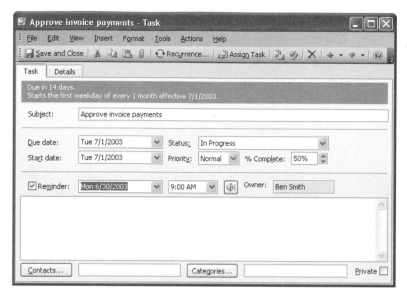

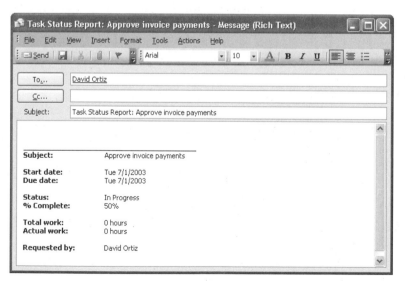

Send Status Report

5 On the toolbar, click the **Send Status Report** button.

The Message form appears, containing the current status of the task.

6 If the task requester's name or e-mail address is not entered in the **To** box for you, enter it now.

Send

7 In the body of the message, above the existing text, type **Approved payments marked in accounting program**, and click the **Send** button.

The Message form closes, sending the status report to the task requester.

8 In the Task form, click the **Save and Close** button.

The Task form closes. The updated task is saved to your Tasks list.

Tip You can quickly create an appointment from a task. Simply drag the task to the Calendar button on the Navigation Pane, and then complete the Appointment form.

9 Double-click the **Approve invoice payments** task.

The Task form appears.

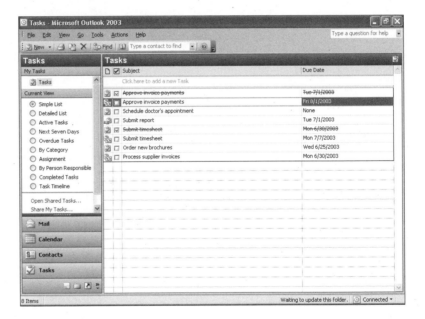

10 On the toolbar, click the **Mark Complete** button.

Mark Complete

The Task form closes. A status report is automatically sent to the task requester. The task appears as completed in your Tasks list, and because this task is recurring, the next month's task is added to your list.

Tip You can quickly mark a task as completed in the Tasks list in Simple List view or in the TaskPad in the default Calendar view. Simply select the check box that appears to the left of the task.

11 In the **Tasks** list, double-click the new **Approve invoice payments** task.

The Task form appears.

12 Click the **Details** tab.

13 Click the down arrow to the right of the **Date completed** box, and then click the task's due date, **8/1/03**.

14 Click in the **Actual work** box, delete the existing text, type **8**, and then press the ⌨Tab key.

Outlook converts the 8 (hours) you entered to *1 day*, because one workday is eight hours long.

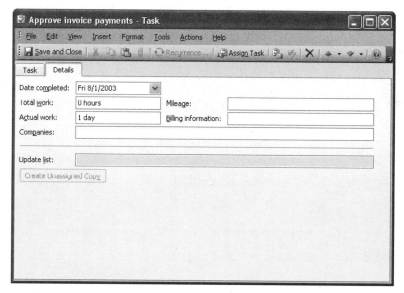

15 Click the **Save and Close** button.

The Task form closes. A status report is automatically sent to the task requester. The task appears as completed in your Tasks list, and the next month's task is added to your list.

16 In the **Tasks** list, double-click the new **Submit timesheet** task.

The Task form appears.

17 On the toolbar, click the **Recurrence** button.

The Task Recurrence dialog box for this task appears.

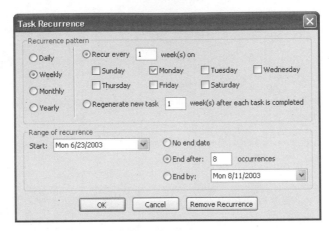

18 Click the **Remove Recurrence** button.

The Task Recurrence dialog box closes, and you return to the updated Task form.

19 On the Task form's toolbar, click the **Save and Close** button.

The Task form closes. The updated task is saved in your Tasks list.

20 In the **Tasks** list, click the new **Submit timesheet** task to select it.

Delete

21 On the toolbar, click the **Delete** button.

The task is removed from your Tasks list.

22 In the **Tasks** list, click the **Approve invoice payments** task to select it.

23 On the toolbar, click the **Delete** button.

A message box asks if you want to delete all occurrences of this task.

24 In the message box, select the **Delete all** option, and click **OK**.

The task is marked as completed in the Tasks list, and no further tasks are created.

Creating and Updating Notes

Microsoft Office Specialist

You can use Outlook's Notes feature to record questions, ideas, reminders, messages, or anything else that you might otherwise write down. Because you can leave notes open on your screen even while Outlook is minimized, they are especially useful for storing small bits of information that you might need as you work. For example, you might open a Note form to record your notes during a phone conference, or you might use a note to jot down useful references you find while doing research on the Web.

In this exercise, you will create and edit notes.

BE SURE TO start Outlook before beginning this exercise.

Maximize

1 If the Outlook window is not already maximized, click the **Maximize** button.

Notes

2 In the **Navigation Pane**, click the **Notes** button.

Your Notes folder opens.

New Note

3 On the toolbar, click the **New Note** button.

The Note form appears, showing the current date and time at the bottom.

4 In the body of the Note form, type **Conference Call to Italy**, press the Enter key twice, and then type **Sent invoice Monday**.

Close

5 To save your note, click the **Close** button.

Your note is saved in the Notes folder, and the first line appears as the note's title.

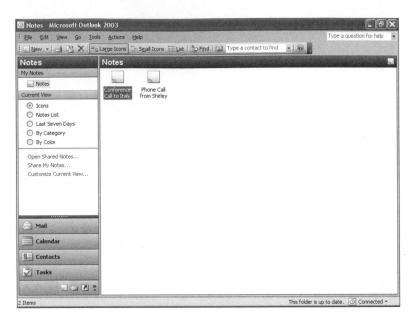

6 Double-click the note you created.

The Note form appears.

7 Edit the contents of the note by clicking at the end of the second line, pressing [Enter],
and typing **Sent payment date and check number by e-mail**.

8 To save the note, click the **Close** button.

The updated note is saved in the Notes folder.

9 On the toolbar, click the **New Note** button, type **Meeting Agenda**, press [Enter], and then
type **Current project status**, **Roadblocks**, and **Next steps**, pressing [Enter] after each.
Finish by clicking the **Close** button.

The updated note is saved in your Notes folder.

Delete

10 In the Notes folder, click the **Conference Call** note, and on the toolbar, click the **Delete** button.

The note is deleted.

Organizing and Managing Notes

*Microsoft
Office
Specialist*

It doesn't take long before you accumulate a variety of notes from different days and about different topics. When this happens, it can become increasingly difficult to find that crucial bit of information you jotted down last week. But Outlook makes it easy to view, sort, organize, and manage your notes to help you find the information you need when you need it. You can view notes as large icons, as small icons, or in a list. You can organize notes by date, category, and color. For example, you might view all the notes on a given date to find the notes you took during a conference call, or you might assign all notes related to personal issues to the Personal category and then view only those notes when taking time to handle personal items. You can also forward notes to others and link notes to contacts. For example, after a phone call with a client, you might link a note you created during that call to the contact information for that client. You can also forward that note to a co-worker who is working with the same client.

In this exercise, you will change view options, sort notes, color-code notes, forward a note, and link a note to a contact.

USE the *SBSTracking* data file in the practice file folder for this topic. This practice file is located in the *My Documents\Microsoft Press\Outlook 2003 SBS\Tracking* folder and can also be accessed by clicking *Start/All Programs/Microsoft Press/Outlook 2003 Step by Step.*
OPEN the Notes folder.

1 On the toolbar, click the **List** button.

The notes are displayed as icons in a list.

2 On the **View** menu, point to **Arrange By**, point to **Current View**, and then click **Notes List**.

The notes are displayed in a list, with the contents of the notes visible. They are sorted by the Created column, with the newest at the top.

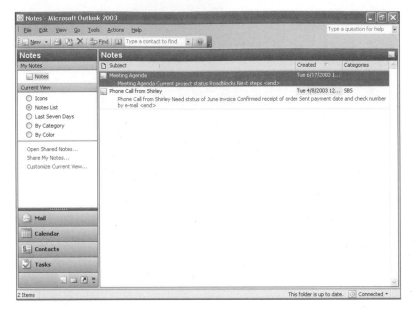

3   Click the **Subject** column heading.

The notes are sorted alphabetically by subject.

4   Right-click the **Phone Call from Shirley** note, click **Color** on the shortcut menu, and then click **Green**.

The Phone Call from Shirley note changes color.

5   Double-click the **Meeting Agenda** note.

The Note form appears.

6   In the top left corner, click the **Note** icon, and then click **Categories** in the drop-down list.

The Categories dialog box appears.

7 Click in the **Item(s) belong to these categories** box, type **To Do**, and then click the **Add to List** button.

The category is added to the Available categories list.

8 In the **Available categories** list, scroll down to see the new category.

The To Do check box is selected.

9 Click **OK**.

The Categories dialog box closes. The To Do category is added to the Meeting Agenda note, although the appearance of the note in this view does not change.

Close

10 Close the note by clicking its **Close** button.

11 Double-click the **Phone Call from Shirley** note.

The Note form appears.

12 In the top left corner, click the **Note** icon, and then click **Categories** in the drop-down list.

The Categories dialog box appears.

13 In the **Available categories** list, select the **Business** check box, and click **OK**.

The Categories dialog box closes. The Business category is added to the Phone Call from Shirley note, although the appearance of the note in this view does not change.

14 Close the note by clicking its **Close** button.

The categories are now visible.

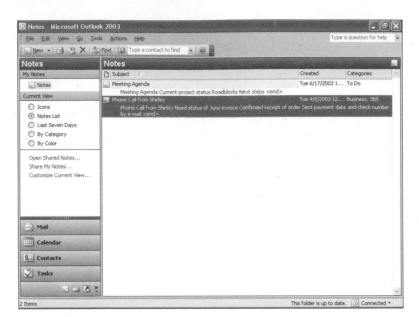

15 On the **View** menu, point to **Arrange By**, point to **Current View**, and then click **By Color**.

The notes are grouped by color.

16 On the **View** menu, point to **Arrange By**, point to **Current View**, and then click **By Category**.

The notes are grouped by category.

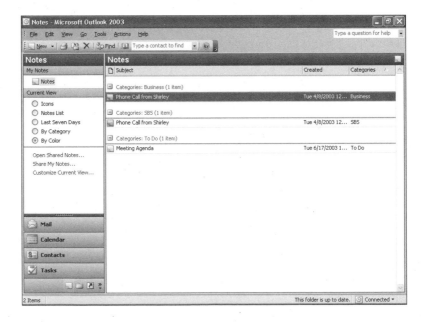

17 If the **To Do** category is not displayed, click the plus (+) sign to its left.

The Meeting Agenda note is displayed under the To Do category.

18 On the **View** menu, point to **Arrange By**, point to **Current View**, and then click **Notes List**.

The notes are displayed in a list, with the content of the notes visible.

19 Double-click the **Phone Call from Shirley** note.

The Note form appears.

20 In the top left corner, click the **Note** icon, and then click **Forward** in the drop-down list.

A new Message form appears, with the Phone Call from Shirley note attached.

21 In the **To** box, type kim@gardenco.msn.com.

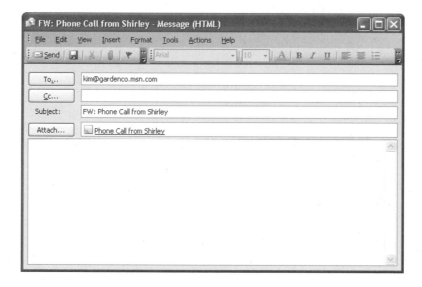

Tip Microsoft Word is used as the default editor throughout this book. If Word is not your default editor, your screen will look slightly different from this one.

22 Click in the message body to the right of the Note icon, type **For your information**, and then click the **Send** button.

The message is sent.

Important The e-mail addresses used in these exercises are not valid, so any messages you send to them will be returned as undeliverable. You can delete the returned messages at any time.

23 In the top left corner of the *Phone Call from Shirley* note, click the **Note** icon, and then click **Contacts** in the drop-down list.

The Contacts for Note dialog box appears.

24 Click the **Contacts** button.

The Select Contacts dialog box appears.

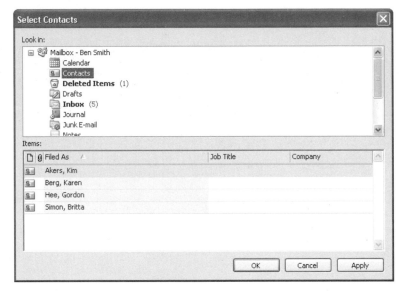

25 In the **Items** list, click the **Akers, Kim** contact entry, and click **OK**. If your Contacts folder does not contain an entry for Kim Akers, click any other contact, and then click **OK**.

The Select Contacts dialog box closes. The contact's name appears in the Contacts for Note dialog box.

26 Click the **Close** button.

The Contacts for Note dialog box closes.

27 On the Note form, click the **Close** button.

The updated note is saved.

28 In the **Navigation Pane**, click the **Contacts** button.

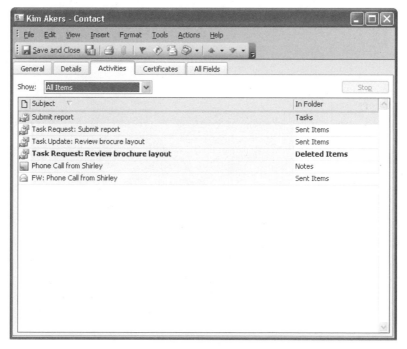

Contacts

The contents of the Contacts folder are displayed.

29 Double-click **Kim Akers** or whichever contact you linked to the Phone Call from Shirley note.

The Contact form appears.

30 Click the **Activities** tab.

The Phone Call from Shirley note appears in the Activities list.

Subject ▽	In Folder
Submit report	Tasks
Task Request: Submit report	Sent Items
Task Update: Review brocure layout	Sent Items
Task Request: Review brochure layout	**Deleted Items**
Phone Call from Shirley	Notes
FW: Phone Call from Shirley	Sent Items

31 Click the **Phone Call from Shirley** note, and press the [Del] key.

The Activities list indicates that the note is now in the Deleted Items folder. When the Deleted Items folder is emptied, the note will no longer appear in the Activities list for this contact.

32 Click the **Save and Close** button.

The Contact form closes.

33 In the **Navigation Pane**, click the **Notes** button.

Notes

The contents of the Notes folder are displayed. The Phone Call from Shirley note no longer appears here.

34 Close any open notes, appointments, or messages. Then in the **Navigation Pane**, click the **Inbox** icon, and on the **File** menu, click **Exit** to quit Outlook.

Inbox

CLOSE the *SBSTracking* data file. If you are not continuing on to the next chapter, quit Outlook.

Key Points

- You can create tasks for yourself and assign tasks to contacts. You can view and sort tasks in various ways, and group tasks by category.

- When you assign tasks, Outlook sends a task request to the person, who can accept or decline the task, and Outlook sends a notification message back to you. When you assign a task you can keep a copy, which will be automatically updated when the person you assign the task to updates the original.

- You can update tasks assigned to you and send status reports to the person who assigned the task. A task can have a status of Not Started, Deferred, Waiting, Complete, or any percentage completed.

- You can create one-time or recurring tasks. Outlook creates a new occurrence of a recurring task every time you complete the current occurrence. You can set a reminder message to display before a task is due.

- You can create notes in which you track various pieces of information. You can view and sort the notes in a variety of ways, and send the notes to other people.

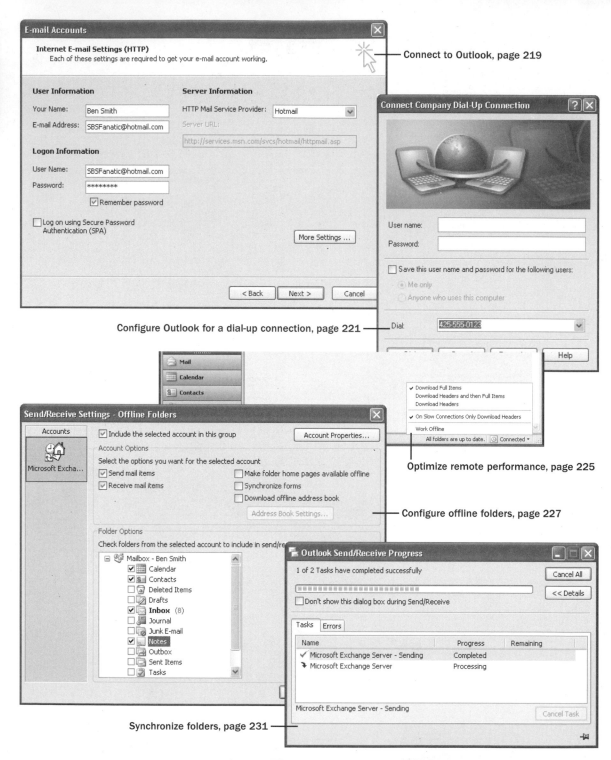

Connect to Outlook, page 219

Configure Outlook for a dial-up connection, page 221

Optimize remote performance, page 225

Configure offline folders, page 227

Synchronize folders, page 231

Chapter 8 at a Glance

8 Working from Multiple Locations

In this chapter you will learn to:
- ✔ Connect to Outlook.
- ✔ Configure Outlook for a dial-up connection.
- ✔ Optimize remote performance.
- ✔ Configure offline folders.
- ✔ Synchronize folders.

In today's workplace, communication, efficiency, and mobility are crucial. Microsoft Office Outlook can help you with each of these. If you have an Internet connection, and your organization provides remote connection capabilities or is running Outlook Web Access, you can access Outlook from home or when you're traveling. If you will be traveling without an Internet connection, you can create offline copies of any or all of your Outlook folders so you can access your e-mail even when you can't stay connected to your mail server. You can manage and synchronize your offline folders yourself, or let Outlook handle them and your connection status for you.

See Also Do you need only a quick refresher on the topics in this chapter? See the Quick Reference entries on pages xlvi–xlviii.

 Important Before you can use the practice files in this chapter, you need to install them from the book's companion CD to their default location. See "Using the Book's CD-ROM" on page xiii for more information.

Remote Connection Methods

Outlook helps you stay connected while you are away from the office. For example, you might need to stay in touch with staff at the office while visiting out-of-state clients, or you might need to access your e-mail while working from home.

There are several ways to remotely connect to e-mail servers through Outlook. The method that works for you depends on your organization's software setup and the type of connection available to you at your remote location. Available remote connection methods include:

- *Dial-up*. You can connect to the Internet through a phone line, and then connect over the Internet to your Outlook server. When using *dial-up networking*, you can connect to your e-mail server and *download* message header information (sender name, subject, date received, size, and so on) before downloading the messages themselves. Then you can choose to download only the messages you need, shortening download time. For example, you might choose to download only High Priority messages or opt not to download a message with a large attachment.

- *Broadband*. You connect to the Internet through a high-speed connection such as DSL or cable modem, and then connect over the Internet to your Outlook server.

- *Virtual Private Network (VPN)*. You establish a secure connection to your organization's network, over the Internet. Once connected to your network, you have access to all the network resources and connect directly to Outlook. Your organization might require that you use special hardware, such as a smart card, to prove your identity in order to maintain network security standards.

New in Office 2003
RPC over HTTP

- *Exchange Server access through the Internet (RPC over HTTP)*. If your organization is running Microsoft Exchange Server 2003, and your Exchange administrator has enabled this feature, you can remotely access your Outlook account over the Internet without going through a special connection or using special connection hardware.

To connect Outlook to your Exchange server using RPC over HTTP:

1 On the **Tools** menu, click **E-mail accounts**.

2 In the **E-mail accounts** dialog box, select the **View or change existing e-mail accounts**, option and then click **Next**.

3 Select the Microsoft Exchange Server e-mail account, and then click **Change**.

4 Click **More Settings**, and then click the **Connection** tab.

5 Under Exchange over the Internet, select **Connect to my Exchange mailbox using HTTP**.

6 To specify a proxy server, click **Exchange proxy settings**.

Connecting to Outlook

The exercises included in this book assume that you already have an active connection to an e-mail server. From time to time, you will want to set up a new connection when, for example, you are connecting from home to an account on your organization's server, or when connecting to your Hotmail, MSN, or other e-mail account.

If you don't have an accessible account set up in Outlook, there is a simple method of setting one up, through the Windows Control Panel.

In this exercise, you will set up a new Outlook account on your computer without a current Outlook connection.

Tip In this exercise, we set up a Hotmail account as an example. You can follow these basic steps to set up any type of account: Microsoft Exchange Server, POP3, IMAP, HTTP, or another type of mail server. If you set up a non-HTTP account, you might need to complete additional pages of the E-mail Accounts Wizard.

BE SURE TO start your computer, but don't start Outlook before beginning this exercise. You will need an active Internet or network connection in order to access your mail server.

1　Click the **Start** button, and then click **Control Panel**.

2　In Control Panel, switch to Classic View if necessary, and then double-click **Mail**.

　　The E-mail Accounts wizard starts.

3　On the **Server Type** page, select the type of server to which you are connecting.

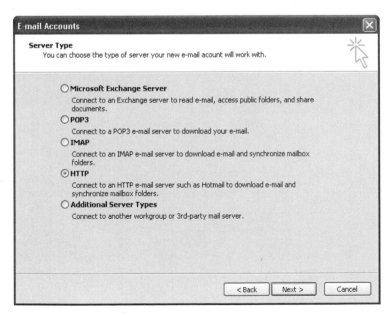

4 Click **Next**.

5 On the **Internet E-mail Settings** page, enter the user information for the account you're setting up.

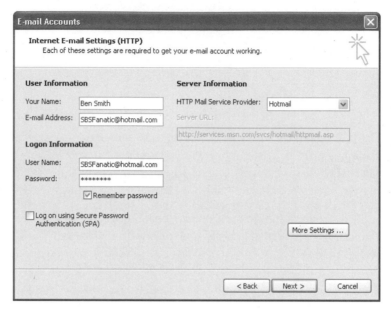

6 Click **Next**, and then click **Finish**.

The Mail Setup dialog box appears.

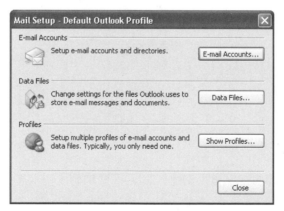

7 If you are finished setting up accounts, click **Close**. Alternately:

■ To set up a new e-mail account or change an existing account, click **E-mail Accounts**.

■ To change the location in which Outlook stores your data files, click **Data Files**.

■ To set up multiple user profiles or change an existing profile, click **Show Profiles**.

For the purposes of this exercise, we clicked Close.

8 When you are done, close Control Panel and start Outlook.

Your new account is displayed and accessible.

Configuring Outlook for a Dial-Up Connection

A dial-up connection is a connection from your computer, through an internal or external modem, to the Internet, over a standard telephone line. Although broadband connections are becoming more prevalent, many people still use dial-up connections when a broadband connection is unavailable, for instance, when staying at a hotel.

The maximum connection speed over a dial-up connection is limited by your modem, usually to 56-kbps, but sometimes to as little as 28.8-kbps. It takes much longer to download and upload information over a dial-up connection; therefore, it is to your benefit to avoid downloading unnecessary or unwanted information.

See Also For information about blocking external content, refer to "Protecting Your Privacy" in Chapter 9, "Customizing and Configuring Outlook."

Important The following exercise instructs you to set up a dial-up connection. If you are already connecting to your e-mail server through a dial-up connection, you completed these steps when you set up Outlook, and can skip this exercise. *If you do not want to configure your Outlook installation to connect through a dial-up connection, do not complete this exercise.*

In this exercise, you will configure Outlook to connect to the server through a dial-up connection and download messages for remote use.

BE SURE TO start Outlook before beginning this exercise, and be sure you have a properly configured modem and the phone number, user name, and password of a valid dial-up account. Your network administrator or *Internet service provider (ISP)* can provide the information you need.

Important This procedure assumes that you are using Microsoft Exchange Server. If you are not using Exchange Server (for example, if you are on a dial-up or other stand-alone computer), your screens and dialog boxes might look different from the ones pictured. However, by following the instructions on your screen, you should easily be able to work through the procedures.

1 On the **Tools** menu, click **E-mail Accounts**.

The E-mail Accounts Wizard appears.

2 Select the **View or change existing e-mail accounts** option, and click **Next**.

The next page of the E-Mail Accounts Wizard is displayed, showing the configured e-mail accounts.

3 In the **Outlook processes e-mail for these accounts in the following order** list, click your e-mail account, and then click **Change**.

The Exchange Server Settings page is displayed, showing the account settings.

4 Click the **More Settings** button.

5 In the dialog box that appears, click the **Connection** tab, and select the **Connect using my phone line** option.

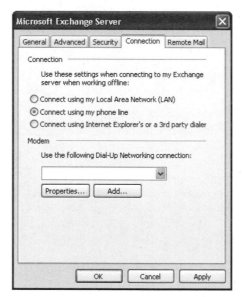

6 In the **Modem** area, click the **Add** button.

The New Connection Wizard appears.

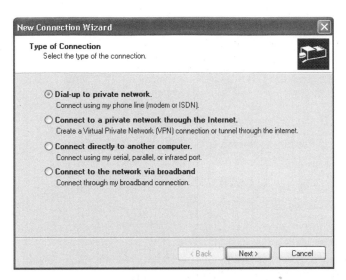

7 On the **Type of Connection** page of the wizard, select the **Dial-up to private network** option, and click **Next**.

8 On the **Phone Number to Dial** page, type the phone number of your ISP in the **Phone Number** box.

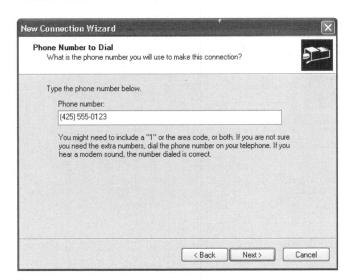

If your computer has been configured for use with a smart card, you can configure the dial-up connection to use your smart card.

Tip If you configure the dial-up connection to use a smart card, you will not be prompted for a user name and password when you connect.

9 If appropriate to your situation, select the smart card option you want, and then click **Next**.

10 In the **Type a name you want for this connection** box, type a meaningful name for the connection you are creating (For example, *Company Dial-Up Connection*), and click **Finish**.

The Network Connection Wizard closes.

11 In the **Use the following Dial-up Networking connection** list, click the connection you just created, and then click **OK**.

12 In the **E-mail Accounts Wizard**, click **Next**, and then click **Finish**.

The E-mail Accounts Wizard closes, saving the new account settings.

 13 On the toolbar, click the **Send/Receive** button.

Outlook begins checking for new messages using the new dial-up connection. The dial-up connection dialog box appears.

Troubleshooting If you configured the dial-up connection to use a smart card, you are not prompted for a user name and password, only to confirm the phone number.

14 Type your user name and password, and then click the **Dial** button. Or, if you have configured the dial-up connection to use a smart card, ensure that the card is in the smart card reader and the reader is connected, enter your smart card PIN, and then click **OK**.

Tip If you want Outlook to store your user name and password (so you don't have to enter them each time you use this dial-up connection), select the "Save this user name and password" check box and select the user option you want.

Outlook connects to your e-mail server using your modem and sends and receives messages.

Optimizing Remote Performance

New in Office 2003
Cached Exchange Mode

If you use a laptop, you probably aren't always connected to your mail server, but with Outlook's remote capabilities, you can read and write messages and other items no matter where you are. *Cached Exchange Mode*, a new feature in Outlook 2003, makes switching from working online to offline and back a snap.

Tip Cached Exchange Mode is not compatible with Outlook's Remote Mail feature. Cached Exchange Mode provides much broader capabilities than Remote Mail, which works only with your Inbox.

When you enable Cached Exchange Mode, Outlook creates a local copy of your mailbox on your computer. While your computer is connected to your Exchange server, your local mailbox is kept up to date. If your connection is interrupted, for example, because you take your laptop on a bus or plane, you can read all the messages you received before you started working offline and write new ones. When your connection is restored, Outlook automatically sends any messages in your Outbox, copies new incoming messages to your local mailbox, and displays them in your Inbox.

You can choose from several Cached Exchange Mode connection settings:

■ The *Download Full Items* setting downloads all your messages and their attachments one at a time. If you keep Outlook open and your computer connected to a network, this is the best option because it uses the least bandwidth to download all your messages. If you have a slow connection or receive messages with large attachments, messages might be slow to appear in your Inbox when you reconnect to your server.

■ The *Download Headers and then Full Items* setting downloads all the *message headers* quickly, and then downloads all the message bodies and attachments. This option uses only slightly more bandwidth than Download only headers.

■ The *Download Headers* setting does not download the body of a message or its attachments until you preview or open the message. This is the best option if your connection is very slow or you pay for every byte you download.

In addition, you can choose to download only the message headers when you are working on a slow connection.

Important This exercise requires that you be connected to a Microsoft Exchange Server network.

In this exercise, you will turn on Cached Exchange Mode, switch between working online and offline, and access the available connection modes.

BE SURE TO start Outlook with an active network connection before beginning this exercise.

1 On the **Tools** menu, click **E-mail Accounts**.

2 In the E-mail Accounts Wizard, select the **View or change existing e-mail accounts** option, and then click **Next**.

3 In the **Outlook processes e-mail for these accounts in the following order** box, click **Microsoft Exchange Server**, and then click the **Change** button.

4 On the Exchange Server Settings page, select the **Use Cached Exchange Mode** check box.

5 If a message appears saying you must restart Outlook for the changes to take effect, click **OK**.

6 In the **E-mail Accounts Wizard**, click **Next**, and then click **Finish**.

7 Exit and restart Outlook.

8 On the Outlook status bar in the lower-right corner of the Outlook window, click **Connected**.

A shortcut menu displays your connection options.

Online indicator

You can click any of the options on the shortcut menu to change the way Outlook downloads items.

9 On the shortcut menu, click **Work Offline**.

The Outlook status bar shows that you are now working offline. You still have a network connection to your Exchange server, but Outlook will not upload or download any items until you turn the Work Offline feature off.

Offline indicator

10 Click the Offline indicator, and then click **Work Offline** again.

The Outlook status bar shows that you are working online.

Configuring Offline Folders

If you choose to not use Cached Exchange Mode, you can use *offline folders* to access your Outlook information when you are not connected to your e-mail server. For example, if you want to catch up on messages while traveling, you might configure a folder containing the messages you want to read so that they are available offline on your laptop. Note that offline folders contain only messages that you received before you started working offline.

Tip It is not necessary to create an offline folder if you use Cached Exchange Mode.

If you created items, deleted messages, or made any other changes to the contents of an offline folder while you were not connected to your e-mail server, you need to connect to your e-mail server and update the corresponding folder on the server to make the contents of the two folders identical. This process is called *synchronizing* offline folders. Be sure to synchronize your offline folders whenever you make changes to the folder—whether working offline or online. Otherwise, you could be working with obsolete or missing items that were added while you were offline.

Important This exercise requires that you be connected to a Microsoft Exchange Server network.

In this exercise, you will create an offline folder file, configure a folder for offline use, and switch between online and offline use.

BE SURE TO turn off Cached Exchange Mode before beginning this exercise.

1 On the **Tools** menu, click **E-mail Accounts**.

2 In the E-mail Accounts Wizard, select the **View or change existing e-mail accounts** option, and then click **Next**.

3 In the **Outlook processes e-mail for these accounts in the following order** list, click **Microsoft Exchange Server**, and then click the **Change** button.

4 On the Exchange Server Settings page, click the **More Settings** button.

The Microsoft Exchange Server dialog box appears.

5 Click the **Advanced** tab, and then click the **Offline Folder File Settings** button.

The Offline Folder File Settings dialog box appears.

6 Click the **Browse** button.

Tip If the Browse button is disabled, click the Disable Offline Use button, click Yes, and then click the Offline Folder File Settings button again.

The New Offline Folder File dialog box appears.

7 On the Places bar, click **My Documents**.

8 Make sure *outlook* appears in the **File name** box and **OST Files** appears in the **Files of type** box, and then click the **Open** button.

In the Offline Folder File Settings dialog box, the path to the .ost file appears in the File box.

9 Click **OK**. If Outlook prompts you to create the *outlook.ost* file, click **Yes**.

10 In the **Microsoft Exchange Server** dialog box, click the **General** tab, and in the **When starting** area, select the **Manually control connection state** option and the **Choose the connection type when starting** check box.

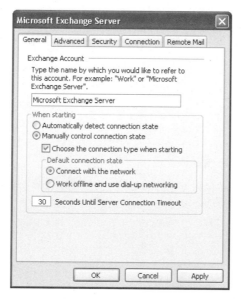

11 Click **OK**.

The Microsoft Exchange Server dialog box closes.

12 In the **E-mail Accounts Wizard**, click **Next**, and then click **Finish**.

13 In the **Navigation Pane**, click your **Inbox**.

14 On the **Tools** menu, point to **Send/Receive**, point to **Send/Receive Settings**, and make sure the **Make This Folder Available Offline** option is selected. If it isn't, click it.

15 On the **Tools** menu, point to **Send/Receive**, and then click **This Folder**.

Outlook synchronizes the selected folder.

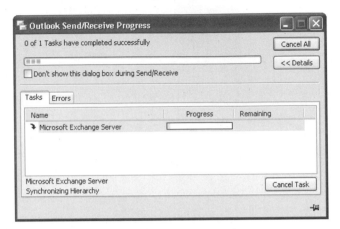

16 Exit and restart Outlook.

Outlook opens, prompting you to choose to connect or work offline.

17 Click the **Work Offline** button.

Outlook opens. The contents of your Inbox are visible and available, but no other content is, including your Calendar, Contacts, or Tasks. You need to synchronize each of the folders you want to have available before working offline.

18 Exit and restart Outlook.

19 When Outlook prompts you to choose to connect or work offline, click the **Connect** button.

Outlook opens with all folders available.

Synchronizing Folders

After working with an offline folder, you must synchronize it with the corresponding folder on the server to make the contents identical. Be sure to synchronize offline folders whenever you make changes to the folder—whether working offline or online. Otherwise, you could be working with obsolete items or be missing items that were added while you were offline.

You can synchronize folders manually, or you can synchronize them automatically at a specified time or time interval.

Important This exercise requires that you be connected to a Microsoft Exchange Server network. To complete this exercise, you must have completed the preceding topic, "Configuring Offline Folders," which ensures that you will have an .ost file on your computer that is configured for offline use.

In this exercise, you will manually synchronize an offline folder, create a group of folders to be synchronized together, and configure Outlook to automatically synchronize the group of folders.

BE SURE TO start Outlook before beginning this exercise.

1 On the **Tools** menu, point to **Send/Receive**, point to **Send/Receive Settings**, and click **Define Send/Receive Groups**.

The Send/Receive Groups dialog box appears.

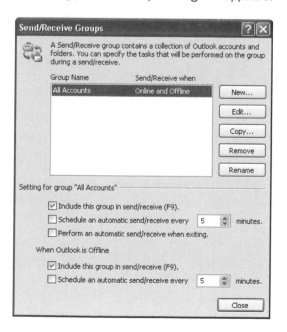

2 Click the **New** button.

The Send/Receive Group Name dialog box appears.

3 In the **Send/Receive Group Name** box, type **Offline Folders**, and click **OK**.

The Send/Receive Settings – Offline Folders dialog box appears.

4 Select the **Include the selected account in this group** check box.

5 In the **Check folders from the selected account to include in send/receive** list, select the check box next to the **Calendar**, **Contacts**, **Inbox**, and **Notes** folders.

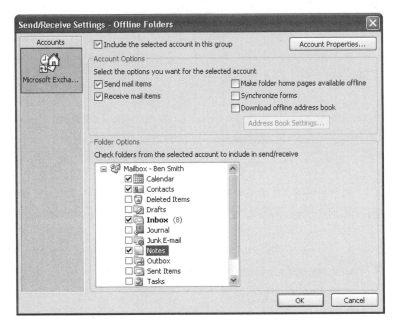

6 Make sure the **Send mail items** and **Receive mail items** check boxes are selected, and click **OK**.

The Send/Receive Settings – Offline Folders dialog box closes.

7 In the **Group Name** list, be sure that **Offline Folders** is selected.

8 In the **Setting for group "Offline Folders"** area, select the **Perform an automatic send/receive when exiting** check box, and clear the **Include this group in send/ receive (F9)** check box.

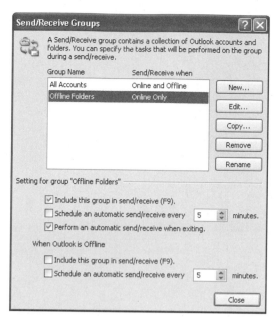

9 Click the **Close** button.

The Send/Receive Groups dialog box closes, and the Offline Folders group is created. Your Offline Folders group will be automatically synchronized when you close Outlook, or when you choose to manually synchronize.

10 On the **Tools** menu, point to **Send/Receive**, and click "**Offline Folders**" **Group**.

Outlook synchronizes the contents of the Calendar, Contacts, Inbox, and Tasks folders with the corresponding folders on your mail server.

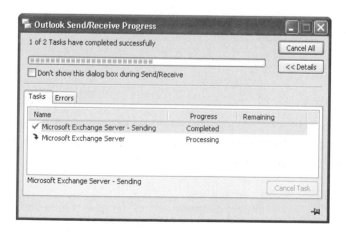

11 On the **Tools** menu, point to **Send/Receive**, point to **Send/Receive Settings**, and click **Define Send/Receive Groups**.

12 In the **Group Name** list, click **Offline Folders**.

13 In the **Settings for group "Offline Folders"** area, select the **Schedule an automatic send/receive every** check box, click in the **minutes** box, delete the existing number, and type **15**.

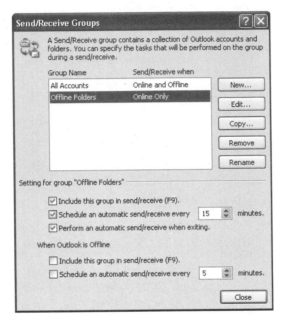

14 Click the **Close** button.

The Send/Receive Groups dialog box closes. When you are working online, your Offline Folders group will be automatically synchronized every 15 minutes.

15 Exit and restart Outlook.

16 When Outlook prompts you to choose to connect or work offline, click the **Work Offline** button.

Outlook opens if Offline mode. Your Calendar, Contacts, Inbox, and Tasks folders are available. Any changes you make will be synchronized with the server each time you exit Outlook.

BE SURE TO set your offline settings the way you want.
CLOSE any open messages, and if you are not continuing on to the next chapter, quit Outlook.

Viewing Contacts While Offline

If Cached Exchange Mode is enabled, Outlook downloads a copy of the *Global Address List* along with your mailbox. If your network connection is slow, you might not want to do this, because it could take a long time and, if you are paying for your connection by the minute, be costly. If you prefer, you can manually download the Global Address List whenever you want to update it.

To manually download a copy of the Global Address List:

1   On the **Tools** menu, point to **Send/Receive**, and then click **Download Address Book**.

2   Select the information you want to download, and then click **OK**.

To update your Global Address List every time you synchronize a send and receive group:

1   On the **Tools** menu, point to **Send/Receive**, point to **Send/Receive Settings**, and then click **Define Send/Receive Groups**.

2   In the **Send/Receive Groups** dialog box, click the group of accounts and folders, and then click the **Edit** button.

3   Select the **Download offline address book** check box, and then click the **Address Book Settings** button.

4   Select the information you want to download, and then close the open dialog boxes.

Key Points

■   Cached Exchange Mode keeps a copy of your mailbox on your computer so you can keep working even when you are away from your network.

■   Cached Exchange Mode handles connecting and synchronizing your local mailbox for you. You can set it to cache all messages or just headers, to save bandwidth.

■   If you prefer, you can manually create and synchronize your offline folders.

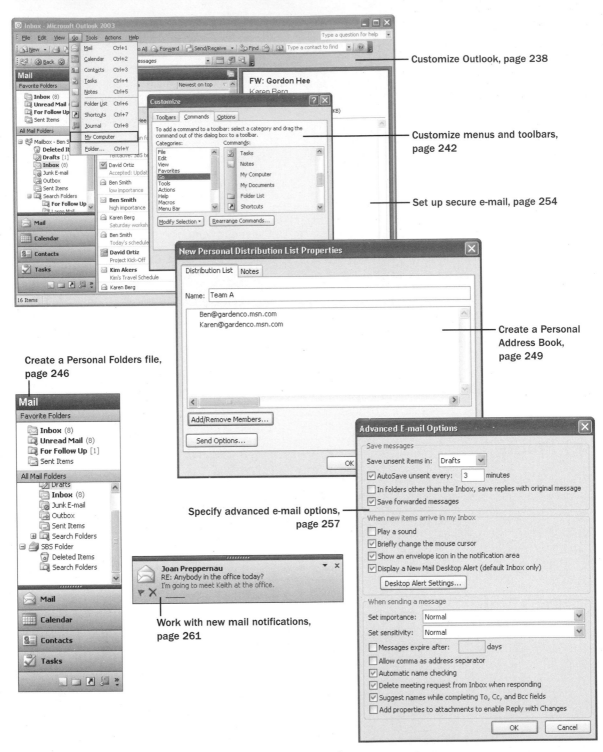

Customize Outlook, page 238

Customize menus and toolbars, page 242

Set up secure e-mail, page 254

Create a Personal Address Book, page 249

Create a Personal Folders file, page 246

Specify advanced e-mail options, page 257

Work with new mail notifications, page 261

Chapter 9 at a Glance

9 Customizing and Configuring Outlook

In this chapter you will learn to:

✔ Customize Outlook.

✔ Customize menus and toolbars.

✔ Create a Personal Folders file.

✔ Create a Personal Address Book.

✔ Set up secure e-mail.

✔ Specify advanced e-mail options.

✔ Work with new mail notifications.

There are a host of configuration and customization options that you can use to make the most of Outlook. You can customize the way Outlook starts, the appearance of Outlook Today, and the content of Outlook menus and toolbars. You can use Outlook's encryption and restricted permissions options to send messages securely and confidentially.

Consolidating your contacts, calendar items, e-mail messages, and other information using the tools provided by Outlook is the key to staying organized.

See Also Do you need only a quick refresher on the topics in this chapter? See the Quick Reference entries on pages xlviii–li.

 Important Before you can use the practice files in this chapter, you need to install them from the book's companion CD to their default location. See "Using the Book's CD-ROM" on page xiii for more information.

Customizing Outlook

As you work with Outlook, you will find that certain configurations are more useful to you. For example, you might find that you need to review your schedule and work with your calendar at the beginning of each day. So you might configure Outlook to start with your Calendar folder displayed. Or you might find Outlook Today very useful but want to fine-tune the appearance to meet your needs. You can also change the contents of your Shortcuts pane to add items that you use frequently, and remove those that you don't.

In this exercise, you create a desktop shortcut, and customize the way Outlook starts, the available toolbars, the appearance of the Outlook Today page, and the available shortcuts.

BE SURE TO start Windows, but do not start Outlook before beginning this exercise.

1 Open Windows Explorer, and size the window so you can see part of your Windows desktop.

2 In Windows Explorer, navigate to the Outlook program file, which is usually located in the *C:\Program Files\Microsoft Office\Office11* or *C:\Program Files\Microsoft Office \Office 2003* folder.

> **Tip** If your computer is set to display file name extensions, the Outlook program file will appear as OUTLOOK.EXE.

3 Right-click the **Outlook** program file, drag it to your desktop, and click **Create Shortcuts Here** on the shortcut menu.

The shortcut appears on the desktop.

Close

4 In the Windows Explorer window, click the **Close** button.

The Explorer window closes.

5 Right-click the shortcut you just created, and click **Properties** on the shortcut menu.

The Shortcut tab of the "Shortcut to OUTLOOK Properties" dialog box appears.

6 To set Outlook to display the Calendar when it opens, press ⒺⓃⒹ to move to the end of the path entered in the **Target** box, type a space after the displayed path, type **/select outlook:calendar**.

Tip You can use command-line switches such as this to instruct Outlook to display your preferred page, or to carry out a variety of tasks on startup. For a full list of command-line switches, search for *command-line switches* in the Microsoft Office Outlook Help file.

7 In the **Run** drop-down list, click **Maximized**.

8 Click **OK**.

The shortcut is saved with your changes.

9 On the desktop, double-click the shortcut you created.

Outlook starts in a maximized window, displaying the Calendar.

10 On the **View** menu, point to **Toolbars**, and then click **Advanced**.

The Advanced toolbar appears at the top of the Outlook window.

Advanced toolbar

Outlook Today

11 On the Advanced toolbar, click the **Outlook Today** button.

The Outlook Today page is displayed.

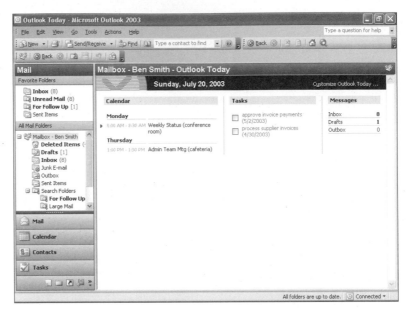

12 In the upper-right corner of the Outlook Today pane, click **Customize Outlook Today**.

The Customize Outlook Today page is displayed.

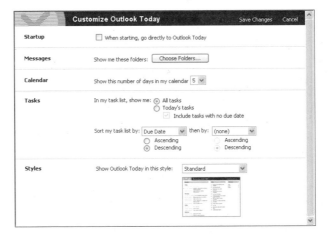

13 In the **Startup** area, select the **When starting, go directly to Outlook Today** check box.

14 Review the options in the **Messages**, **Calendar**, and **Tasks** areas. Change any options you want.

15 In the **Styles** area, in the **Show Outlook Today in this style** drop-down list, click **Summer**.

A preview of the selected style is shown.

16 In the upper-right corner, click **Save Changes**.

Outlook Today is displayed in the selected style.

17 On the **File** menu, click **Exit**.

Outlook closes.

18 On the **Start** menu, click the **Microsoft Outlook** icon (don't click the desktop shortcut you created).

Outlook starts, displaying Outlook Today.

Shortcuts

19 In the **Navigation Pane**, click the **Shortcuts** button.

The Shortcuts pane is displayed.

20 In the **Shortcuts Pane**, click **Add New Shortcut**.

The Add to Navigation Pane dialog box appears.

21 Click the plus (+) sign to the left of **Mailbox** to expand its list of folders.

22 In the list of folders, click **Deleted Items**, and click **OK**.

A shortcut to the Deleted Items folder is added to the Shortcuts pane.

23 In the **Shortcuts** pane, click **Deleted Items** to display the Deleted Items folder.

24 In the **Shortcuts** pane, right-click the **Deleted Items** shortcut.

Tip To delete a shortcut, right-click it and then on the shortcut menu, click Delete Shortcut.

Notice that you have full access to this folder from the Shortcuts pane, including the ability to empty the folder.

25 Click away from the shortcut menu to close it.

Customizing Menus and Toolbars

Microsoft Office Specialist

You will most likely find that you use certain menus and toolbar buttons quite frequently and that you never use others. To make Outlook more effective, you can customize your menus and toolbars to contain the items you use and display them in the way that you use them. You can add and remove items from both menus and toolbars, hide or display toolbars, move toolbars, and create your own toolbars. For example, if you frequently use dial-up networking, you might create a toolbar containing commands you use to mark message headers. Or if you don't use custom forms, you might remove the Forms command from the Tools menu.

New in
Office 2003
Go menu

Microsoft
Office
Specialist

When customizing the Outlook 2003 interface, take advantage of the new Go menu. This menu links to all the panes that can appear in the Navigation Pane, allowing you to quickly switch between them.

In this exercise, you select which toolbars are displayed, set options for how menus appear, add and remove items from menus, and add and remove items from toolbars.

BE SURE TO start Outlook before beginning this exercise.

Mail

1 In the **Navigation Pane**, click the **Mail** button, and then click the **Inbox**.

The Inbox is displayed.

2 On the **View** menu, point to **Toolbars**. The displayed toolbars are indicated on the submenu.

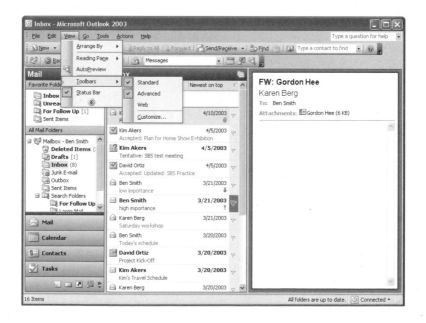

3   Click **Customize**.

The Customize dialog box appears with the Options tab displayed.

Troubleshooting   If the Options tab is not displayed, click it now.

4   In the **Personalized Menus and Toolbars** area, select the **Always show full menus** check box.

5   In the **Other** area, click the down arrow to the right of the **Menu animations** box, and then click **Slide** in the drop-down list.

6   Click **Close** to save your selections.

7   Click the **Tools** menu.

Because you selected the "Always show full menus" check box, the menu opens fully, displaying all its commands.

8   On the **Tools** menu, click **Customize**.

9   In the **Customize** dialog box, click the **Commands** tab.

10   In the **Categories** list, click **Go**.

The list of commands in the View category is displayed in the Commands list.

11   In the **Commands** list, click **My Computer**, drag it to the **Go** menu, which expands, and drop it just below **Journal**.

The command is added to the Go menu.

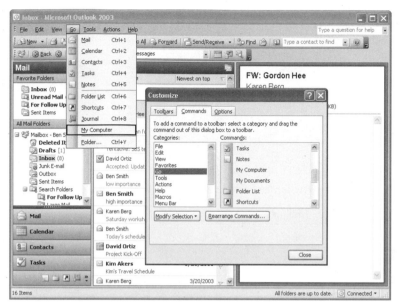

12 In the **Customize** dialog box, click **Close**.

13 On the **Go** menu, click **My Computer**.

The contents of the My Computer folder are displayed in a separate window.

14 Close the My Computer window.

15 On the **Tools** menu, click **Customize**.

The Customize dialog box appears. When this dialog box is open, you can add and remove items from visible menus and toolbars, using the menus and toolbars themselves.

16 On the **Go** menu, right-click **My Computer**, and then click **Delete**.

The command is removed from the menu.

17 In the **Customize** dialog box, click the **Commands** tab.

18 In the **Categories** list, click **Advanced**.

The list of commands for the *View* category is displayed.

19 In the **Commands** list, drag **Outlook Today** to the right end of the standard toolbar.

The Outlook Today button appears on the toolbar.

New Outlook Today button

20 In the **Customize** dialog box, click **Close**.

Outlook Today

21 On the Standard toolbar, click **Outlook Today**.

Outlook Today appears.

22 On the **Tools** menu, click **Customize**.

23 In the **Customize** dialog box, click the **Toolbars** tab.

24 In the **Toolbars** list, click **Standard**, and then click the **Reset** button.

The Standard toolbar is reset to its default state, and the Outlook Today button is removed.

25 Close the **Customize** dialog box.

Creating a Personal Folders File

Microsoft Office Specialist

The items you create and receive in Outlook—including messages, appointments, contacts, tasks, notes, and journal entries—are kept in a data file either on a server on your network or on the hard disk of your computer.

■ If your information is kept on a server, which is the case when you are working on a network that uses *Microsoft Exchange Server*, it is part of a file called a *private store*. You can access this store only when you are connected to your server.

New in Office 2003
New Data File Type (.pst)

■ If your information is kept on your computer, it is stored in a *Personal Folders file* that has a .pst file extension. Personal Folders files created for Outlook 2003 offer a greater storage capacity than those created for previous versions, and support multilingual Unicode data.

Whether you are working on a networked or a stand-alone computer, you can create Personal Folders files to store Outlook items on the hard disk of your own computer. If you are working on a network, you might want to do this so that certain items are available whether or not you are connected to the server—for example, if you work on a laptop that you use both in the office and at home. If you are not working on a network, you might want to do this so that you can keep items related to a particular project in a separate Personal Folders file. Then you can back up that file separately from your other Outlook items, or you can copy that file to another computer.

In this exercise, you will create a Personal Folders data file, move messages and folders to it, and learn how to open and close data files from within Outlook.

BE SURE TO start Outlook before beginning this exercise.

1 On the **File** menu, point to **New**, and then click **Outlook Data File**.

The New Outlook Data File dialog box appears.

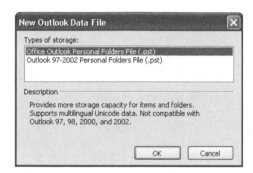

2 If you run an older version of Outlook on another computer, and you might want to open this personal folder in that version, click **Outlook 97-2002 Personal Folders File**, and then click **OK**. Otherwise, with **Office Outlook Personal Folders File** selected, click **OK**.

Tip Outlook 2003 uses a new Personal Folders file format with improved support for international Unicode character sets and large items. However, if you want to export a Personal Folders file to a computer that uses an older version of Outlook, you must export the file in the older Personal Folders file format.

The Create or Open Outlook Data File dialog box opens. The default personal folder location is within your Outlook profile folder, but you can save the personal folder anywhere you want.

3 On the Places bar, click **My Documents**.

4 In the **File name** box, type **SBSFolder**, and then click **OK**.

The Create Microsoft Personal Folders dialog box opens.

If you want, you can change the encryption level or assign a password to the file to keep it secure.

5 In the **Name** box, type **SBS Folder**.

6 Click **OK**.

The new Personal Folders file is visible in the Navigation Pane, at the same level as your Inbox.

7 Click the plus sign to the left of the *SBS Folder* file to expand it, and then scroll down to view its contents.

By default, the Personal Folders file contains only a Deleted Items folder and a Search Folders folder. You must create any other folders you want saved in this file.

8 Right-click and drag your Inbox folder to the *SBS Folder* file. When you release the mouse button, click **Copy** on the shortcut menu.

Your Inbox and all its contents are copied to the Personal Folders file.

9 Click the Inbox that now appears in the SBS Folders file. Verify that the contents are identical to your original Inbox.

10 Right-click the **SBS Folder** file, and on the shortcut menu, click **Close "SBS Folder"**.

The Personal Folders file disappears.

11 On the **File** menu, point to **Open**, and then click **Outlook Data File**.

12 If necessary, browse to the *My Documents* folder. Click the **SBS Folder** data file, and then click **OK**.

The SBS Folder file re-opens in Outlook. In this way, you can open any date file from within Outlook and access its contents.

Creating a Personal Address Book

You might want to create a *Personal Address Book* to store e-mail addresses and distribution lists separately from your Contacts folder. Personal Address Book files have a *.pab* file extension and can be stored on your local computer.

You can share the information in your personal address book by e-mailing it to other people, who can then open it in Outlook on their own computers.

In this exercise, you will create a Personal Address Book and a personal distribution list.

BE SURE TO start Outlook before beginning this exercise.

1 On the **Tools** menu, click **E-mail Accounts** to display the **E-mail Accounts** dialog box.

2 Select the **Add a new directory or address book** option, and click **Next**.

The Directory or Address Book Type page appears.

3 Select the **Additional Address Books** option, and click **Next**.

The Other Address Book Types page appears.

4 In the **Additional Address Book Types** list, click **Personal Address Book**, and then click **Next**.

The Personal Address Book dialog box appears.

5 In the **Name** box, type **SBS Addresses**.

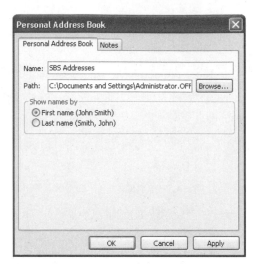

6 Click the **Browse** button to open the **Use Personal Address Book** dialog box.

7 In the **File name** box, type **SBS Addresses**.

8 Click **Open**, and in the **Add E-mail Account** message box, click **OK**.

The address book is added, but you must restart Outlook to use it.

9 Click **OK** to close the message.

10 On the **File** menu, click **Exit**.

11 On the **Start** menu, point to **All Programs**, point to **Microsoft Office**, and click **Microsoft Office Outlook 2003**.

12 On the **Tools** menu, click **Address Book**. Then click the down arrow to the right of the **Show Names from the** box, and click **SBS Addresses**.

The new, empty, personal address book appears.

13 On the toolbar, click the **New Entry** button.

New Entry

The New Entry dialog box appears.

14 In the **Put this entry** area, click the down arrow to the right of the **In the** box, and then click **SBS Addresses** in the drop-down list.

15 In the **Select the entry type** list, click **Personal Distribution List**.

16 Click **OK**.

The New Personal Distribution List Properties dialog box appears.

17 In the **Name** box, type Team A, and click the **Add/Remove Members** button.

The Edit Members of Team A dialog box appears.

18 In the **Show Names from the** list, click **SBS Addresses**.

The empty Personal Address Book appears.

Tip You can also add contacts to your personal distribution lists. In the Edit Members dialog box, in the "Show Names from the" list, click Contacts, and then click the names you want.

19 In the **Members** box, type Ben@gardenco.msn.com;Karen@gardenco.msn.com and then click **OK**.

If Ben and Karen are in your address book from previous exercises, their names now appear on the Distribution List tab. If not, they are listed by e-mail address.

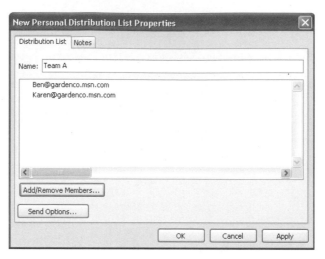

20 Click **OK**.

The new distribution list appears in your personal address book.

Expanding Distribution Lists

A new feature in Outlook 2003 is the ability to expand and edit distribution lists in an e-mail message. You can then add or remove individual message recipients, without having to edit the distribution list itself.

New in Office 2003
Expand Distribution Lists in an e-mail message

For example, if you want to send a surprise birthday party invitation to all the employees of your organization other than the person whose birthday it is, you can type the name of the employee distribution list in the To box, then click the plus sign that appears to the left of the name to expand the distribution list so that all the individual members are listed. You can then delete the birthday person's name from the To box, and send the message.

Reading Newsgroups Using Outlook Express

A *newsgroup* is a collection of messages that are focused on a particular topic, like a sports team, a hobby, or a type of software. Messages to a newsgroup are posted to a *news server*. Anyone with access to the newsgroup can read messages posted to the newsgroup, respond to existing messages either through the newsgroup or directly to the person who posted the message, and post new messages. A newsgroup can be private, such as an internal company newsgroup, or open to the public. You can access newsgroups through a news server maintained either on your organization's network or by your Internet service provider (ISP).

You use a *newsreader* program to download, read, and reply to newsgroup messages. You can reply to the person who originally posted a message, post your reply to the entire newsgroup, or forward the message to someone else. Outlook is not a newsreader program; instead it utilizes the newsreader capabilities of Outlook Express, which comes with Windows. To access newsgroups from within Outlook, you can add the News command to the Go menu. When you click the News command, Outlook Express starts.

To add the News command to the Go menu:

Toolbar Options

1   On the Standard toolbar, click the **Toolbar Options** button.

2   Point to **Add or Remove Buttons**, and then click **Customize**.

3   In the **Customize** dialog box, click the **Commands** tab.

4   In the **Categories** list, click **Go**.

5   In the **Commands** list, drag **News** to the **Go** menu, and drop it where you want.

6   Close the **Customize** dialog box.

The first time you start Outlook Express, it leads you through the process of setting up your information. Then you can subscribe to the newsgroup you want.

For more information about Outlook Express, refer to *Microsoft Windows XP Step by Step*.

Setting Up Secure E-Mail

Your e-mail messages are vulnerable to interception by hackers and others who are intent on viewing them as they travel from server to server en route to you or your recipients. You can use Outlook to send e-mail securely by *encrypting* and *digitally signing* your messages. Encryption ensures that only the intended recipients can read the messages you send, and a digital signature provides your recipients with proof that a message is really from you. To use either of these features, you must have a *digital ID* stored on your computer.

You can encrypt an individual e-mail message or instruct Outlook to encrypt all your outgoing messages. To encrypt a single message, click the message's Options button, click the Security Settings button, and then select the "Encrypt message contents and attachments" check box. To encrypt all outgoing messages, on the Tools menu, click Options, and on the Security tab, select the "Encrypt contents and attachments for outgoing messages" check box.

To digitally sign an individual e-mail message, click the message's Options button, click the Security Settings button, and then select the "Add digital signature to this message" check box. If all your message recipients don't have *Secure Multipurpose Internet Mail extensions (S/MIME)* security, select the "Send this message as clear text signed" check box. To receive verification when your message arrives, select the "Request S/MIME receipt for this message" check box.

Digitally signed messages contain a Signed By status line, which displays the digital signature name and either a Valid Signature icon or an Invalid Signature icon. An invalid signature is also indicated by a red underline. Click either button to see more information about the signature.

For additional security, you can use *security zones* to control whether *scripts* (a list of commands executed without user interaction) or other active content can be run in HTML messages you send and receive. Microsoft Internet Explorer uses security zones to categorize Web sites so that you can set a suitable security level for them. When visiting a Web site, you can tell which zone it is in by looking at the right end of the Internet Explorer status bar. There are four zones—Internet, Local intranet, Trusted sites, and Restricted sites. You can select from four pre-defined security levels—High, Medium, Medium-Low, and Low—for each security zone. Each level is described in the Security dialog box. You can also customize security levels for any zone.

New in Office 2003
Information Rights Management

If you don't want the recipient to forward, copy, or print your message, you can send it with restricted permissions. You can use Information Rights Management, a new feature in Microsoft Office 2003, to control who can read your messages and what they can do with them.

You can only send a message with restricted permissions from an Exchange Server account, and you must have a digital ID for that account. To read a message with restricted permissions, recipients must have Outlook 2003 or the Rights Management Add-on for Internet Explorer. If recipients have Internet Explorer but not the add-on, they will be prompted to download the add-on for free when they open a message with restricted permissions.

To send a message with restricted permissions:

● On the message form's Standard toolbar, click the **Permissions** button.

Obtaining a Digital ID

If you want to digitally sign messages, you must obtain a digital ID. If your organization is running Microsoft Exchange Server 2000 or earlier, you can obtain an Exchange Digital ID from the server itself. Your Exchange server administrator can provide the information you need.

To send digitally signed messages over the Internet, you must obtain a digital ID from an external company that provides certification services, such as VeriSign, Inc., GlobalSign, British Telecommunications, or Thawte Certification.

To obtain a digital ID to send messages over the Internet:

1 On the **Tools** menu, click **Options**.

2 In the **Options** dialog box, click the **Security** tab, and then click the **Get a Digital ID** button.

The Microsoft Office Assistance Center Web page opens in your default Web browser.

3 Click the name of one of the available providers. If a message appears warning you about viewing pages over a secure connection, click **OK**.

Follow the instructions on the Web page to register for a digital ID. Most certifying authorities charge a small fee for IDs, but some offer free IDs or a free trial period.

You can have more than one digital ID on your computer, and you can select which one to use for each message. For example, you might have one ID for business use and one for personal use. You can also copy digital IDs from one computer to another by importing and exporting ID files.

To export or import a digital ID:

1 On the **Tools** menu, click **Options**.

2 In the **Options** dialog box, click the **Security** tab, and then click the **Import/Export** button.

3 In the **Import/Export Digital ID** dialog box, select the option you want, fill in the information, and then click **OK**.

Protecting Your Privacy

E-mail is increasingly being used as a means of delivering marketing information to customers and potential customers. Many companies include pictures in their marketing messages to help explain their product or to make the message more attractive and noticeable, but these pictures can make e-mail messages large. To avoid this problem, some companies include links to pictures that are hosted on their server. When you preview or open the message, you can see the pictures, but they aren't actually part of the message.

Some junk mail senders have utilized this new technology to include Web beacons in their messages. Web beacons are small programs that notify the sender when you read or preview the e-mail message. This confirms that your e-mail address is valid, and might result in more junk e-mail being sent to you.

New in Office 2003
Enhanced privacy features

To help protect your privacy, Outlook 2003 includes new features that block external content such as pictures, sounds, and Web beacons. In addition to helping ensure your privacy, this provides the opportunity to save bandwidth resources, as you can choose to view images when you want.

By default, Outlook 2003 blocks external content to and from all sources except those defined in the Safe Senders and Safe Recipients lists, and from Web sites in your Trusted Zone.

To change the way Outlook handles external content:

1   On the **Tools** menu, click **Options**.

2   In the **Options** dialog box, on the **Security** tab, click **Change Automatic Download Settings**.

3   In the **Automatic Picture Download Settings** dialog box, select the check boxes for the options you want.

4   Click **OK** in each of the open dialog boxes to save your settings.

To view the blocked content in an individual e-mail message:

1   In the message, click the **InfoBar**.

2   On the shortcut menu, click **Show Blocked Content**.

Specifying Advanced E-Mail Options

Microsoft
Office
Specialist

Outlook includes a selection of advanced options so you can manage your e-mail most effectively. To avoid losing your work, you can choose to have Outlook automatically save messages you have created but not yet sent. When new messages arrive, you can choose to have Outlook alert you by playing a sound, briefly changing the mouse pointer to an envelope icon, showing an envelope icon in the system tray, or any combination of these. You can also set default options for sending a message. For example, if you are concerned about privacy, you might choose to set the sensitivity of all new messages to Private.

In this exercise, you specify how Outlook saves messages, what happens when new messages arrive, and which options are used when sending messages.

OPEN your Inbox before beginning this exercise.

1   On the **Tools** menu, click **Options**.

The Options dialog box appears. From this dialog box, you can open several other dialog boxes that control the settings and appearance of Outlook's features, including E-mail, the Calendar, Tasks, Contacts, the Journal, and Notes.

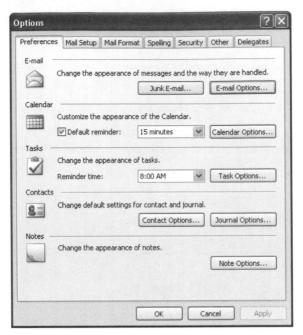

2 In the **Options** dialog box, click the **E-mail Options** button.

The E-mail Options dialog box appears.

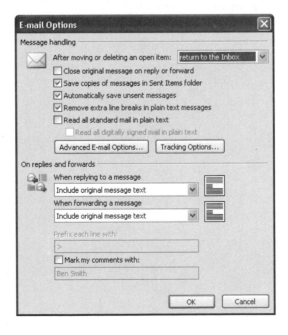

3   Study the available options, and then click the **Advanced E-mail Options** button.

The Advanced E-mail Options dialog box appears.

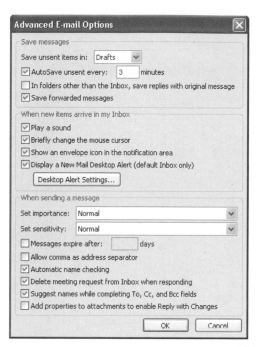

4   In the **Save messages** area, be sure the **AutoSave unsent every** check box is selected, and in the **minutes** box, type **1**.

Outlook will save any messages that you are composing, but have not yet sent, in your Drafts folder after one minute.

5   Clear the **Save forwarded messages** check box.

Outlook will not save a copy of messages that you forward to others.

6   In the **When new items arrive** area, clear the **Briefly change the mouse cursor** check box.

Outlook will play a sound, display an envelope icon in the system tray, and display a desktop alert when new messages arrive, but the mouse pointer will not change.

7   Select the **Allow comma as address separator** check box.

Outlook will recognize commas as well as semicolons in the *To*, *Cc*, or *Bcc* boxes as separators between names or addresses.

8   Click **OK** in each of the open dialog boxes to close them and save your changes.

New Mail
Message

9 On the Standard toolbar, click the **New Mail Message** button.

A new message appears. In the message form, the toolbar indicates that the message is marked as High priority.

High priority indicator

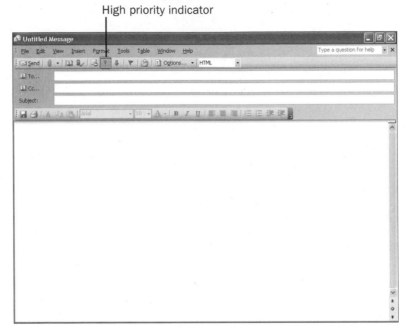

10 Close the message. If prompted to save it, click **No**.

11 On the **Tools** menu, click **Options**, click the **E-mail Options** button, and then click the **Advanced E-mail Options** button.

The Advanced E-mail Options dialog box appears.

12 In the **Set importance** list, click **Normal**.

All new messages will be set to Normal priority.

13 Select or clear any other options you want, and click **OK** in the open dialog boxes to save your changes.

Working with New Mail Notifications

There are several ways Outlook can notify you when you get new messages, even if you're working in another application. When a new message arrives, a letter icon appears in the system tray. You can also set Outlook to play a special sound or display a *desktop alert* on your screen for a few seconds.

New in Office 2003
Desktop Alerts

Desktop alerts are a new feature in Outlook 2003, intended to subtly notify you when you receive new e-mail messages. When the message arrives, a small, transparent box appears on your screen, displaying the name of the sender, the subject, and the first few words of the message (approximately 125 characters). From the desktop alert, you can open the message, mark it as read, flag it for action, respond to it, or delete it. Desktop alerts are enabled by default. You can change their position, transparency, and the length of time for which they appear, or you can choose to not display them.

In this exercise, you will customize your desktop alert settings and mark and delete messages using desktop alerts.

OPEN your Inbox before starting this exercise.

1 On the **Tools** menu, click **Options**.

The Options dialog box appears.

2 On the **Preferences** tab, click the **E-mail Options** button.

The E-mail Options dialog box appears.

3 Click the **Advanced E-mail Options** button.

The Advanced E-mail Options dialog box appears.

4 In the **When new items arrive in my Inbox** area, clear the **Play a sound** check box.

Tip To turn off desktop alerts, clear the Display a New Mail Desktop Alert check box.

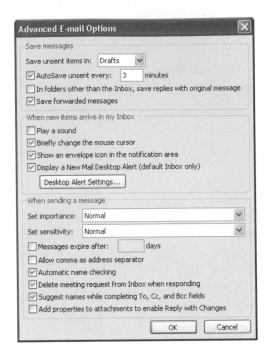

5 Click the **Desktop Alert Settings** button.

The Desktop Alert Settings dialog box appears.

Tip To quickly access the Desktop Alert Settings dialog box, when a desktop alert arrives, click the Options button and then click Desktop Alert Settings.

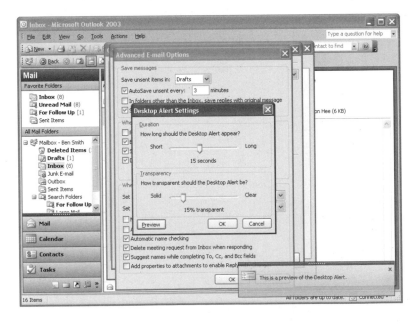

6   Drag the **How long should the Desktop Alert appear** slider to 30 seconds (the far right end of the slider bar), and click the **Preview** button.

A sample desktop alert appears on your desktop.

The sample alert doesn't include all the functionality of a real desktop alert, which looks like this:

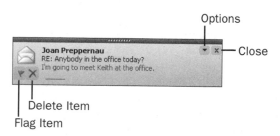

Options

Close

Delete Item

Flag Item

7   Drag the sample desktop alert to the lower-left corner of your screen.

8   In the **Desktop Alert Settings** dialog box, drag the **How transparent should the Desktop Alert be** slide to 0% transparent (the far left end of the slider bar) and click the **Preview** button.

The sample desktop alert appears where you placed the previous sample, and darkens until it is opaque.

9   In the **Desktop Alert Settings** dialog box, set the duration and transparency as you want, previewing your changes and moving the desktop alert as necessary, and then click **OK**.

10   Click **OK** in each of the three open dialog boxes.

New Mail
Message

11   On the Standard toolbar, click the **New Mail Message** button.

A new message form appears.

12   In the **To** box, type your e-mail address.

13   In the **Subject** box, type Alert test 1.

14   In the message body, type This is a test.

15   Click the **Send** button.

The message appears in your Inbox, a letter icon appears in the system tray, and a desktop alert appears on your screen.

16   Position the mouse pointer over the desktop alert to keep it open.

Options

17 In the desktop alert, click the **Options** button, and then on the shortcut menu, click **Mark as Read**.

The desktop alert closes, and the message in your Inbox is marked as read.

18 On the Standard toolbar, click the down arrow to the right of the **New Mail Message** button, and then click **Meeting Request**.

A new Meeting Request form appears.

19 In the **To** box, type your e-mail address, in the **Subject** box, type **Alert test 2**, and click the **Send** button.

A message appears in your Inbox, and a desktop alert appears.

20 In the desktop alert, click the **Delete Item** button.

Delete Item

The message disappears from your Inbox, and the desktop alert closes.

Windows SharePoint Services Alerts

New in Office 2003

Create and manage alerts

If you use a *Windows SharePoint Services* Web site hosted on a server that is configured to send e-mail, you can have that Web site send you an e-mail message whenever the content changes. You can receive alerts about changes to individual documents, tasks, events, or whole folders. You can have an alert sent immediately after each change, or you can receive daily or weekly summaries of changes.

To create a Windows SharePoint Services alert:

1 Open the SharePoint Web site in your Web browser, and browse to the document library or list for which you want to set up an alert.

2 To create an alert for the entire library or list, under **Actions**, click **Alert me**. To create an alert for a single item, point to the item's name, click the down arrow that appears, and then click **Alert me**.

The New Alert page opens.

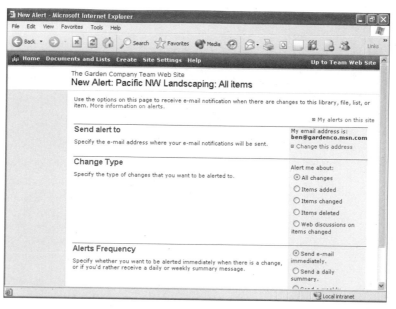

3 If you want the alert sent to an address other than the one you are signed in as, in the **Send alert to** area, click **Change this address**. Then in the **E-mail Address** box, type the address, and click **Save and Close**.

4 If the alert is for a list or folder, in the **Change Type** area, select the **All changes**, **Items added**, **Items changed**, **Items deleted**, or **Web discussions on items changed** option, depending on the events to which you want to be alerted.

5 In the **Alerts Frequency** area, select the **Send e-mail immediately**, **Send a daily summary**, or **Send a weekly summary** option, depending on how frequently you want to receive alerts.

6 Click **OK**.

To manage your Windows SharePoint Services alerts through Outlook:

1 On the **Tools** menu, click **Rules and Alerts**. If a dialog box appears telling you that HTTP e-mail accounts cannot be filtered using Outlook rules, click **OK**.

2 In the **Rules and Alerts** dialog box, click the **Manage Alerts** tab.

The Rules and Alerts dialog box lists your alerts. Here you can examine your alerts, delete them, create new ones, and create rules to play special sounds when they arrive or move them to a special folder.

Key Points

- You can customize what is shown in Outlook Today. Outlook Today can open every time you start Outlook, or you can create Outlook desktop shortcuts that open the Calendar or other components. You can add shortcuts to the Shortcuts pane, and organize those shortcuts into groups.

- You can customize how menus show or hide rarely used items, add or remove items from toolbars and menus, and choose which toolbars to hide or display.

- You can use desktop alerts to flag, mark as read, or delete e-mail messages as they arrive in your Inbox. You can choose where and for how long they appear, and you can turn them off entirely. You can also use Outlook to create, modify and delete Windows SharePoint Services alerts.

- You can organize your e-mail messages and contact entries by creating personal folders, a Personal Address Book, and personal distribution lists.

- You can digitally sign your messages so that recipients will know they haven't been tampered with; encrypt them so that only intended recipients can read them; and set permission so that recipients can't copy, forward, or print them. You can also block the display of external HTML content when you read messages to help keep your e-mail address off junk mail lists.

Glossary

address book A collection of names, e-mail addresses, and distribution lists used to address messages. An address book might be provided by Microsoft Outlook, Microsoft Exchange Server, or Internet directory services, depending on how you have set up Outlook.

address card Contact information displayed in a block that looks like a paper business card.

All Mail Folders The list that displays the folders available in your mailbox. If the Folder List is not visible, on the Navigation Pane, click Folder List.

appointment An entry in your Outlook Calendar that does not involve inviting other people or resources.

archiving Moving old or expired items out of your Inbox and other message folders to an alternate location for storage.

attachment A file that accompanies an e-mail message.

AutoArchive An Outlook feature that archives messages automatically at scheduled intervals, clearing out old and expired items from folders. AutoArchive is active by default.

AutoPreview A view which displays the first three lines of each message in your Inbox, making it easy to scan for your most important messages.

Cached Exchange Mode A feature of Outlook that creates local copies of your mailbox and address book on your computer and keeps them synchronized. Cached Exchange Mode monitors your connection status and speed and optimizes data transfer accordingly.

Calendar The scheduling component of Outlook that is fully integrated with e-mail, contacts, and other Outlook features.

category A keyword or phrase that you assign to Outlook items so that you can easily find, sort, filter, or group them.

client rules Rules that are applied to messages stored on your computer.

contact A person, inside or outside of your organization, about whom you can save information, such as street and e-mail addresses, telephone and fax numbers, and Web page URLs, in an entry in your Contacts folder in Outlook.

Date Navigator The small calendar that appears next to the appointment area in the Outlook Calendar. The Date Navigator provides a quick and easy way to change and view dates.

Day view   The Calendar view displaying one day at a time, separated into half-hour increments.

delegate   A person given permission to read, reply to and delete your messages in one or more folders.

desktop alert   A notification that appears on your desktop when a new e-mail message, meeting request, or task request appears in your Inbox.

dial-up networking   A component of Windows with which you can connect your computer to a network server through a modem.

digital ID   A private key that stays on the sender's computer and a certificate that contains a public key. The certificate is sent with digitally signed messages.

digitally signing   Proving one's identity by attaching a digital certificate to an e-mail message. The certificate is part of the sender's digital ID.

directory server   A computer on which a directory is stored.

distribution list   A collection of e-mail addresses combined into a single list name. All members of the list receive the e-mail message sent to the list name.

downloading   Moving or copying items from a server to a local computer.

draft   A message that has not yet been sent.

e-mail   Electronic mail.

e-mail address   The information that identifies the e-mail account of a message recipient, including the user name and domain name separated by the @ sign. For example, someone@microsoft.com.

e-mail server   A computer, on a network, that routes and stores e-mail messages.

encrypting   Encoding data to prevent unauthorized access. An encrypted message is unreadable to all but the recipient, who has a public key that will decrypt it.

event   An Outlook Calendar entry for an activity that lasts 24 hours or longer.

filtering   A way to view only those items or files that meet conditions you specify.

Folder List   The list that displays the folders available in your mailbox. If the Folder List is not visible, on the View menu, click Folder List.

follow-up flag   An icon associated with a message indicating a need to act on the message.

form   The feature in Outlook in which the user can define how items will be displayed. For example, the Outlook Message form defines how messages are displayed on the screen.

Global Address List An address book, provided by Microsoft Exchange Server, that contains all user and distribution list e-mail addresses in your organization. The Exchange administrator creates and maintains this address book.

HTML Hypertext Markup Language, the authoring language used to create Web pages and other documents on the Internet.

HTML format The default format for Outlook e-mail messages. This format supports text formatting, numbering, bullets, alignment, horizontal lines, pictures (including backgrounds), HTML styles, stationery, signatures, and Web pages.

HTTP HyperText Transfer Protocol, a protocol used to access Web pages from the Internet.

IMAP Internet Message Access Protocol, a protocol that organizes messages on the server and you choose messages to download by viewing their headers.

import The action of reading and using data produced by a different program.

importance The urgency of a message. Messages can be of High, Normal, or Low importance.

Inbox The default message folder in Outlook. Typically, incoming messages are delivered to the Inbox.

instant messaging A method of communication in which you send electronic messages that appear on the recipient's screen immediately.

Internet mail A type of e-mail account that requires that you connect to the e-mail server over the Internet. POP3, IMAP, and HTTP (for example, Hotmail) are examples of Internet mail accounts.

Internet Service Provider (ISP) A business that provides access to the Internet for such things as electronic mail, chat rooms, or use of the World Wide Web.

Journal entry An item in the Journal folder that acts as a shortcut to an activity that has been recorded. You can distinguish a Journal entry from other items by the clock that appears in the lower left corner of the icon.

label A color and short text description you can apply to meetings and appointments to organize your Calendar.

live attachments See *shared attachments*.

local area network (LAN) A network that connects computers in a relatively small area, typically a single building or groups of buildings. Generally, all computers in an organization are connected to a LAN. Organizations might have multiple LANs that are connected to each other.

meeting request   An e-mail message inviting its recipients to a meeting.

message header   Summary information that you download to your computer to determine whether to download, copy, or delete an entire message from the server. The header can include the subject, the sender's name, the received date, the importance, the attachment flag, and the size of the message.

Microsoft Exchange Server   An enterprise-level e-mail and collaboration server.

Microsoft Office Internet Free/Busy Service   A Web-based service that you can use to publish your schedule to a shared Internet location.

Month view   The Calendar view displaying five weeks at a time.

NetMeeting   A program that enables Internet teleconferencing.

news server   A computer, in your organization or at your Internet service provider (ISP), which is set up specifically to host newsgroups.

newsgroup   A collection of messages related to a particular topic posted to a news server.

newsreader   A program used to read messages posted to a newsgroup.

notes   Outlook items that are the electronic equivalent of paper sticky notes.

offline folder   A folder you use to access the contents of a server folder when you are not connected to the network. It is important to update the folder and its corresponding server folder to make the contents of both identical.

Out of Office Assistant   An Outlook feature that helps you manage your Inbox when you're out of the office. The Out of Office Assistant can respond to incoming messages automatically, and it enables you to create rules for managing incoming messages.

Outlook Rich Text Format (RTF)   A format for Outlook e-mail messages that supports a host of formatting options including text formatting, bullets, numbering, background colors, borders, and shading. Rich Text Format is supported by some Microsoft e-mail clients, including Outlook 97, Outlook 2000, Outlook 2002, and Outlook 2003.

Personal Address Book   An address book for personal contacts and distribution lists, rather than work-related contacts. The e-mail addresses and distributions lists in this address book are stored in a file with a .pab extension

Personal Folders file   A data file in which Microsoft Outlook saves messages, appointments, tasks, and journal entries on your computer.

Plain Text   A format for Outlook e-mail messages that does not support any text formatting but is supported by all e-mail programs.

POP3   A common protocol used to retrieve e-mail messages from an Internet e-mail server.

print style　A combination of paper and page settings that determines the way items are printed. For most items, Outlook provides a set of built-in print styles, and you can create your own.

private　A property of an appointment or meeting that prevents other users from seeing its details even if they have permission to view your calendar.

private store　A database for storing public folders in an Exchange sever.

profile　A group of e-mail accounts and address books configured to work together in Outlook.

Reading Pane　One of the ways you can read an e-mail message. In this pane you can view a message without opening it.

recurring　Describes items that occur repeatedly. For example, an appointment or task that occurs on a regular basis, such as a weekly status meeting or a monthly haircut, can be designated as recurring.

reminder　A message that appears at a specified interval before an appointment, meeting, or task, announcing when the activity is set to occur. Reminders appear any time Outlook is running, even if it isn't your active program.

Rich Text　See *Outlook Rich Text Format*.

rules　A set of conditions, actions, and exceptions that process and organize messages.

scripts　A list of commands executed without user interaction.

search folder　A virtual folder that contains a view of all e-mail items matching specific search criteria.

Secure Multipurpose Internet Mail extensions (S/MIME)　A standard specification for authenticating and encrypting e-mail.

security zone　A feature that you can use to assign a Web site to a zone with a suitable security level.

sensitivity　A security setting of an e-mail message that indicates whether a message should be treated as normal, personal, private, or confidential.

server rules　Rules that are applied to messages as they are received or processed by the Exchange server.

shared attachments　Attachments saved on a SharePoint Document Workspace Web site, where a group can collaborate to work on files and discuss a project. Also called live attachments.

signature　Text and/or pictures that are automatically added to the end of an outgoing e-mail message.

spam　Electronic junk mail.

stationery   A preset or automatic format for e-mail messages that specifies fonts, bullets, background color, horizontal lines, images, and other design elements.

synchronizing   Copying changed items between a mailbox or address book on a server and it corresponding offline folder so that both are up-to-date.

task list   A list of tasks that appears in the Tasks folder and in the TaskPad in Calendar.

TaskPad   The list of tasks that appears on the right side of the Outlook Calendar window.

tasks   Personal or work-related activities you want to track through to completion.

theme   A set of unified design elements and color schemes used to automatically format e-mail messages. Themes offer more formatting options than stationery.

Uniform Resource Locator (URL)   Represents the address of Web pages and other resources available on the Internet.

vCard   A standard text-based format for storing contact information.

virtual folders   Folders that that look like and link to an original folder.

Web browser   A program that retrieves web pages over the World Wide Web and displays the pages as hypertext, with embedded images.

Week view   The Calendar view displaying one full week at a time.

Windows SharePoint team Services   Microsoft's server application for team Web sites that are used for information sharing and document collaboration.

work week   The days you are available for work-related appointments and meetings each week. Outlook displays the days outside your selected work week as shaded, to indicate that you are normally not available on those days.

Work Week view   The Calendar view displaying only the work days of one week in columnar format. You can define your work week as whatever days and hours you want.

Index

Learning solutions for *every* software user

Microsoft Press learning solutions are ideal for every software user—from business users to developers to IT professionals

Microsoft Press® creates comprehensive learning solutions that empower everyone from business professionals and decision makers to software developers and IT professionals to work more productively with Microsoft® software. We design books for every business computer user, from beginners up to tech-savvy power users. We produce in-depth learning and reference titles to help developers work more productively with Microsoft programming tools and technologies. And we give IT professionals the training and technical resources they need to deploy, install, and support Microsoft products during all phases of the software adoption cycle. Whatever technology you're working with and no matter what your skill level, we have a learning tool to help you.

The tools you need to put technology to work.

Microsoft®

microsoft.com/mspress

Learn how to get the job done every day— faster, smarter, and easier!

Faster Smarter Digital Photography
ISBN: 0-7356-1872-0
U.S.A. $19.99
Canada $28.99

Faster Smarter Microsoft® Office XP
ISBN: 0-7356-1862-3
U.S.A. $19.99
Canada $28.99

Faster Smarter Microsoft Windows® XP
ISBN: 0-7356-1857-7
U.S.A. $19.99
Canada $28.99

Faster Smarter Home Networking
ISBN: 0-7356-1869-0
U.S.A. $19.99
Canada $28.99

Discover how to do exactly what you do with computers and technology—faster, smarter, and easier—with FASTER SMARTER books from Microsoft Press! They're your everyday guides for learning the practicalities of how to make technology work the way you want—fast. Their language is friendly and down-to-earth, with no jargon or silly chatter, and with accurate how-to information that's easy to absorb and apply. Use the concise explanations, easy numbered steps, and visual examples to understand exactly what you need to do to get the job done—whether you're using a PC at home or in business, capturing and sharing digital still images, getting a home network running, or finishing other tasks.

Microsoft Press has other FASTER SMARTER titles to help you get the job done every day:

Faster Smarter PCs
ISBN: 0-7356-1780-5

Faster Smarter Microsoft Windows 98
ISBN: 0-7356-1858-5

Faster Smarter Beginning Programming
ISBN: 0-7356-1780-5

Faster Smarter Digital Video
ISBN: 0-7356-1873-9

Faster Smarter Web Page Creation
ISBN: 0-7356-1860-7

Faster Smarter HTML & XML
ISBN: 0-7356-1861-5

Faster Smarter Internet
ISBN: 0-7356-1859-3

Faster Smarter Money 2003
ISBN: 0-7356-1864-X

To learn more about the full line of Microsoft Press® products, please visit us at:

microsoft.com/mspress

Get a **Free**
e-mail newsletter, updates,
special offers, links to related books,
and more when you

register online!

Register your Microsoft Press® title on our Web site and you'll get a FREE subscription to our e-mail newsletter, *Microsoft Press Book Connections.* You'll find out about newly released and upcoming books and learning tools, online events, software downloads, special offers and coupons for Microsoft Press customers, and information about major Microsoft® product releases. You can also read useful additional information about all the titles we publish, such as detailed book descriptions, tables of contents and indexes, sample chapters, links to related books and book series, author biographies, and reviews by other customers.

Registration is easy. Just visit this Web page and fill in your information:

http://www.microsoft.com/mspress/register

Microsoft®
